Praise for P~~~

1

'A fine adv

The Irish Times

'A compulsive, educational, laugh-out-loud read, and one of the most gloriously daft yet irresistible books I have ever read.'
Ferdia MacAnna, *Sunday Independent*

'For sheer pleasure, nothing I read beat *The Height of Nonsense*.'
Jan Morris, *The Observer*

'A book about turning off the motorway and heading for history and legend. Take it in your car and you will discover parts of Ireland you never dreamed of.'
Irish News

'A fascinating journey around the hidden corners of Ireland.'
BBC Radio

Burren Country

'Finely wrought language, lively engagement with interesting people.'
Michael Viney, *The Irish Times*

'Written in a carefree style, this is a love letter to the Burren that digs deeper into the history, mystery and mythology of the region – the author's avid fascination shines through.'
Belfast Telegraph

'A wonderful book that will brighten any day.'
Belfast News Letter

'A breath of fresh air, informative, funny and sensitive.'
Irish News

BY THE SAME AUTHOR
Bookshops of Belfast
Burren Country: Travels through an Irish Limestone Landscape
Insight Guide Belfast
Irish Shores: A Journey Round the Rim of Ireland
Jan Morris: A Critical Study
Romancing Ireland: Richard Hayward, 1892–1964
A Walk through Carrick-on-Shannon
*Wandering Ireland's Wild Atlantic Way: From Banba's Crown
        to World's End*

AS EDITOR
*The Blue Sky Bends Over All: A Celebration of Ten Years of the
        Immrama Travel Writing Festival*
*Jan Morris, Around the World in Eighty Years: A Festschrift
        Tribute*
*Legacy: A Collection of Personal Testimonies from People
        Affected by the Troubles in Northern Ireland*

AS CONTRIBUTING WRITER
Fodor's Ireland
Insight Guide Ireland
Rough Guide to Ireland

THE ULTIMATE IRISH ROAD TRIP

PAUL CLEMENTS is a journalist, broadcaster and writer. He is the author of a trilogy of travel books about Ireland: *Burren Country* (2011), *The Height of Nonsense* (2005 & 2016) and *Irish Shores* (1993). Originally from County Tyrone, he lives in Belfast and spends part of each year in the west of Ireland researching, writing, walking, and seeking inspiration. A former BBC journalist, he now contributes to newspapers, magazines and to travel guides to Ireland He is a Fellow of Green-Templeton College, Oxford. His latest book is *Wandering Ireland's Wild Atlantic Way* (2016).

I dedicate this book to my son Daniel,
for providing love and inspiration

THE HEIGHT OF NONSENSE

THE ULTIMATE IRISH ROAD TRIP

PAUL CLEMENTS

The Collins Press

PUBLISHED IN 2016 BY
The Collins Press
West Link Park
Doughcloyne
Wilton
Cork

First published 2005

© Paul Clements 2005, 2016

Paul Clements has asserted his moral right to be identified
as author of this work in accordance with the Irish Copyright and
Related Acts 2000.

All rights reserved. The material in this publication is protected by
copyright law. Except as may be permitted by law, no part of the
material may be reproduced (including by storage in a retrieval system)
or transmitted in any form or by any means; adapted; rented or lent
without the written permission of the copyright owners. Applications
for permissions should be addressed to the publisher.

A CIP record for this book is available from the British Library

ISBN 13: 98-184889-265-1

Typesetting: The Collins Press

Font: Palatino, 11 point

Printed in Sweden by Scandbook AB

Contents

The men of Ireland are mortal and temporal,
but her hills are eternal.
G.B. Shaw

Preface

The Call of the Hindquarters

By any standards it was an ambitious venture. The 'it' in question was a back-burner project that simmered gently for a while, boiled over occasionally, then settled again in the back of my mind before resurfacing at other times; it simply refused to go away.

The project was a trip I wished to make into the heart of Ireland: a journey in which I would visit each county, travelling the mountain roads in search of the highest point. The county tops – whether the summits of grand mountains or the peaks of mere molehills – would be my goal.

My solo route, by car and on foot, would take me across the length and breadth of the country, with the mountains as companions for the entire trip. Zigzagging along back roads, I resolved to keep the hills in view, surround myself with them, feel their presence constantly and learn their secrets. As well as reaching the summit, I wanted to talk to local people about the lore and the cult of these high places. It was a trip, I felt, that could not be made in one continuous sweep. My plan was to undertake the journey in separate sections, with breaks for reading, writing and reflection.

As a Capricorn I was used to being called 'a mountain goat'. It is said that the qualities of people born under the sign of the goat include stubbornness, severe criticism of others (plus thyself) and a dogged determination. Several mountain ranges were familiar to me but I longed to know them better. I admired the description of the Irish mountains by Daphne Pochin Mould:

> The pattern of the heights is rather of a monotonous repetition of rock and boggy moorland in rounded massive haunches, with a certain majesty like the hindquarters of an elephant.

In advance of my journey to explore these hindquarters, I set out a number of Rules of the Road: avoid motorways, dual carriageways and national primary routes; steer clear of the so-called 'Trans-European routes' and 'roundabout heaven' linking cities, and at all costs avoid the 'key strategic diagonal corridors'. No wide, fast, six-lane highways for me; instead, the Great Mountain Roads – the GMRs – would be my aim. Forsaking the twenty-first-century Celtic superhighways, my quest would take me along the 'Hibernian songlines', the boreens, turf-cutter roads and mail-coach roads.

To family and friends it appeared an outlandish project. A work colleague said it was something I should think about for retirement; I told him I could not wait that long. I also had another plausible reason: 2002 was designated by the United Nations as 'International Year of Mountains'.

A final personal note. I was fortunate to secure some lengthy leave from my job to allow me to make the trip in an unhurried way. Domestically and financially I could not afford to take a long time off, but when I turned it over in my mind I could not afford not to. I had agreed on homecomings and regular family meetings, and promised to keep in touch with friends. My chosen mode of travel by car – a fourteen-year-old Nissan Bluebird with over 100,000 miles on the clock – was well up to the task of travelling the mountain roads. I pack some books, maps and field guides, a collection of music tapes and an eight-hour audio tape of Henry David Thoreau's *Walden*.

That's enough by way of background. I am anxious to get on the road; the time has come to drive somewhere, climb some hills, and see some stars and sky.

PAUL CLEMENTS
Belfast 2004

Acknowledgements

I am indebted to all those who opened their doors and helped me along the way. Many people provided support, supplied navigational tips, drinks, meals and accommodation, and suggested roads to follow as well as hills to climb. Members of local walking clubs gave me advice and eased the path to the summits. With one exception landowners and farmers showed hospitality, often opening their gates to allow me to roam freely with unimpeded access.

This book is partly the product of other people's knowledge and erudition. Special thanks are due to the unsung band of local historians who shared with me their wisdom; these sages of Irish life gave unselfishly of their time, anecdotes and information. I profited enormously from their generosity and local researches, and I hope I have done them justice.

On wet days I spent time in libraries. Librarians and archivists in many towns went out of their way to find books, journals and publications long out of print. Frequently they suggested titles that might help. In later research I used the services of the Central Library in Belfast and wish to acknowledge the supremely helpful staff for whom my innumerable enquiries were never too much trouble. I also wish to place on record my thanks to staff in tourist information offices and heritage centres in the towns and villages through which I passed.

Some people read the manuscript, or sections of it, and gave unending encouragement, often suggesting improvements. Particular thanks to my father-in-law, James Hughes, for meticulously reading an early draft with his homophone-spotting, gimlet eye and for correcting spelling discrepancies, dangling modifiers and mismatches. With similar care and keen observation, Ivor McDonald enthusiastically checked the ornithological references, making invaluable suggestions, and I am grateful to him. Special thanks are due to the indefatigable Marty Johnston, a fellow-lover of the hills and a computing guru. He skilfully produced the map and gave unstinting help and advice on the manuscript layout.

It is impossible to name all those who helped or guided me but I would specifically like to express gratitude to the following: Bill Bailey, Fiona Bonner, Fionuala Boyd, Paddy Boylan, Emma Caffrey, Anne Carpenter, Percy Clendennen, John Connole, Catherine Elliott, Jim Gibney, Marie Harvey, Harry Hume, Seán Kierse, Jane King, Mike Leane, May McClintock, Michael McGrath, Pauline McKenna, Father Nivard, Raymond Piper, Brian Roberts, Natasha Sayee, Faith White and Willie White. I would like to thank my agent, Jonathan Williams, who was unfailingly helpful and believed in the project. The faults that remain are all my own work. I am grateful to BBC Northern Ireland for accommodating my sabbatical leave. I would also like to thank all those authors and poets from whose books I have quoted extracts. The lines from the Patrick Kavanagh poem 'Monaghan Hills' are reprinted by kind permission of the Trustees of the Estate of the late Katherine B. Kavanagh, through the Jonathan Williams Literary Agency. Every effort has been made to trace and contact copyright holders. If notified, the publisher will rectify any errors or omissions at the earliest opportunity.

Finally, my love and thanks to my wife Felicity and son Daniel for their forebearance, support and ceaseless encouragement. Although they were not with me for the trip, they were always part of the journey through the obsidian stone. They have been more than generous in putting up with my long absences and in tolerating their writer-in-residence.

Author's Note

I forced my way into some people's lives and they gave generously of their time and knowledge. In several instances the names of places and identities of people have been disguised to respect their privacy.

As far as possible I have chosen to spell place-names in accordance with modern Ordnance Survey maps. However, the metrication of mountains has never appealed to me. In listing their heights, I have stuck to the imperial measurements. To me, 3,000 feet will always sound more attractive than the prosaically precise 914 metres.

Any brand names mentioned in this book should not be interpreted as an endorsement of the product. The views expressed are entirely my own; they do not represent those of my agent, publisher, editor or employer.

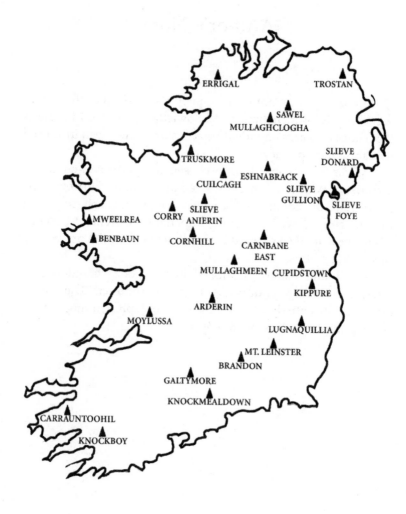

The County Tops of Ireland.

PART I

The Mountain of
Shape-shifting Sexuality

But to live near mountains is to be in touch with Eden, with lost childhood. These are the summer pastures of the Celtic people. On the darkest of days there is that high field, green as an emerald. This is the precious stone that a man sells all his goods to possess.

R.S. Thomas, *The Mountains*

The sweet aroma of turf smoke filters into the Bluebird as I drive with the windows down along one of the greatest mountain roads in Ireland. The route from Falcarragh to Gweedore in the north-west Donegal highlands is one of the best from which to view mountain scenery. Inland lies a chain of mountains stretching from the broad flat summit of Muckish in the north through Crocknalaragagh, Aghla Beg and Aghla More to Errigal which queens over all. Isolated and unchallenged, it is easily ahead of any rivals as the county's highest peak. It sticks up razor-sharp beneath a deep blue sky. Its conical shape, a porcelain colour, its summit – at 2,466 feet – my ultimate Donegal destination.

I drive along daffodil- and dandelion-drenched roadsides with an uninterrupted view of Errigal. The hedges are high with bright yellow gorse, the emblematic plant of Donegal and, at the beginning of April, the most ubiquitous. Birds dart from tree to tree. In one morning I see robin, bullfinch, mistle thrush and blackbird. The countryside is shaking off the last vestiges of a bleak winter. I browse the audial junk on the car radio: a snatch of Mozart, an Elton John song followed by The Corrs. On Highland Radio's Country Music Show they're playing the hits of Merle Haggard, Dwight Yoakam, Dolly Parton and Roly Daniels: three-minute stories telling tales of love and heartbreak.

Donegal is a huge county with an unfairly disproportionate number of hills. From its most northerly summit on the Inishowen peninsula at Ardmalin Hill, to the most southerly point at Bundoran, the county boasts hundreds of small, medium and large-sized peaks. They are, uncharacteristically for mountains, hidden out of the way in numerous ranges. In fact, the county has more than 100 peaks over 1,000 feet.

Daphne Pochin Mould summed it up neatly when she said that 'perhaps the essence of Ireland for the mountaineer is that clearness and purity of line and colour that is typical of Donegal … the white cone of Errigal rising from the roads edged with the gold of the gorse, the small white cottages set amongst their stone-walled fields under the line of the high ridges'.

She was writing 50 years ago. Today some small white cottages can still be seen in the landscape but you have to look hard to find them. They've given way to enormous mock-Tudor mansions and ugly houses set up on heights. Every few hundred yards a half-finished Spanish-style hacienda sits in perfect alignment to the road. The cottages of the 1950s and the shoe-box bungalows of the 1960s have been transformed into huge homes with Gaudi-esque flourishes. They all contain the essential accoutrements and must-have add-ons: conservatories, porches, double garages, satellite dishes, security gates, intruder lights and burglar-alarm boxes.

In the library in Letterkenny a woman tells me the best person to speak to for information about Errigal is Cathy Rea who knows the folklore, especially the fairy folklore, surrounding the mountain. Carefully distancing herself, she says Cathy is regarded by some people as 'an enigma'.

Several others also mention Cathy. One man says she is a self-proclaimed witch who has her own consultations between this world and the next. Other descriptions range from 'eccentric' to 'revered' and 'notorious'. With such a build-up of mystery I feel it would be remiss not to contact this woman of many adjectives. I check the phone book but she is ex-directory.

When I arrive in Dunlewy, the nearest village to Errigal,

I realise there is no point in going directly to her cottage door. I decide to employ the services of the staff at the Dunlewy Centre. The receptionist gives me Cathy's number but the line is dead; she has changed it. She phones her husband – the Dunlewy postman – and tries her new number. After a short exchange of words, she hands the phone to me.

A voice crackles down a bad line: 'I don't want to talk to journalists. I've had a horrible time with you people.'

Before I have a chance to speak she hangs up. I call the number again and introduce myself saying I want to speak to people who live near Errigal about what it means to them. I add that I am doing research on the fairy paths of Ireland – a subject on which, I understand, she is an expert. Compliments usually pay off, and this one clinches my entry.

'If you come now I'll give you fifteen minutes,' she says, 'but no longer as I have a busy schedule.'

I abort my Saturday afternoon plan to climb Errigal and drive the short distance to Cathy's house. Her cottage is hidden down a lane enclosed in a ring of mountain ash, holly and alder. Before I've climbed out of the car, a collie rushes up the path barking furiously. When I step out it snaps at my heels. I contemplate jumping back into the car and revving off at speed but instead make my way nervously past a 'No Trespassing' sign on the gate. A woman is standing at the door and calls the dog off. We shake hands and she sizes me up with apprehensive eyes. She repeats what she has said on the telephone about being wary of having a stream of journalists, then asks, 'Tea or coffee?' Inside the cottage the dog is still snapping and licking

round my trainers. She gently rebukes him: 'Moisteen …
Moisteen … come here.' The name, she tells me, is spelt
Maistín in Irish and means 'rascal'.

Cathy Rea has a cherubic face with a happy-go-lucky
countenance. She has small round glasses and flowing ginger hair. She wears a heavy green jumper with a brown patterned skirt. In the early 1970s she was a journalist. As she
pours the tea I feel a sense of her warming to me. I crack a
couple of jokes and explain my mission. Her eyes shine. She
nods, smiling benignly.

From her front door she has a grandstand view of
Errigal. Although she has never climbed it, it is a special
place for her. She giggles. 'I used to be built for speed and
now I am built for comfort, so I don't go up mountains. But
anybody who lives in its shadow cannot fail to be affected
by it. I definitely have been.

'It is a mystical place. There is an important ley line that
goes through the cottage to Errigal and on to a standing
stone with a cross on it. It is spiritually uplifting and in a
basic way cleansing. You just feel clean being close to the
mountain. I feel very protective of it; it is protective of me
and therefore I am protective of it. You'll find that most
people who believe in earth religions are at heart environ-
mentalists. Balance is important for us. Where balance
exists things are all right and where it doesn't exist then
things go out of kilter.

'If you see Errigal in the quiet of the full moonlight, with
the quartzite glistening, it is ethereal. It is not of this world.
It is a place between the worlds.'

Cathy believes local people take the mountain for granted because they live close to it.

'The strange thing is when people return from America, they only realise then how much they miss the mountain. I think people are very much part of the clay they come from. There is a magnetic pull with the clay and the earth drawing people back.'

Partly to please her, I raise the subject of fairy folklore. She says there are several realms of fairies with connections to Errigal, and she has been on some fairy paths, describing them as beguiling, inspiring and frightening.

Cathy admits to being a witch and says she is not ashamed of it. She practises an earth religion called Wicca. Her theory is that fairies were a genetic experiment and have survived in greatly reduced numbers.

She beams at me. 'You're gonna think I am nuts when I tell you this, but I think they were a mixture of humans and mushrooms. Sometimes I can smell fairies before I see them. They smell of mushrooms. If millions of people all over the world believe a God can mate with a human and reproduce, then why should it be so outrageous that a mushroom could be mated with a human?'

'How are they dressed?'

'The first ones I ever saw were dressed in small brown cowls like tiny monks with cowled hoods. I've seen them in trousers and jerkins. But I've never seen any with a red pointy hat.'

I decide it's time to ask about documentary evidence; where are the photographs?

'One didn't have the time to run for one's camera,' she counters. 'Fairies are careful about who they allow to see them. They learned to be careful and not to show themselves for long. Sometimes there are fleeting glimpses, but other times they stay around. Not all fairies are sweet and kind. Some are fed up with humans. There are good and bad ones. I have had to do exorcisms in houses where there are bad fairies and bad spirits.'

'There will be people who doubt everything you say.'

'Yes, I know people will doubt it. They should talk to the older people here. There are several old men who have brewed poteen in the bog and told me they saw fairies and that was before they sampled their wares.'

This is Cathy's cue to offer me a drink. She gives me a sweet cake made with honey and 'fairy juice' served in a crystal shot glass with a drawing of Errigal etched on the side. It is a mixture of poteen (supplied to her by an unnamed source from the Gaeltacht) and sloe berry fruits. To be fully appreciated it has to be sipped slowly. It has been a long fifteen minutes. Two hours after arriving she shows me to the door, giving me a guided tour of the garden. A fairy circle of eight stones about two feet tall stands in one corner to help bring balance to her life. Crystals dangle from trees glinting in the afternoon sunshine.

She blows me a parting kiss as I make my way back down the garden path, running the gauntlet of a snarling rascal.

The April sunlight streaming into my bedroom awakens me. I pull back the curtains to see Errigal bathed in early morning sun, its top shrouded in a thin veil of mist, casting a strange filigree of light. The easiest approach to climbing the mountain is from Dunlewy, a scattered settlement of 100 people. The Lakeside Hostel, a substantial two-storey building at the side of the road, is the perfect location for launching my first assault on the hills.

Dunlewy consists of a petrol station, community centre, church, post office, a bar, and several dozen farmhouses and bungalows strung out over two miles. There is an incongruous green steel tower that used to be a peat-burning power station but it closed in 1996. The woman in the hostel says there are plans to turn it into an art gallery.

When I reach the car park a handful of people are making their way uphill. I exchange pleasantries with a French woman sitting in a car. In broken English she says her husband and daughter have gone to climb the mountain but she hasn't the energy.

I carry out a final rucksack check, running through a newly-minted rhyme:

camera, binoculars, money,
mobile phone and obsidian stone.

The day before setting off, my wife had given me a small rectangular Capricorn crystal. I planned to take it with me into the mountains, trusting it would bring me good fortune. It would be my talisman for the trip. A piece of card attached to it describes obsidian as volcanic lava used to improve poor eyesight:

It is said to help those embarking upon a spiritual quest, keeping energies stable and clearing blockages, and bringing an experience and understanding of silence, detachment, wisdom and love.

Crossing some of Errigal's obstinate stones, I join a path beside a stream, taking my first tentative steps into the heart of Donegal's highest mountain. After several weeks of sun the terrain is dry. In places there are a few bog pools but I make my way round these and quickly reach rocky ground. Twenty minutes later I begin perspiring. I notice a man basking on his foam bedroll beside a rocky outcrop. His boots are resting by his side, along with a walking stick and binoculars. He looks the picture of contentment. He introduces himself as Joe. He comes to the hills for peace and to get away from people. In the past six years, he says, he has climbed Errigal 300 times.

'I am 73 and if I don't keep these bones active I'll stiffen up with pains.'

I follow a well-worn zigzag path of white quartzite stones. Near the top a dedicated walker is armed with trekking poles and moves with a swift methodical approach. Brendan Devine has just returned from Kerry where he spent a week camping. He is climbing all Ireland's mountains over 2,000 feet in preparation for a summer walking trip to the Pyrenees. He has a fascination for the mountains of Ireland which matches mine. He has also climbed in Scotland and is slowly building up his collection of Munros – all the Scottish mountains over 3,000 feet.

Brendan is wearing a flashy yellow watch, which he calls a 'wristop computer'. Eagerly he shows me what it can do. It gives details of how far he has walked, the height he has reached, and the time it has taken him. It produces a cumulative total of successive climbs.

'It's also a barometer, compass, watch, altimeter and heart rate monitor, so you can keep an eye on your ticker. You should get one for your walk.'

We discuss the merits of trekking poles and walking sticks, neither of which I use. Folksy conversations, interrupting the serious business of getting to the top, are part of the social culture of hillwalking. There is a bond between people with rucksacks which often leads to friendships, but I feel I am living out the Bord Fáilte cliché: 'In the hills of Donegal there are no strangers, just friends who haven't met.'

On the summit two cairns about 30 yards apart are connected by a narrow path called One Man's Pass. Two men and a woman arrive just before me, and sit on the rocky shoulder, drinking in the air. On windy days, one of the men says, the Pass can be hazardous. Today there is not a breath of wind. A heat haze restricts the views but it is still possible to appreciate the scale, quantity and distribution of the surrounding hills. To the south are the peaks that make up the bare rocky mountains of the Derryveagh range, with Dooish and Slieve Snaght rising prominently. Looking northwards with my binoculars I pick out the islands of Inishbofin, Inishdooey and Inishbeg. Scores of houses and small farmsteads are dotted across Bloody Foreland. Most cottages are white but every so often a bright yellow, cerise or red walled house stands out. Below me, Altan Lough shimmers in the sun.

During the steep descent I think about the mountain and its symbolism. Errigal has captivated landscape artists, painters and professional photographers. It has been captured on canvas in its many moods, and portrayed from every angle under blue, purple, crimson and yellow light. In art galleries, craft shops, hotels, restaurants and bars, I have seen its image on paintings, sketches, photographs and postcards – sometimes glittering in the snow or sun, sometimes in melancholy or misty mood. Often a turf-cutter or donkey features in the foreground. In Falcarragh, the gable wall of the Errigal Bar is decorated with a huge mural of the mountain and a toucan urges drinkers to 'Drop in for a Guinness'. Errigal adorns book covers, walking guides, maps and tourist board literature. It can be found on T-shirts, caps, badges, matchboxes, calendars, wine glasses, mugs and coasters. Its distinctive profile has been exploited for all its commercial potential, fulfilling the tourist demand for kitsch. But there is no escaping Errigal's grip on the imagination as a potent symbol of the Donegal psyche. In three days driving around the roads of the northern highlands, I have seen it in different physical guises: jagged, rugged, serrated, conical.

On Saturday evening, for another perspective, I had contacted a poet who lives beside the mountain. Cathal Ó Searcaigh said I would be welcome to visit him the next afternoon. 'Don't come too early,' he warns. 'I work through the night and don't get up most days until late'.

When I finish my walk I return to the hostel, change my clothes and take a narrow road to Cathal's farmhouse. He lives four miles from Dunlewy on the road to Gortahork in the townland of *Mín a Leá*. He had told me I would have no trouble finding the house; just look out for the prayer flags or bunting hanging outside. It's a traffic-choked road: choked with hens, sheep and gaggles of geese that refuse to budge. I stop to allow a sheep to escort two new-born lambs across. Stone walls line both sides of the road for a short stretch. Turf stacks are piled high in the yards of houses. Concentrating all my efforts on animal dodging, I drive past his white bungalow, mistakenly thinking the bunting is an ordinary Donegal family's weekly laundry.

Cathal's is no ordinary Donegal home. He explains that the small pink, yellow and blue handkerchief-size flags hanging on the clothesline are Tibetan mantras from Nepal. He brought them back from his travels in the Himalayas. Each winter he spends several months in Nepal, living with the Sherpas and writing. Cathal has a boyish face. He could pass for being in his early thirties. His Nepali hat makes him look younger than his 46 years. A gifted Irish-language poet, his work has been translated into English. He is renowned for a lyric intensity and sensuality in his poems. In his native Donegal Gaeltacht he is called *Guru nCnoc*, the 'Guru, or wise man, of the Hill'.

Over coffee in the warm sun he gushes with rapture about the mountain across from us. He speaks a precise, high-pitched, clipped and articulate Donegal-English. *Mín a Leá*, he tells me, means 'the little plain of flagstones in the mountain'. It takes little prompting to get him talking about it. Looking at it as a child, he recalls, Errigal was just a mound of rocks but over the years it has become a mysterious entity.

'When I was a young boy it was there as a tangible presence but later it became more withdrawn and I am much more curious about it. I love its mysteriousness and sense of awe which is part of its magic – all those hidden crevices and the changes that happen to it.'

The Irish translation, *Aireagál*, means an 'oratory'. Cathal knows it intimately, having climbed it more than 30 times.

'The mountain is there in my front garden like an installation glinting grey in the foreground. I am obsessed with it and aren't all of us who live at the foot of mountains obsessed with them? It is sacred. Going up gives me a wonderful surge of blood through the body. Every time I climb it I feel enlightened, which I know sounds southern Californian, but it is a power surge towards the divine. It is a spiritual presence and I feel there has to be respect and a sense of humility when climbing it.'

For Cathal, his side of the mountain is the most beautiful. I had noticed its differing shapes seen from different approaches. He says it looks unbalanced from some directions. He compares it to other mountains that he knows in Asia.

'Errigal has that sort of triangular symmetry about it which is very similar to the Japanese mountain Fujiyama, especially from this side. I also think it looks like Mount

Ararat in Armenia. I love the connections it has with other mountains. Each year I spend a substantial amount of time in Nepal where the mountains are sheer and huge, but I've never told Errigal that there are higher mountains than it in the world. It thinks it's the pinnacle of loftiness and I don't want to deflate its ego.'

I ask which is his favourite season for contemplating the mountain. Cathal stares across again at the conical peak, pondering its beauty. He switches gear, moving into poetic turbo-drive.

'In the winter it glistens in its negligee of snow; in the autumn it has a beautiful russet homespun of heather that I love. It can be quite gloomy at times and that affects people who live underneath it, especially in the winter. But I think this time of year – the spring – is my favourite because we have this wonderful clear light that changes all the time. It seems to creep along the hills and is close to the earth. Suddenly there is a whole transformation of mountains and scenery going on. Another strange aspect of it that I love is its shape-shifting sexuality. It is both male and female. The top is female, the bottom is male, or vice-versa. I love how it changes. At other times of the year I love the fieriness of it. When you see it in the amber glow of twilight or under stars it is an incredible spectacle. I have never become accustomed to it. It constantly amazes me and I find it nourishing for the spirit. I have a million views of it.'

Cathal has been trying to write a long poem that would embody the ethos of Errigal but the muse has so far not permitted him to produce it to his satisfaction. Apart from his eloquent thoughts on the mountain there is also a practical side to his love for it. He is fighting against what he believes may lead to its desecration: a proposal to plant trees, which he calls 'cash-crop conifers', at the foot of the mountain. He has written letters of protest to the local paper about 'this landscape outrage'.

His new poem, simply called 'Errigal', is about his father and his obsession with the mountain, both physical and psychic. Before leaving, I want to find out what Cathal feels the mountain means to the people who live around it. I tell him about an elderly woman I stopped to talk to along the road on the way to his house. She said she had last climbed it 55 years ago and found it terrifying.

Cathal says this is fairly normal. 'It is a witnessing presence to our lives but for lots of people it is just there, y'know, just out there,' he points animatedly. 'I am surprised at the amount of people around here who have not climbed it. I am amazed they have not got the adventurousness to walk up to the top out of sheer curiosity.'

I had spent an absorbing couple of hours in Cathal's company. He had generously shared with me his knowledge and enthusiasm, as well as his passionate and poetic love for Errigal. I thank him for his time and leave him to the million views of his sacred transsexual icon.

Over a beer in McGeady's in Dunlewy I reflect on the day. My first county summit is safely tucked under my rucksack. A man drinking a pint tells me the story of two doctors from Scotland who married in Donegal the previous summer. After the wedding, the entire party of 70, including the bride clad in her wedding dress and newly-shone Brasher walking boots, trooped to the top of Errigal.

A woman behind the bar snorts. 'I've never climbed that mountain in my life and wouldn't go up there on my wedding day. I would have better things to do. I am sure I never will climb it now, even though I drive past it every day.'

I tell her I had met a man who had climbed it 300 times.

'Well, y'see, that's part of the problem. No wonder the mountain is so badly eroded and walkers are complaining. It's people like him who are causing those problems.'

By midnight Dunlewy has drifted into a deep sleep. As I walk back along the road, adapting my eyes to the dark, I survey the night sky lit up by thousands of stars. A tapestry of jewels, resembling a star city, is woven into the blackness. I make out the shape of the plough and a trio of bright stars, Lyra, Deneb and Aquila, forming a triangle. Clusters of other scintillating stars – some virgin white, others with a bluish tinge – fill the sky. The silhouette of Errigal sticks up in the clear night. On the other side of the road Dunlewy church presents a theatrical floodlit spectacle. I walk along the central white line. It is eerily quiet. There is no traffic. There are no nocturnal creatures abroad; not even a Donegal fairy moves.

Early the next morning, when the stars have been switched off again, I leave Dunlewy and drive through Creeslough, completing the final section in the circuit of the Errigal jigsaw. I content myself that I've seen its different faces from all sides. For about two miles I catch the solitary mountain in my offside wing mirror. Its top is covered in a veil of cloud creeping slowly down one side. After another mile I lose sight of it in a trail of dust billowing up from road repairs. I drive over to Lifford, leaving behind the secretive hills of Donegal, feeling I have got to know them a little better, and have at least scratched their quartzite surfaces.

2

Sperrin's Hospitable Dunghills

Does the road wind uphill all the way?
Yes, to the very end.
Will the day's journey take the whole long day?
From morn to night, my friend.

Christina Rossetti, 'Uphill'

The young woman in the tourist information centre in Strabane freely admits she does not have a clue where Tyrone's highest point is. She asks a friend sitting beside her who is at an equal loss. The shelves are brimming with historical tourist information. A literary sub-culture has grown up around the past. She swamps me with leaflets, booklets, guides, maps and a newspaper listing everything

I could ever want to know on cycling, fishing, golfing and walking in the Sperrin Mountains.

The tree-shadowed road out of Strabane towards Plumbridge twists up into the Sperrins and runs parallel with the River Mourne. A crooked, hand-painted sign nailed to a tree advertises 'Fresh dug new potatoes'. Other signs say 'Duck Eggs', 'Farm Fences for Sale', and, curiously, 'Mature Manure'. I am so busy reading the agricultural signs, I miss the turn for Plumbridge and end up in Douglas Bridge. As I study the map, the school-crossing patrolman comes over to help me. He discusses the permutations and combinations that I could take to get to 'the Plum'.

'There are several ways to go but the best is to drive along this road and when that tapers out you meet the main Omagh to Newtownstewart road at a staggered junction which you cross, but on no account go into Newtown – if you do, you're done for. You want to taper off into the …'

His voice tapers away as I study the map. He looks at my boots in the back of the car and asks what I'm doing.

'Coming from mountains and going to mountains. Travelling around, talking to people. I am searching for the highest place in Tyrone. Do you know it?'

'I should know that, you know, let me see, let me see.' His eyes rove round the countryside. 'Tyrone … Tyrone … Tyrone,' he mutters to himself, his voice tapering away again, just like the roads.

'I don't know for certain but I think it might be the Bing Rock above Castlederg. There's a graveyard there that is higher than the church and, in fact, higher than the church spire.'

20

He's off again: 'Tyrone … Tyrone … Tyrone … it would-n't be Bessy Bell or Mary Gray over towards Baronscourt … or there's a place called Beauty Hill. They're all quite high but I think it might be somewhere in the Sperrins. Mind you, you'd need a good head for heights to be going up there.'

The afternoon is wearing thin. I've booked two nights at an activity and accommodation centre in Gortin and need to check in before five o'clock. I am still a bit topographi-cally confused. I have seen signposts for Victoria Bridge, Douglas Bridge, Plumbridge and even one saying 'Weak Bridge'. I had always thought the county's slogan was 'Tyrone among the Bushes' but somehow 'Tyrone among the Bridges' has a more appealing ring. Despite the instruc-tion to avoid Newtownstewart, I end up 'tapering' into it and discover that the road to Plumbridge is closed because of bridge-strengthening repairs. I take the road straight to Gortin. The Sperrins come into view. Compared to the mountains of Donegal, they are on a different scale and are more rounded and hummocky.

I lie on a soft bed in my room leafing through the liter-ature. The Sperrin Mountains, I learn, mean 'pointed hills'. They first appeared on the Ordnance Survey map in 1833 and took their names from the village of Sperrin. I am intrigued to discover that the Sperrins used to be called the Munterloney Mountains – *Muintir Luinigh* – family of O'Looney. At one time they were the dominant tribe in the district. I check the phone book to see if any O'Looneys still live in the area. The name has been corrupted and I find some O'Loans, six O'Loanes, several O'Lones, and, appropriately enough, just one Olone … all alone and living in Ballymena.

The Sperrins Visitor Guide is packed with information. There's a new walk called Hudy's Way, a seven-mile circuit of the village of Moneyneena. According to local legend, Hudy McGuigan once famously attempted to fly using home-made wings and leapt off one of the neighbouring peaks. He failed miserably. Straddling the border with County Derry and dominating mid-Tyrone, the Sperrins are a sprawling range. At least fifteen hills take the Mullagh (meaning 'hilltop') prefix. Sawel Mountain, at 2,240 feet, is the highest peak but it is not clear from my map if Tyrone or Derry has ownership of it.

The 'Flavour of Tyrone' brochure quotes the poets W.F. Marshall and John Montague on the front and back covers. The tourism spin-doctors have been working overtime. Superlatives, puns and alliteration are sprinkled throughout its pages and the county is described as the friendliest in Ulster. The guide recommends that in Tyrone you should 'choose to do only those things you cannot experience in Tenerife, Tampa or even Tralee'. The gushing clichés flow, just like the 'breathtaking' waterfalls west of Omagh.

For those who like quizzes and with respect to the renowned Tyrone writer, Flann O'Brien and his 'Catechism of Cliché', here's a quick test to see who's paying attention:

What are the Tyrone traditions?
Timeless.
To where do they transfer you?

Back in time.
Of what stuff are the landscapes made?
Legendary.
To what do the ancient artefacts, standing like millennium milestones, bear witness?
The wealth of our heritage.
What will you find in the bars?
A large helping of craic.
In the restaurants of Tyrone, what will the chefs be eager to please?
The discerning palate.
What is the air as clear as?
Tyrone Crystal.
What do you see before your very eyes at the heritage centres?
History come alive.
Where in Tyrone will you find the scent of wildflowers and the sweet sounds of birdsong?
Everywhere.
And finally, where is there no better place to hit the trail?
Tyrone.

Having replenished my cliché album and with darkness descending, I check out the 'fleshpots' of the village. Gortin is an unpretentious place. A notice-board says its name means 'the little field'. The village is in the parish of Badoney, and the original church was founded by St Patrick during the fifth century. In 1837 Gortin comprised 'one irregular street, containing 82 houses indifferently built'. Looking along that same irregular street 165 years later, it's hard to see how that description could be updated. Take away a handful of cars parked higgledy-piggledy, a few satellite television dishes, three neon signs, and you could easily be back in the nineteenth century, and the Ireland of the Tyrone novelist, William Carleton.

For no particular reason, other than the name was in my head, I choose the Badoney Tavern for a nightcap. Peter McKenna runs the pub. He is a Sperrins man in his early forties, coming originally from Gorticashel Upper, 'the post office and pub', in the centre of the mountains. He describes them as a vast range and says he had no idea of the hold they had on him until he left them.

'In 1986 I went to work in Essex and I remember feeling a physical pain at the flatness. I was happy in my work but there was no reference point in the landscape and when I was driving around I felt lost. I was transferred to Devon and worked in a factory that backed on to Exmoor. The round soft brown slopes of the mountain settled me again. I realised it was the nearness and the comfort of the mountain that was important to me.

'The Sperrins are very old mountains. What's left is just the tree stumps after erosion and glaciation. There were several distinct episodes of glaciation; it's thought three were of Irish origin and one was of Scottish origin. The attractions are the rivers, tributaries and burns running up and punctuating the mountains which round them off and give them their interest.'

Talking to Peter is like releasing a mountain spring, or turning on a gushing tap. Like one of his cherished Sperrin rivers in spate, the words flow from him in an unstoppable deluge. From the glimpse I've seen of the countryside, the fields and hills seem remarkably well maintained, a result, he says, of over-grazing.

'I had some Americans here last year. One guy said he owned 24,000 acres in Texas and he couldn't get over how clean our fields are. I told him most of the farms here are 24 acres and that is an awful lot easier to keep clean. He said if a tree fell down on his farm he wouldn't bother lifting it, whereas here it would be taking up too much ground and causing a hazard. The important thing to remember about the Sperrins is that they are hospitable mountains. Unlike parts of Donegal or Kerry which have vast tracts of unin-habited land that man never conquered, these mountains have always been lived on. The valleys provided a place for food and the mountains provided a place for grazing. The animals went up for a bellyful of rough pasture and when they came down at night the manure was saved. A man's dunghill, or 'doughill', was prized at the front of his house as much in those days as a BMW is today.'

Peter has thought deeply about the human history of his immutable Sperrins. He takes another sip of his coffee. He talks about the customs and attitudes of the people, or what he refers to as 'the pebble-dash of previous generations'. The tincture of the people's speech fascinates him; the area has an arcane vocabulary with its own lingua franca, accu-mulated over hundreds of years.

'We have an interwoven mix of Tyrone Irish, Scottish, and Elizabethan English with some colourful expressions. For example, people talk about "wrought" instead of "worked" – that used to be a description of what you did all day, whereas now it means describing what you do with iron. There's another saying, "we doubt" or "we suppose", when we don't either doubt or suppose, we are absolutely sure – as in "I doubt if he'll survive another week or two". The old people I grew up with had a very different way of speaking compared to the way people speak today.'

Peter has even studied the physiognomy of the people. He can tell at a glance which side of the Sperrins someone is from simply by their physical features.

'The people who live in this part of the southern Sperrins have a commonality in that they tend to be taller, more angular and have less fat on them; they are bony-featured, square-jawed and prominent-browed. But if you go into south Derry – above the county march – you will find a much fairer-haired, rounder-faced, fatter and fleshier people. You can easily see the difference in them; they are as different as day and night. They have another trait: the north Sperrin people – from the foothills and valleys – grow bald in their twenties, but in this area they are black-haired, hold their hair and turn grey. There was an awful lot of inter-breeding amongst the people of the valleys so that partly explains the facial characteristics.'

'Would most people be aware of these physical differences?'

'They would, but they wouldn't know that they'd said it. They may have passed a comment about a man such as, "he looks like a boy from the Plum, or from Park", or wherever he's from. We can tell people's ancestors for four or five generations. That's not learnt; it's absorbed on the way up.'

After returning from England, Peter began an inquisitive search for his origins, his place and his identity. He wanted to find out about the events that had shaped them and the people who occupied them before his family. We spread the map over a bar room table.

'To the biggest majority of people the Sperrins are just home. I have more of an acknowledged attachment to them because I was away. When I came back I set about the task of looking at them, getting to know them and linking the topography to the people. As far as I am concerned you can see them as well on a wet day as a dry day. When the sky is down, the mountain is near and the air is clear. On bright days everything is hazy and far away, but on a murky day, they become more relevant.'

As we finish our chat, I ask him to single out the most special thing about the Sperrins.

'It's the fact that I live in a place that has been ignored by the outside world. Yet it is a place of tremendous history and antiquity as well as great human involvement, struggle and development, not necessarily on a national or world stage. We have jewels under our feet that even we don't particularly know about. I like the continuity and the fact that we are the next generation in a place that has always been inhabited happily. It is a place of complementary human marks where people have toiled and where nature is in charge.'

By his own admission Peter McKenna is a man of the mountains. He is defined, sheltered and influenced by them – a man in love with the glens, fields and rivers, and whose

27

world revolves around them. He is content with everything he finds in them: solace, reassurance, comfort, seclusion, and even wet weather. He has delivered a Sperrins spring soliloquy. As I leave, he wishes me good luck for the walk with a parting thought.

'Don't forget what I said. The best day for the Sperrins is a wet day; it's much better than a hot day and more nourishing for the soul.'

Peter's wish for rain is fortunately unfulfilled. My first sight of the high Sperrins comes on the road to Plumbridge. Fluffy clouds march playfully along the summits of the main range, moving east, leaving the tops shining clear in the golden spring sun. On my GMR-ometer I grade the road from Plumbridge to Cranagh as at least a seven. The manicured fields of the Glenelly Valley look like the smooth green baize on billiard tables, more Tyrolean than Tyrone.

The built environment is made up of smallholdings, spick and span bungalows alongside derelict two-storey farmhouses surrounded by trees for shelter. Long-forgotten farms stand alone, with abandoned tractors or ancient rusting cars the only blot on the landscape. But these are inhabited hills full of life and this is a working countryside. I pass several houses halfway through construction. Builders' vans are parked with back doors open. It's only seven miles to Cranagh, but it takes me an hour to get there, pausing as I drive through the townlands of Eden, Castledamph, Glenroan and Meenacrane. Across the ladder farms, on the other side of the Glenelly River, I pick out small tracks –

hardly even roads – skirting up into the high hills and, in the best Tyrone tradition, 'tapering off' into fields.

When he came this way in the 1940s, the travel writer Richard Hayward was gushing in his description of the Sperrins: 'A veritable fairyland of mountain grandeur', he rhapsodised. At Cranagh I ask a tall, thin farmer, standing chatting to a man in a white van, about Mullaghclogha. He pauses, with an owl-like expression, as the Sperrin Rambler bus races past. He repeats his directions.

'The place you want is Conway's farm,' he says, throwing out a long arm.

Instantly I recognise him as a south Sperrins man, one of Peter's lean angular types, over six feet tall, and in need of fattening. His face is narrow, his cheeks hollow, his chin pointed, his nose aquiline; his features are chiselled by the Sperrins wind, his skin caulked by the rain. Leaning over the open van door, he looks skywards.

'They own that whole mountain; every blade of grass on it is theirs. Go back along that road and take the first on your right. Keep going till you hit a mountain – you can't miss their farmhouse.'

Several rounded hills rise to my left as I drive towards Conway's. They look similar. At the end of the road a woman emerges from a sheep house. Mary Conway says she's glad to have a break from lambing. Eagerly she helps me work out the lie of the mountain land. She points me a guided tour.

'That's Dart, next is Mullaghclogha – our mountain – and then Sawel which is in County Derry. Dart is the highest mountain in Tyrone; I've lived here 30 years and it has always been the highest.'

I tell her I had been told it is Mullaghclogha.

'As far as I am aware, it is Dart. You'll be wasting your time going up Mullaghclogha.'

We spread the map over the bonnet. I show her the heights of each. She guffaws, saying on her map Dart is definitely listed as being higher.

'Unless Mullaghclogha has grown in recent years. It certainly has changed its appearance, although mind you my map is a few years old.'

Her son joins us by quad bike. Eamon Conway is beefier than the average south Sperrins man. He's been distributing nuts and meal into sheep troughs. He offers me a lift uphill on the quad. I hesitate. Wouldn't it be cheating? I haven't made any rules to say I must walk up every hill and it would speed my progress. Without further ado, I put my boots on, tie the rucksack with bailer twine to the front and hop on the back of his Big Red Honda. It's my first time on a quad and I am uncertain about the road – or rather the mountain – ahead. Eamon warns me to hold on 'good 'n' tight' as we could be in for a bumpy ride. Gambolling lambs run ahead of us; two dogs follow our trail.

Mullaghclogha is, in Eamon's words, 'a big lump of a hill'. We set off down a mucky track. The engine putters as he opens two gates before we make our way via a route he calls 'the long ditch'. Sweeping round the side, he skilfully avoids rocks and bog pools. He has ridden this machine for ten years and is an old hand. As we gain higher ground, the ride gets bumpier. I cling on tight to wooden brackets at each side behind me. My seat is a bag of hay in a position normally occupied by his dog Spot, who looks on forlornly as we speed uphill. He avoids the hollow depressions of water, driving between the tussocks and hummocks. We shout to make ourselves heard over the engine.

After a twenty-minute white-knuckle ride by a track that Eamon often travels and is known only to him, we reach Tyrone's little-known crowning height of 2,088 feet – in my case slightly dazed. It is an invigorating way to scale a mountain, even though my hands are numb. We climb off and survey features of the countryside. No mountain furniture marks the summit. We look across to Dart, Sawel and other peaks. Loose clusters of farms dot the landscape. He points out the tower of Altnagelvin Hospital in the distance.

Eamon's family has farmed in the Sperrins for many generations. They have over 1,200 acres on this farm and some on adjoining land. They own all Mullaghclogha, which is about 1,000 acres. The Conways are one of the last hill-farming families in the area. Eamon worked in Belfast and Dublin but never took to city life. His heart is at home in the Sperrins, close to the earth, smelling it, walking it, 'quadding' it, and working the land.

'I never knew my way round the streets of the cities and kept getting lost,' he says. 'But I know my way round the circuit of this mountain. These are my roads and streets.'

He has quartered these tracks many times. He knows how to avoid the dips, depressions and streams, and how to find the sheep paths. The descent is even bumpier. Eamon is in his element. As we contour downhill we cross rough terrain. We lurch over a stream called the Oughtdoorish Burn, our boots and legs soaked. He roars back to me, 'Who needs bridges in Tyrone?'

If any man was ever happy in his job and in his hills, then it is Eamon Conway. But he's still pleased to have a break from the bleating ewes for an hour because he was up all night helping with the lambing. We go through an open gateway, arriving safely back in the yard to a ripple of applause from his family.

He smiles. 'We've done what I call the vicious mountain circle and you've survived to tell the tale.'

Four people have corrected my pronunciation of Sawel after I had said 'Saul'; the phonetic pronunciation is 'Saa-waal'. The woman in the Sperrin Heritage Centre becomes the fifth to set me right as she explains how to get there. I had knocked off one county top in the morning, albeit aided by quad, and after a break for a strong pot of coffee, it is time for my second of the day, this one in County Derry. The road to Sawel is single track, treeless and houseless. The mountain is swathed in afternoon sun. From the car it looks well rounded and finely proportioned – a bit like the people on the Derry side – fatter and fleshier. I have the whole place to myself. Passing the remains of several discarded cars, I climb a barbed wire fence, tearing my trousers. I jump across bog pools, soaking my boots, but manage to keep my torn trousers dry and follow a line of posts uphill.

After 40 minutes the triangulation pillar comes into

view. Sitting on rocks beside the pillar at 2,240 feet, I enjoy a late lunch. Never mind Peter's nourishment of the soul, my stomach needs to be nourished by a flask of tomato soup and ham sandwiches. From the top I look across a kaleidoscope of scenery. It is a contented picture, a wind-free 360-degree view of hills in all their infinite variety. My ringside seat looks out over a range of broad summits, sharp pointed hills, elongated ridges, undulating peaks and lower hills flanked with sitka spruce.

Looking across to Mullaghclogha – only a stone's throw away and where I had been four hours ago – I appreciate the extent of the huge gash cut out of the mountain. Eamon had told me that in his grandfather's time a devastating flood had, in one night, washed away part of the inner section of the hill, leaving it with a gouged out centre.

On the County Derry side, sitting on the high ground above Claudy (where the rounded, heavily-jowled and fair-haired Sperrinites live) are the mandatory windmill turbines that cover the countryside, turning slowly in a gentle breeze. A wheatear accompanies me for part of my descent. Hopping up and down, it moves from post to rock. After a few minutes it obligingly poses on a rock, giving me a close-up view with my binoculars of its flashy white rump, contrasting bright black wings and grey back.

As I reflect on my luck so far, I feel happy. It is day six on the road and I have not seen so much as a dark or threatening cloud, never mind a spit of rain. I touch my obsidian stone; I have not killed two birds, but with the help of one small gemstone, I have conquered two mountains in one day.

I had heard Peter McKenna talk about a music session in a pub in the nearby village of Mountfield. He had recommended it as a good venue for traditional music. It is after 10.30 p.m. when I arrive and I still manage to get there before some of the musicians. Three men are tuning fiddles in a corner of the lounge and another is fondling an accordion. With typical Tyrone straight talking, a wizened man beside me thinks my trip is a load of codswallop. He looks and sounds under the weather and swiftly disappears to take a waiting lift.

After he leaves, Michael, the owner, bolts the front door. Five minutes later it is unbolted with the arrival of Joe, the bodhrán player. I can tell that he's a south Sperrins man: long limbed, lank and thin, to the point of emaciation. He slips in sheepishly and settles himself awkwardly in a corner as he searches for his bones – the musical ones. Another ten minutes elapse and two tubby tin-whistlers arrive: most likely north Sperrins men, although I would need Peter beside me to pinpoint the exact townland. They keep coming in ones and twos; north, south, east and west Sperrin people, until no fewer than nineteen musicians occupy four tables and three-quarters of the bar space: fresh-faced fat fiddlers, gaunt and gangling guitarists, portly poets and scrawny singers, plus a meaty melodeon player.

Michael is a noted fiddler. Between pulling pints he runs round from the other side of the counter, lifts his fiddle and plays a couple of slow airs, before rushing back to attend to the needs of his thirsty customers. Platters of salmon, chicken salad, and ham and cheese sandwiches appear out of nowhere and are circulated. A pudding-faced woman beside me munches her way through a double helping of chicken salad and taps her brand new bright red and yellow trainers rhythmically to the music. She tells me the session is a regular gathering held on the first Tuesday of each month. It attracts all sorts of performers. Some nights a lot more musicians turn up; the numbers are smaller tonight. By 12.30 a.m. the *céili* is in full torrent, with no sign of abating. There are more musicians than instruments; the squeezeboxes are passed around faster than the sandwiches and readjusted to suit the temperamental musical quirks of each performer. Two young girls wait their turn for the fiddles. The tunes pour forth: 'The Nervous Man', 'The Whistler from Roscrea', 'Slieve Gallion Brae', and 'The Flower of Sweet Strabane'.

My new friend with the dazzling trainers shows two visitors from Liverpool how a four-hand reel goes. She explains the intricacies involved by using a box of matches and a packet of twenty Rothmans lying on the table. The dancing has now started in earnest and volunteers are sought. I take a new-found interest in my own trainers. A few willing dancers step forward and a man marshals them into a semblance of order. They take off at great gusto. In a broad Tyrone accent, he delivers the courtship instructions:

Couples Advance – Change Ladies
Couples Advance – Change Ladies

It is all clean fun. The Liverpudlian women and two

other brave souls attempt 'The Siege of Ennis' with little success. They give up after a few minutes of mix-ups. Two round dances – 'The Stack of Barley' and 'The Bonfire Dance' – attract some accomplished locals. The evening ends with the entire ensemble playing their hearts out, accompanied by much feet-tapping, hand-clapping, table-rapping, and head-nodding. Michael twiddles with two fiddles, choosing a smaller one to play a couple of closing airs. He hints that the hour is getting late. Someone asks what time he closes.

'The thirty-first of December and you have to be up early on New Year's Day.'

3

The Rolling Jungle Drumlins

Monaghan hills,
You have made me the sort of man I am
A fellow who can never care a damn
For Everestic thrills.

Patrick Kavanagh, 'Monaghan Hills'

'You must be the chap about the mountains,' Mrs Rooney says. Her eyes glide over me for a moment, then look heavenward. 'You'll not find too many of them in this part of the world. It's flat as a pancake here.'

I had phoned the day before to make a booking in her B&B in Clones. I mentioned I was looking for hills, saying I would be glad of any help. It is late afternoon when I arrive.

I leave my bag in my bedroom and go off in search of information. A sign in The Diamond informs me that the town's name means *Cluain Eois*, 'The Meadow of Eos'. The ancient town grew up around a monastery 1,000 years ago. Fish was an essential item in the diet of monks, therefore they built their monasteries where the fishing was good. An adjoining map lists no fewer than fifteen lakes for anglers.

Mrs Rooney is right. Mountains and Monaghan are not synonymous. The two words are rarely seen in the same sentence. Ironically, the name of the county means 'a place of little hills'. On the way across from Clogher I had seen scores of small hills or drumlins. It is also a watery landscape with dozens of lakes covering the county from Glaslough in the north to Lough Egish in the south. On my first evening in Clones I resolve to try to find out where the highest point is. The men sitting at the bar in McGurk's are watching Manchester United playing Deportivo La Coruña in a Champions' League game. I study the map, listening to the Monaghan idiom. The bar owner, Mary, asks if she can help. When I tell her what I am looking for, she suggests the answer might be the spire of St Tiernach's Church. She winks.

'We'll see if any of these learned gentlemen know the answer, provided we can drag them away from watching the match.'

She turns my question into an unexpected pub quiz and vox pops the five drinkers at the bar. Left to right, she calls out the name of each of the men sitting on high stools: Micko, Tam, Conor, Paddy, Seán; they shake their heads in silence. She admonishes them in a stiff tone. 'You're all Monaghan men good and true and you should know the answer to that.'

Their reserve begins to melt. Mary's gaze is directed firstly at Micko. He rolls a dead match between his fingers but does not offer anything. Tam shrugs and has a quiet sip of his frothy stout, looking up at a piece of goalmouth action: 'I am more of a passive spectator, more of an indoors man than an outdoors one, but am I allowed to phone a friend?' Conor brays like a donkey. In his defence he pleads that he was born in Cavan, has lived in Nottingham for 43 years and is a bit out of touch with things locally. Paddy is slightly more analytical; he says he does not climb hills for the sake of it, spitting out the word 'sake', but he agrees people take them for granted. Seán chews his bottom lip, shifts on his stool, refuses to take his eyes off the television set, and mutters something *sotto voce* in unintelligible Monaghan-speak.

The referee has stopped play. David Beckham has injured his foot and is being carried off to applause and the amusement of the drinkers. Mary thinks the answer may be somewhere in Slieve Beagh but she has heard of other high points in the south of the county. Another man, Seamus, is drawn into the discussion. Without a second thought, he says the answer is Mullyash near Castleblaney.

'I'll swear my life by that,' he insists, 'and I've lived here all of it. Even though I'm not a gambling man I would put money on that.' He places his hand on my shoulder, 'but don't let me stop you doing your research or thesis or whatever you're doing.'

It is half-time in the match. The other men suddenly take an interest in the map, running their fingers along yellow lines marking third-class roads. Cigarette ash and beer spills on to the map. Areas of greenery are scanned; they consult each other, speaking in hushed tones as if planning a bank robbery. The Beckham injury is being replayed several times from different camera angles. After much deliberation, they agree that the highest point lies to the southeast of the county, near Castleblaney. I can't verify it since no height is given for Mullyash on my map.

Ole Gunnar Solskjaer scores again for United. Seamus, who is standing beside me, advises me to go over to Castleblaney in the morning. 'It's Big Tom Country over there; y'know the singer? Ask him, if you don't believe me. He lives near Mullyash.'

I am still not convinced about Mullyash. Mary has given the matter more thought and is swung by Seamus's conviction.

'It's Mullyash Mountain,' she exclaims, ''tis a fierce height.'

More drinks are bought and the questions start to flow. There are cheers as Manchester United score a third through Giggs, winning the match 3-2. I feel I have also won my game, or at least am on the way to achieving my own Monaghan goal.

A finch-feeding frenzy is underway in Mrs Rooney's back garden. Goldfinches vie with chaffinches and greenfinches for sustenance from the seed feeder hanging from a chestnut tree. A wire mesh has been put around it to protect the birds from sparrowhawks. A blue tit noses its way in, adding to the melée, and ransacks the feeder. I embark on my own feeding frenzy, tackling a table groaning with orange juice, grapefruit, cornflakes, pancakes, scrambled eggs and bacon. My head throbs from the alcoholic excesses of the night before, but I feel jubilant, having found what appears to be the answer to the Monaghan leg of my trip. After breakfast Mrs Rooney casts some doubt.

'I am not sure about Mullyash,' she says. 'Some people say Corcaghan Hill near Monaghan town is the highest point, but I don't know, although I should. Geography is not really my strong point. Isn't it awful that a man like you has to come all this way and nobody knows the answer?'

She suggests the names of a couple of people in Clones who may be able to help me. I head for the library in search of authenticating the previous night's information. The Monaghan County Library is an imposing building in the town centre. To my dismay it's locked, but a man says if I ring the bell at the side door someone will answer. When the door is opened a woman in her mid-fifties politely says they are closed and no exceptions are allowed. I protest that I have travelled more than 100 miles to see her books. She says she cannot break the rules about opening hours and asks me to come back in the afternoon.

I persist. 'I am looking for important information about the hills. I want to find out about the soul of the landscape and talk to people about high places.'

Perhaps it's the urgency in my voice or the fact that my foot is blocking any possible closure of the door but something stops her shutting it firmly in my face; in fact she opens it wider. She gives me an incredulous look and asks if I am sure I am in the right county.

'International Year of Mountains … high places … Monaghan …'

We stand for a few moments. I sweet-talk my way into her good books.

'I know Monaghan is mostly drumlins, but I am on a quest for the highest place, which seems to be a matter of dispute. Do you know?'

Her face erupts in a wide grin. 'Oh Lord above! Now that's a question. What are you looking for on your quest – the Holy Grail? I suppose you'd better come in.'

Reluctantly, and against all the ground rules of librarianship, she leads me down a dimly-lit corridor lined with boxes of books into the inner sanctum. I am ushered into the bright main library. She has been thinking about the question and reckons that it might be Fincairn Hill, but she wouldn't 'swear by it'. Then she tells me that a new Ordnance Survey map for Monaghan is about to be launched. In less than 24 hours I've had three suggested locations volunteered as being the highest place in the county: Mullyash Mountain, Corcaghan Hill and Fincairn. Confusion is setting in. Three a day means that by Friday – if I am still here – I'll have collected the names of nine hills, all as possible contenders. Mention of the Ordnance Survey sparks off the name of a book. She disappears upstairs. Five minutes later she returns with a copy of *Ordnance Survey Memoirs of Ireland, Counties of South Ulster, 1834-1838*.

In the stillness of the library I delve hungrily into the linguistic roots of the Monaghan hills. Several hills in the parish of Ematris, I discover, are named after a peculiarity of soil or because they produced certain vegetables. The prefix 'Cor' (as in Corcaghan) is applied to some hills, and points to a conical or dome-like form, having a protuberance towards its summit. Coravacan means the 'mushroom hill', Cordiessigo 'the briar hill', Coragarr 'the garden hill' and Cortubber 'the fountain hill'. There's no indication as to what or where the county's highest point might be. I find references to some hills: Fincairn, Mullyash and Corcaghan which by now seem old friends; in another section the principal points in the Slieve Beagh Mountains are mentioned as Bragan, Carricknabrock, Greagh and Eshnaglough; the problem is that some of the Slieve Beagh range crosses the county border into Fermanagh.

I feel I am getting hot, or perhaps frustration is setting in. I call at the Canal Stores. The jungle drums, or in Monaghan's case the jungle drumlins, have been beating. Kevin Gavin is expecting me. Mrs Rooney had phoned and asked him to point me in the right direction. He is a Clones man who knows Monaghan inside out. He buttonholes me immediately and gives a potted history of the building as we walk towards the café. It opened in 1840 as the distribution centre for goods coming via the Ulster Canal. The main products brought in were coal, tobacco, tea, wine and iron. The outgoing goods included flax and unbleached linen.

We spread the map on a table. In typical no-nonsense Monaghan fashion Kevin quickly gets to the heart of the matter.

'The highest point in Monaghan is Corcaghan in the parish of Aghabeg,' he states emphatically. 'I know that for a fact and I'll tell you how. About 30 years ago a man came from Tipperary to erect a television mast for Telefís Éireann. The place they chose was Corcaghan Hill. A few years later they put up a booster station beside it which greatly improved reception.'

Kevin warms to his theme. 'I know for a fact that those people do their research thoroughly because they have to place the masts in the highest point in the entire county. It makes sense, doesn't it? Why would they go anywhere else?'

I express some scepticism and mention Slieve Beagh in the northwest of the county.

'If you don't believe me then call the people in the Phoenix Park in Dublin and ask them because they were heavily involved with the mast.'

We look at Corcaghan on my beer-stained and torn map. There are no contours or indications that there is any kind of hill in the area. Our discussion is suddenly interrupted by the receptionist, Christine, who comes running into the café calling 'mountain man ... mountain man'.

'You should know this,' she shouts to me. 'They're asking on the radio where the Appalachian Trail is – have you any idea? ... and it's such a lovely name I would like to know what it means. Can you help me?'

'It's in the eastern US,' I reply. 'The whole range covers

44

quite a large area, but I don't know what the name means. Are you going to phone in?'

Christine rushes off laughing. Kevin continues his Monaghan monologue as if we have never been interrupted.

'I think you should trust me and believe what I say. I know my facts. Why don't you go over there and take a look for yourself? I think the man who maintains the mast lives beside it.'

I agree that it sounds plausible. Kevin gives me directions, saying I won't be disappointed.

'You g'out that road and head for Newbliss, turn left at Swan's Cross, then take the road straight for Monaghan town. God bless you.'

Along the road to Corcaghan I startle two fat magpies into a tree. Criss-crossing Monaghan is a simple pleasure; uncluttered roads, quiet single tracks, high hedges. No road rage, no road warriors, no road hogs; in fact, there are no other cars on the road, only a tractor coming from Newbliss up to its back axles in mud. I pull in to the side to let it pass. A few miles along a couple of sheep in the back of a prehistoric Datsun stare out at me.

Swarms of drumlins accompany my route. The term drumlin is derived from the Irish *droimnin*, meaning 'small ridge'. It refers to the shape of the hills formed under glaciers, and not to their composition. Drumlins are low, hogbacked mounds of soil, usually between 50 and 100 feet high and up to half a mile long. Monaghan has hundreds of them. My eyes search the horizon; no sign of any peaks, just drumlins – ahead of me, behind me, to the right and to my left, uniform in appearance but, like pizza, all with different toppings: drumlins with lounging Charollais cattle, drumlins with trees, drumlins without trees, drumlins with primroses, drumlins with mobile phone masts, drumlins with flags, drumlins with dozing sheep, drumlins with telegraph poles, drumlins with fences and hedges running across them, drumlins with motte mounds, and drumlins dressed in nothing but short grass.

I crane my neck for anything vaguely resembling a view. Only occasionally does the land lift to a hillside of any size. The road to Corcaghan climbs gently, almost imperceptibly, for two miles until I reach the masts. They stand beside a locked-up water treatment plant. The first one, built 30 years ago, is free-standing; there is no one around. The newer one bristles with antennae and half a dozen satellite dishes. It is surrounded by a high fence with a padlocked gate. Afternoon mist has closed in and shuts down long-range views. I can just make out the spire of Monaghan Cathedral. I walk down the road to a farmhouse with an open front door. A woman, bringing in shopping bags from her car, says she doesn't know much about the masts. She invites me in.

Maggie Traynor says there is no doubt in her mind that Corcaghan is the highest place in Monaghan. Her husband, who knew the hills well, died several years ago.

'It's a pity he isn't here,' she sighs, 'because he would have known all that sort of stuff. I remember him saying it is 610 feet above Monaghan town. Would you like Earl Grey or Barry's?'

She pours me a mug of strong thick tea. There's a pause in the conversation. She points through the window.

'Children have also come from the local schools to get information. They were doing a project and their teachers brought them up to look at Corcaghan Hill, so for them it's certainly the highest place. On a clear day you can look over to the Slieve Beagh Mountains and you look down on them from here. It used to be called Corcaghan Hill, but it's not called that now. The young crew don't call it a hill. They don't speak like the older people. And they've no interest either in what's going on around them these days – just the television, discos and drink. That's all they want. When I was growing up around here you took an interest in the countryside and in what your neighbours were doing. Now they don't seem to care.'

Maggie is a small, lightly-built woman with black hair. Her red fleece has a chunky zip three-quarters of the way closed up.

'Everybody says it's lovely up here, but I am working all the time and don't get much chance to enjoy it. I am looking after three children and 3,000 hens and it's not an easy task. Sometimes you wonder what it's all about.'

I ask about the work involved in tending the hens.

'They're free-range and I have to check on them at least twice a day. I gather the eggs, change the paddocks, and check the feathers and drinkers, so there's plenty of work. The men from the Department come every so often to check up on them and I have to make sure all the regulations are adhered to.'

Maggie produces an apple tart from the cupboard and cuts me a large triangular slice. She slides it across the kitchen table on a blue-patterned plate. She seems alarmed that I am on my own and asks if I ever feel lonely. She would not have allowed her husband to roam the country.

'I married a farmer,' she confides, 'because I knew he'd have to be here all the time. You can't swan off all over the place in this job.'

It is time for me to be 'swanning' onwards. I glide up to the northern part of the county again. In the library in Clones I'd read about an area known as the 'Seven Hills of McKenna' in Emyvale. I had come across a reference to them in a booklet called *Clann MacKenna* and noticed the name of Seamus McCluskey who lives in the village.

McKennas appear to dominate every facet of local life. In the past few days I had seen signs on white vans advertising their wares. They feature in every realm of business. There are electricians, mechanics and surveyors; they run shops, cafés and pubs; they will fix your teeth, re-heel your shoes, repair your car, sort out your plumbing, paint your house, clean your windows, mend a leaking gutter and cut your grass. Not content with all this, their prowess in sport is renowned: there are celebrated footballers, boxers, rugby players and fishermen.

I join a conga line of vehicles on the way into Emyvale; so much for traffic-free roads. In Holland's hardware store I ask about the McKenna name. A man in the shop smiles at me through broken brown teeth. He says he is known as 'Peter Pat' McKenna but he never 'went backways to look into the history of it'. The owner directs me to Seamus McCluskey: 'He lives across there in a bungalow on the other side of the street. He's an ancient historian and he'll tell you all you want to know about the McKennas.'

Seamus is a retired teacher in his early seventies. He is a softly spoken erudite man with a love of local history.

'You're certainly in the right place,' he laughs. 'Emyvale is the epicentre of McKenna country. Practically everybody is a McKenna. If you're not McKenna, you are descended from one. Although I am McCluskey, my grandmother was a McKenna.'

North Monaghan has hundreds of families with the surname McKenna. Patronymics and nicknames are used to distinguish between them.

'You have to have nicknames,' he explains; 'otherwise it's like looking for a needle in a haystack. Tourists come regularly from America, Australia and New Zealand trying to trace their McKenna ancestors. The first question I ask them is to give me the nickname, and it's half the battle if they have it. There are families known as "the master", "yankee", "thump", "willy harry", "oiney", "mickey joe", "james pat", "the hill", "fig-a-harley", "larry", "crush", "roe" and "pat tammy". There are the McKenna Mores, the McKenna Beggs and the Shan McKennas. They all come from the Irish, and I wouldn't call them nicknames at all but family names.'

The McKennas from north Monaghan went all over the world, leaving their mark, from Chile to New Zealand and from the United States to Australia. I ask about the Seven

Hills of McKenna.

'Well, Rome had its seven hills,' Seamus quips, 'so McKenna had to have them too in Emyvale.'

Without a pause for thought he rattles off the names: Tully, Derrygassan, Scarnageeragh, Cornacreeve, Emy, Pullis and Derrynashallog. They are not big hills, but drumlins. On the vexed question of the county's highest point, he says it's certainly not one of the Seven Hills. He produces a Second World War map that was used by the British Army and came into his family's hands. Seamus is convinced the answer is in the Slieve Beagh range. He is strong on the minutiae of local topography.

'The highest point of Slieve Beagh is actually in Fermanagh,' he asserts. 'So that means if we come across the border on the Monaghan side we find a point called Eshnabrack at 1,190 feet.'

'There you are,' he points triumphantly. 'I would say that is the official highest point and is the spot you want.'

Satisfied I have now found the true county top, I start out from Clones the next morning for Slieve Beagh. I pass through a series of villages that in some cases are no more than post offices at crossroads: Bellanode, Scotstown, Knockatallan, Barratitoppy. At the Slieve Beagh Centre the reception desk is unstaffed. I shout a couple of 'hellos' and eventually find a man carrying trestle tables in an inner room. He's surprised to see me. He asks me to wait for a few minutes, saying the man I want is John Moyna.

'He is big time into walks,' he says, 'big time. There is

not a corner of that mountain he doesn't know.'

He goes off down the main road and arrives back with John ten minutes later.

'That's a powerful day, isn't it?' John says.

I explain my mission and we discuss Eshnabrack. He confirms that it is the highest point in Monaghan. John is keen to show me the mountain. We drive for two miles and turn on to a thin ribbon of a road. He loves the idea of my journey. He laughs raucously. 'Holee Jay-sus that's some trip sir, isn't it?' We continue along the road until it peters out into a dirt track.

'This is you here,' he says, pointing to a small turning area. We seem to be about halfway up the mountain. John is 42. He started hillwalking only in recent years and loves the outdoors. We walk side by side at an even pace along a turf track. He is loquacious and speaks at high speed. Much of the boggy terrain is black and there is a strong burning smell from the peat. The previous week a fire raged for five days. It involved crews from three areas and could be seen for many miles.

We walk across more burnt patches of heather and scrub to the top of Eshnabrack. It is not a steep climb, and takes us only about half an hour. The views are extensive. There is no clearly defined summit but this is the reaffirmation that I need. John says local people call the area 'The Rock'. We look across to Corcaghan Hill. 'Some view this, isn't it? Any time we get snow, Corcaghan also gets it, but we seem to hold it a bit longer which proves we are higher, y'know what I mean?'

I notice how John indulges in what linguists call 'up-speak'. This is the practice, common in parts of Ulster, of introducing an interrogative lift or changing the intonation at the end of some sentences to a rising tone. It often manifests itself with sentences that end on a high intonation with the addition 'you know' tagged on as a question. It is also assertive. Several times in the past week, while travelling through Tyrone and Monaghan, I had come across examples of this speech pattern.

John points out an area known as Shane Barnagh's Stables beside the Three Counties Hollow, the spot where Monaghan, Fermanagh and Tyrone meet. He talks about setting up the Slieve Beagh Centre and about some of the changes that have taken place.

'Within the past two years the turf machines have been put off this area as they were destroying all before them and seriously damaging the blanket bog. Do y'know what I mean? There was a big area of bog where the heather disappeared, but there are still about half a dozen farmers who cut turf here by hand. Years ago each family was allocated a portion of the mountain known as a "turbary" and they were all involved in cutting and drying turf.'

On our return journey we come across a man making notes in his car. Simon Travis is packing up after spending three days looking for rare birds. We stop to talk to him about his work. He is wearing Swarovski binoculars around his neck – the sign of a serious bird-addict since prices for these top of the range optics start at €1,000.

Simon is a conservationist who works as a wildlife

consultant. He's carrying out an environmental impact assessment on the site of a proposed windfarm development on Slieve Beagh. His job is to establish bird numbers throughout the summer. He is focusing on some key species, specifically hen harriers, peregrine falcon and merlin, but also curlew, golden plover and dunlin. When the survey is complete the information will be put on maps and sent to the company proposing the windfarm.

The bird that interests Simon most is the hen harrier, *Circus cyaneus*. On three days in the hills he has had a couple of sightings. It is still early in the season for them but he has seen males setting up territory and displaying. They are trying to attract the female into their habitat and he believes they will set up a site for the summer.

Simon is a professional ornithologist by training and is energised by his job.

'Hen harriers are famous for a food pass,' he explains. 'The male flies in with food in his talons, the female flies underneath, turns upside down and takes the food from him. They also do a thing called sky-dancing, which is like being on a big dipper. They go very high, then drop in an undulating flight. It's all part of the courtship display and is an impressive sight. He is trying to prove to the female that once she is nesting on the eggs in dense heather, he has got to provide food for her and when the chicks hatch he has to provide food for them. The female will come off the nest but tends to stick around the chicks until they are older.'

Starting at seven each morning, Simon reconnoitres the territory from the bottom edges of Slieve Beagh, gradually moving around the contours to the top. Often he will be in the field for up to twelve hours a day. He knows the breeding and feeding habits of the hen harrier as well as John knows the mountain.

'Their flight is fantastic and is almost butterfly-like. They drift along, waiting to see something, and then suddenly pounce. They feed on mice, skylarks and meadow pipits. When you see them at the shore they are entirely different birds. The male is like a Wedgwood blue and sometimes blends into the sky.'

We search the skies for a few minutes but *Circus cyaneus* has slipped back in to his mountain retreat. I say farewell to Simon and John. I had stayed longer than planned, nosing around the jungle of Monaghan's rolling drumlins.

4

No Cheese, No Sheep, No Mushrooms

We have no prairies
To slice a big sun at evening –
Everywhere the eye concedes to
Encroaching horizon,
Is wooed into the cyclops' eye
Of a tarn.

Seamus Heaney, 'Bogland'

Cruising the main street in Longford I had hoped to find a friendly café for a morning coffee. The Longford Cafeteria turns out to be more of a 'smoke-ateria'. I leave without waiting for service. The town has recently had a bad press. Earlier in the year it was labelled the 'worst town' in Ireland. This was the result of a government report that found it was the worst in terms of poverty, education, health and crime, compared to towns of similar size in areas of Ireland which had applied for particular forms of government funding.

It has a certain run-down, honky-tonk, mildly bohemian feel to it. Plastic signs and new buildings mingle with the old; cars and vans sit awkwardly in the main street. It is not hard to see why Longford has been denigrated: parking and traffic problems, decrepit approach roads with dumped cars, litter, filthy signposts and more than its share of dilapidated and scruffy buildings with peeling paint. The River Camlin is awash with cans, bottles and plastic bags. Street and river cleanliness is not a priority in Longford.

In my enquiries I had been pushed from tourist office to post office, and from librarian to priest. The woman in the tourist office said to try the bookshop where the assistant said the owner was out ('he'll be back at five') and directed me to Luke Baxter at the chemists ('he's busy with prescriptions'); he said to ask Mary Reynolds in the library (who wasn't in) but whose colleague suggested Father Casey at Ennybegs (who wasn't answering his phone) and so it went on. I tried other names, all unavailable, at meetings, or otherwise hiding from men on mountain quests. The important information gleaned was that Cornhill, sometimes referred to as Cairn Hill and in the middle of the county, is Longford's highest peak of attainment.

Apart from the fact that no one wants to talk to me, I am discovering that Longford is a strangely inconspicuous county. There are no spectacular views and no great ranges of hills to admire. It has always had what might be termed a low profile, physically and politically. There are few mountains of any size to push the transmission of my car into low gear. There is no easily defined Longford landscape: no cheese, no sheep, no mushrooms, no crafts – what have they been doing? They must have cashed in on something. They don't even make jokes about it.

In Valentine's the acoustic wallpaper is a mix of folk and traditional. Everyone sitting around the horseshoe-shaped bar has a mobile phone and everyone is talking or texting. A woman of about twenty pulls funny faces as she texts on a yellow Nokia; a ginger-haired man leans forward on his stool punching in letters; a group of pony-tailed girls chatter volubly on theirs, and a goateed man opposite me, wearing a navy baseball cap, hugs his close to his ear. He smiles knowingly. I catch gossipy snatches:

– You're a busy bloody bee I am telling ya … how's the big bad world treating you anyway?

– OK see you at the Backstage at eight …

– We'll all go to Slashers later – I can't get away earlier …

– He's a class act that fella, isn't he … ?

– Ah lukid, I was pissed again last night so I am takin' it easy …

The bright-eyed waitress pours me a filter coffee and talks about the mobile phenomenon.

'This used to be called "the happy hour" – between six and seven – it's now called the mobile phone hour, especially as it's Friday night.'

She raises her eyebrows and screws up her nose. 'It's like a symphony. There was a Frenchman here last week and he couldn't believe it. Do y'know the funny thing is they're probably only calling each other from one end of the bar to the other. Now how sad is that?'

A bearded, mobile-phoneless man arrives and stands beside me at the bar. He asks me questions with a delicate but firm insistence. I turn them back on him, responding to his questions with another question. He seems flummoxed. He stares at me with a puzzled look, as though I am on a high-octane substance. He's alarmed that I'm on my own for the whole trip. I am pleased with his curiosity and the fact that he specialises in asking the supreme journalistic question: Why?

'Why am I making this journey?' 'Why did I not bring my family?' 'Why did I not want to travel abroad and see the "real" world?' 'Why am I fascinated so much by mountains?' 'Why do I ask so many questions myself?' 'Why de hell am I in Longford of all places?' and 'Why don't I have a drink?' I answer them all easily, except the penultimate one.

An orange ball of sun is sinking slowly as I drive out to Cornhill behind a cream David Brown tractor. I think there is about an hour of daylight left to make it to the top. From Drumlish, it's ten minutes' drive to within a short walk of the summit. There are no signs but the woman in the bar was specific: 'Follow your nose and when you get to Drumlish you'll see the mast soon enough. It's not a very dizzy height.'

The visitor to Longford does not suffer altitude sickness. There are few lofty summits, few dizzy heights. Vertigo is not a problem. There is no trekking, no mountain skiing, no sweating, no trouble reaching the summit, especially with a road most of the way to the top. Under the fiery light of the sunset, I clamber over a stile of concrete blocks and walk up a tarmac path. A herd of noisy cattle enjoy a grassy supper. They pause and lift their heads, watching me closely. Incongruously, a goat stands in their midst, equally curious at my late presence. Two blackbirds shoot across a field, chuckling as they go. A lane runs along one side of the mast up to the trig point at 916 feet. The view is partially obscured by trees planted en masse to the top of one side of the hill. Like so many Irish hillsides, it is another county top all 'spruced up'.

The landscape is familiar. I watch twilight gently fall over a latticework of small fields, lakes, hedges and more small fields, lakes and hedges. The topography of Longford, like its Ulster neighbours – Cavan and Monaghan – is made up of a large amount of water. Lights flicker and glow in houses. It's lighting up time in half a dozen villages. A red light comes on at the top of the mast. Thin grey threads of smoke trickle from chimneys.

Beside the summit pillar, several stones litter the ground with the names of townlands in coloured paint: Dernacross, Ennybegs, Doorock, Kiltemer. I note unseen noises and reflect on the clarity of sound: a low hum from the shed attached to the mast; the drone of a tractor; the discharge of a shotgun; the bedtime howl of a dog; the shrieks of children playing outside; the honk of a pheasant; avian evensong, including a hooting owl and the hubbub of rooks and jackdaws.

Before darkness envelops the hill, I stroll back to the car where a bushy-eyebrowed man with ears like satellite dishes is locking up his farmyard and tucking up his John Deere for the night. The tractor engine throbs quietly. Three young boys stand around in the yard. The farmer says the local parish priest organises an annual walk to the top of Cornhill. I ask about the goat with the cattle. He says it's a sign of luck, to do with superstition, or *piseog*; the goat stops the cattle eating any poisonous weeds and helps keep them calm. He talks bluntly about the interminable rows of conifers which he regards as a desecration of the landscape. As a boy he can remember that the mountain was bald.

'They're a terrible blot on the countryside and no one wants them. The sitka has darkened the entire face of the country. They've also damaged lakes, rivers and in some places the wildlife habitat. The foresters love them for the money they make. They scatter them over the hillsides because they grow quickly in a wet climate and provide a fast return in about 40 years. A friend of mine felt so strongly about them that he threatened to strike a match and burn them down. He called them "shitka" spruce trees and said they were "rural terrorism". He felt they were taking away something of his soul when they took away that view of one of the few hills that we have. He regarded it as an assault on the Longford landscape.'

Climbing mountains is normally an automatic entry ticket to local society, or at least some bonhomie in a pub; mostly, but not always. There are exceptions. Take later that same night when no one wants to strike up a conversation in the Mountain Tavern in Drumlish. It's Friday night, the end of a busy week for most working people; time for a drink and the cultural highlight of the television week, 'The Late Late Show', which is absorbing the five men supping pints at the bar. They don't even give me a second glance. Nor do they appear to have a single controversial opinion on the endless spread of *Picea sitchensis* on the surrounding hills.

Behind the bar the surly-faced woman with hairs sprouting on her chin doesn't appreciate being interrupted. She glares at me with eyes as colourless as the rain when I mention the coolness of the night. She returns a filthy look when I ask for a hot port. She disappears into the kitchen in search of a kettle and turns on the tap.

Unable to find the charm tap, she shouts out: 'Sugar in that?'

'Just one please.'

'Any cloves?'

'Yes please.'

'Lemon?'

'No thanks.'

She goes off in search of sugar and cloves. I watch the second hand ticking on the Father Canning Gaels clock hanging to one side of the bar. On my café and pub travels I've come across a selection of quotations and sayings contained on 'A Spoonful of Irish' sachets from the Gem sugar company. They provide a sweetener for coffee, and food for thought along the way. I muse over one in the glass dish on the bar counter: 'Beauty does not boil the pot.'

On the television the Irish actor Colin Farrell is being interviewed. The surly one pauses to watch while the world's slowest kettle boils. It takes a total of fourteen minutes to boil, pour, stir, clove, and serve my drink. I browse tourist leaflets: 'Leisurely Longford: relax in the heart of the midlands.'

I ask if she has ever climbed Cornhill. Nope. She sniffs. So this pub has no connection to it? Nope. Tight-lipped, she hoists herself on to her monosyllabic perch, turns stonily to stare up at the screen, arms folded over the word 'Diesel' emblazoned across the front of her T-shirt, the colour of fruit cocktail orange. After ten minutes of television boredom, I order another port which produces a delightful grimace. I didn't really want one, but thought the kettle might take slightly less time to boil: eleven minutes. I return to my literature: 'Charming Longford: a place that retains a welcoming rural magic.'

Like an unhappy parrot, she returns to her perch, settling back to watch the television, without a flicker, smile, tear or laugh. Could it be possible, I silently wonder, to be so bored with everything? The reticent five chatter quietly amongst themselves. One of them asks how they get the audience for the show. She grunts. At least I am not the only one with whom she doesn't want to communicate. I pick up my brochures: 'Friendly Longford: easy to reach, hard to leave.'

It is certainly not hard to leave the Mountain Tavern. I do so immediately after knocking back my second tepid port.

Sometimes, on the road, there's an expectation that things can only get better. In Longford the reverse is the case. The B&B on the outskirts of town is the worst in which it has ever been my sad misfortune to stay. I had heard of 'shabby chic', but never 'shabby nasty'. My room is pure Irish guesthouse: regulation hideously floral-patterned frayed curtains, regulation peeling wallpaper, regulation worn beige carpet (with a hint of stickiness), regulation twelve-inch television on which you can get only two channels (the others always have fuzzy reception), regulation low-wattage light bulbs, and regulation en suite in which it is impossible to dry yourself with the regulation size threadbare towel. The bedroom floor sags gently, just like the old mattress. Not as much as an Impressionist reproduction print adorns the walls. The views are not much better. Through the trees I see the top of a dilapidated greenhouse. A fine-sieved rain, in which the Irish midlands specialise, falls over the countryside. In one corner of a field a single horse stands motionless. Four cows are wreathed in their own breath.

Over the regulation breakfast – cold, hard toast and tar-like tea – I listen to a report on the radio on global population. During the next 100 years the planet will be getting a little less crowded. A team of demographers predicts that the world population will peak in 70 years' time and will be falling by the end of the twenty-first century. The report, sponsored by scientists in Europe, Japan and the United States, says there will be concerns about the population growth for Africa and India where people will still be living in unhealthy conditions and poverty. All this should not present any problems in Longford where the population is only 30,000. In fact, it is one of the few counties in Ireland to have shown a decrease in its population. I ask the young man serving why so many people are leaving.

'There's nothing here,' he says. 'The twenty-first century means nothing here. Longford town missed out on the twentieth century, so they've a lot of catching up to do. It's a dull place this – dull as ditch-water. If you lived here you'd soon discover that. The people are suspicious, mean and unfriendly, and that's the kindest thing I can think to say about them.'

Instinctively, on occasions, you know when it's right to cut and run. I pay up, check out, and rev off, skedaddling out of Longford as fast as my wheels will take me to my eyrie in the mountains of Connemara.

My Saturday morning drive skirts an area the map calls the Plains of Mayo, from where the mountains of north and west Mayo come into view. I have barely left Claremorris when they confront me: Croagh Patrick in the far distance, the Nephin Beg range to the north, and south of me, the Partry Mountains. It is a mixed countryside of stone walls and hedges. The road is narrow, with crests, dips and turns. I drive through a succession of historic hamlets – Ballyglass, Cornanagh, Carnacon, Ballintubber and Killawalla – some of the placid rural communities making up part of the Tóchar Valley. I am on my way to a cottage in northern Connemara to tackle the highest summits of the five counties in the Province of Connaught.

On an elevated site by the side of the road, before it rushes downhill to Ballyglass, the skeletal structure of a partially built two-storey house stands square on to the road, surrounded by scaffolding. The main structure, built of brown bricks, is in place; piles of tiles sit on the roof. There are square and rectangular spaces for the windows. Two white transit vans, cement mixers, and a digger are parked outside. No work is in progress on this Saturday morning. A wheelbarrow stands idle. A five-litre plastic bottle of sparkling water sits on a piece of wood. Long lathes of timber lie up against a side wall. A twelve-foot steel ladder rests against another wall. Small mountains of bricks and concrete pipe sit around beside opened bags of cement and a five-foot castle of sand. An assortment of barrels and tins are strewn around. Jackdaws sniff the ground searching for crumbs. A solitary silent blackbird enters, sitting on an upstairs window lintel, and like a foreman, surveys the site with a look of approval.

Because of its abbey ('lovingly restored with a simple elegance', says my guidebook), all signposts lead to Ballintubber. The village is buzzing with activity. About 150 guests are gathered for a wedding. The car park is lined with BMWs, new Rovers, Jaguars, a Porsche and a magenta open-top Lotus.

I stop to admire the fashionistas of a Tóchar Valley society wedding. The men in their dark Sunday-best suits with buttonholes wield camcorders a CNN cameraman would be proud to possess. A jangle of women dripping with jewellery makes its way across the car park. Their hats boast outlandish designs that could grace lady's day at Ascot: twirling snake-like creations, floppy feathered formations, tall cylindrical affairs, and perched precariously, be-ribboned, swirling numbers. Most wear figure-hugging dresses or long skirts in the season's colours of pink, lemon and champagne white. Delicately, in their high heels, they pick their way over loose stones, uncertain if they'll make the short distance from car park to hotel foyer without tripping, or their hats taking on a life of their own. One young woman struggles in the wind to cope with her impedimenta: hat, camera, handbag and mobile phone held to her ear. She finishes her call on the pavement, sobbing into her phone at the absurdity of it all, and makes her own vows of celibacy to a friend.

'I am never ever, and I mean never ever, gettin' married.'

5

The Grey Bald One

Then there are the grand bare mountains ... with caprices of sunlight playing about their solemn heads, and shining into their dark purple depths; and below are waters untraceable and incalculable.

Harriet Martineau, *Letters from Ireland*

If any county is defined by its hills, then it is Mayo. There is a long and proud mountain-climbing heritage. It is home to the most climbed and arguably most famous mountain in Ireland, Croagh Patrick. Every year, on the last Sunday in July, thousands of pilgrims take part in the annual walk of 2,510 feet to the top. I am not averse to climbing the mountain, but since it is not the highest point in the county, it would be a waste of my time. My target is Mweelrea, a much less-visited mountain, lying twenty miles round the coast on the south-west edge of the county overlooking the sea. The problem for Mweelrea is that it has been outgunned and outshone by Croagh Patrick: '*La montagne sacrée de l'Irlande*', and '*Ireland's Heiliger Berg*' as it is marketed to the French and Germans.

The girl in the newsagents in Westport asks me to spell it again.

'M-W-E-E-L-R-E-A.'

'I've never heard of it,' she admits. She taps the letters slowly into her computer screen … 'ME, sorry, MW …'

I lean across to see what comes up.

'There's nothing listed here. Hold on and I'll ask the man above.'

I wonder what God could possibly know about Mayo's highest mountain that a computer doesn't.

'I mean Joe. He's de boss – upstairs in the bargain books department. Joe! Joe! Somebody here wants to find out something about a mountain. Joe, are you up there? He must've gone for a cuppa.'

I stock up on some basic provisions: bread, butter, milk, tea, coffee, cheese, fruit, soup and newspapers. On the audio cassette in the car, Henry David Thoreau is cogitating on the value of newspapers; he didn't like them: 'I have never read any memorable news in a newspaper.'

I would like to do without them too but my journalistic craving demands a daily fix. I had bought *The Irish Times*, the *Guardian*, and the *Connaught Telegraph*. The last was founded in 1828 (when Thoreau was eleven) and has a proud motto of which he surely would have approved: 'Be just and fear not.' I scan its front-page headlines:

Suicide link to church sexual abuse

Profits and passengers soar at Knock

Measles outbreak causes health concern

Man produced screwdriver when approached by Garda

Henry, you are correct. There is nothing memorable, nothing new under the Connaught sun. I've read it all before.

In the hierarchy of Mayo's hills, Mweelrea narrowly pips Nephin, which lies to the north east, to claim elevational superiority by a mere 42 feet. In *An Irish Journey* in 1941, Seán O'Faoláin ignored it in favour of Nephin, which he called Mayo's 'tutelary mountain'. He said there is no escaping Nephin and Nephin Beg. As I noticed on my drive across, it acts like a guardian over the surrounding countryside. O'Faoláin liked towns with lakes, which he felt 'softened and sweetened' some counties. He conveys a memorable description of what the mountains mean to him:

The farther you get from the really mountainy region the more you need that softening touch. The mountains have force, and they excite. The flat land to the east lies on the mental stomach like a cold pancake, and its towns are flatulent, sour towns, as if they had never been able to digest life. The lakes add lyricism, and give dignity.

Mayo is rich in mountainy roads. Narrow boreens run

up into the hills throughout the county. The Doo Lough Pass leads down to Killary Harbour where I follow the road to Letterfrack. From my base in a small sea-coast cottage on the northern edge of Connemara, my plan is to launch a concentrated attack on the mountains of Connaught. After a week spent driving through the north midlands, the mountains are enormous. It's Saturday evening by the time I arrive. A ten-minute drive along the famine relief road takes me to Rosroe Pier. Local people, in return for food rations, built the road in 1846. Apart from my ride on a quad, all my approaches to mountains so far have been conventional. In climbing Mweelrea, I decide on a different tack, approaching it by boat from across Killary Harbour. My priority is to find a boatman willing to take me across.

The pier is deserted. Five upturned currachs lie tied down with blue and green rope. Secured in place with concrete blocks and resting on Goodyear and Bridgestone tyres, they look as if they have been anchored for the winter. A man called Peter, standing with binoculars at the front gate of his house, advises me to ask at the salmon fishery offices on Monday for information about a boat. He says I should speak to Abdon Ryan, who is in charge of the fish farm.

Peter is a tall, silver-haired man dressed head to toe in black. On his feet he wears a pair of black Wrangler slip-ons. Black hair flows out of his nose and ears. His eyes narrow as he talks to me.

'Lived here all my life and I've never got round to climbing it,' he says, rolling his eyes up the slopes. 'I don't think I'd be fit to now, not at my time of life. I should've done it when I was younger but I was always too busy. Mind you, it's a hardy six-hour slog to the top.'

Peter trains his binoculars on sheep halfway up the eastern slope.

'They can't go much higher than where they are or they'd be needing oxygen.'

We stand side by side looking up at the formidable presence of Mweelrea. He pronounces it 'Mile-ray'.

He looks me over. 'Did you know it's called that because it's a mile across the Killary to the other side and it's a mile to the top of it?'

His rugged face breaks into a mischievous grin.

'I know you don't believe that. Its real name means "the bald king".'

'Has it changed much over the years?'

'Apart from a few landslides that have come down with very heavy rain, I don't think it has changed its appearance at all. It's a big lump of ice really, but it has witnessed some changes. If it could talk about what it has seen and the winds it has suffered, that would be something – but it tells no tales.'

'What's it like in winter?'

'We had six months of rain here one winter. Then it rained non-stop a couple of winters ago. We never got a dry day for the whole season. The winter just past was a hard one too. We went for nine days with no electricity and no telephone.'

He tells me about a suggestion several years ago to put in a cable car to entice people to the top.

'It never got off the ground. It would have cost millions

but it would have brought in the tourists in jumbo loads and would have been a great attraction. It's what the area needs. It was a missed opportunity.'

Peter delivers a salutary warning.

'A man can meet his match on Mweelrea. I've heard of people suffering vertigo and others losing their way in the mist. It can be a place of great beauty but also temperamental, moody and menacing. Watch yourself.'

My alarm clock is set for 7.00 a.m. but I am awakened an hour earlier by a howling gale and lashing rain. I lie restlessly in bed before daring to pull back the curtains. Mweelrea has gone. There is no mountain; the one I am meant to climb today is not there. Enshrouded in a misty cloak from its rock solid feet at the shore to the cusp, it does not exist in physical terms. It has been snuffed out. Fully aware of the vagaries of the Irish weather, I make breakfast and prepare my rucksack.

Streams gush down hillsides in torrents and the heavy rain lashes the windscreen as I drive to the pier to see what the fishermen say. Abdon Ryan leaves the decision to me. If I want to cross Killary Harbour, he'll get someone to take me. He looks up at Mweelrea and says the winds at the top will be 80 miles an hour.

'You'll see absolutely nothing up there and it could get worse. The winds can even get up to 100 on a really bad day. That mountain stands full in the teeth of the Atlantic gales. We call it "cloudland" up there.'

He phones Met Éireann's Weatherdial which provides a

fax forecast service. While we're waiting for the fax, Abdon tells me about an Englishman they brought across several years ago who got hopelessly lost. With his bike, he had hoped to climb Mweelrea, continue through the valley and cycle up to Louisburgh. He had told the gardaí to expect him around five. When he had not shown up by six, the police phoned the fish farm and set out to look for him. After a long search, they found him as darkness fell, stranded on a cliff edge with his bicycle propped by his side.

Abdon is site manager of the salmon farm. The company was set up in 1986 by a Norwegian firm trying to diversify from tobacco production. It sold out in 1992 to an Irish company which owned it until 1999. It was then resold to another Norwegian firm. About fifteen people are employed full-time. At other times of the year another five or six people are brought in to help. Abdon is one of three trained divers. Once a week they carry out a mortality check in each net picking up dead fish.

'We have to find out how they died. They could have been attacked by birds, so there may be a predation problem that needs to be addressed or perhaps some sort of disease, although that is rare. At the moment we could have up to fifteen dead fish a week per cage.'

The average size of the salmon they bring in at the start of each year is 80 or 90 grams.

'We grow them on, feed them and start to harvest them in May the following year, by which time they should have reached an average size of four kilos.'

The finished product – freshly gutted salmon – ends

up in France, Spain and Germany. Some of it is used for smoking. I ask about the state of the industry.

'In 2000 we had probably the best prices ever; 2001 was probably the worst. It has improved slightly for four-kilo fish and above, but the big problem is cheap salmon coming in from Chile and Norway. They have low production costs and their feed and labour is much cheaper.'

The fax chunters into life. Abdon hands me a copy:

Forecast for the Province of Connacht updated at 0600 hours. Cloudy with scattered outbreaks of rain, heavy and persistent in places; highest temperatures 10 to 13 in a fresh south and south-east wind.

The implications of the forecast are clear. It means I'll be spending the day firmly on the ground. I pick up on the word 'fresh' to describe the wind. It's one of those words favoured by meteorologists, which can mean anything from windy conditions to gale force. Abdon peers out through the window and looks up.

'I would say it's heading for a blizzard within the next hour. We'll take you there if you really want to go, but I wouldn't guarantee you'll do much walking or that you'll return in one piece.'

We agree to leave it for the day. Abdon says the best day to try again will be Thursday or perhaps Friday – my last day because I leave on Saturday morning.

Michael O'Toole is preparing to open one of Ireland's most

idyllically sited museums for another day. Sitting hard by the rainy shores of Killary Harbour, the wool and sheep museum in Leenaun focuses on the tradition of hill sheep farming in Connemara. Here you can mingle with the flock and identify the different breeds from photographs. It's the closest I'll be getting to sheep until the weather improves.

Michael is a jovial, moon-faced man with glasses. He is about 70. He wears a blue V-neck jumper over a T-shirt and navy trousers, with shining dark blue shoes. He is a small man with a few wispy strands of hair. His face lights up when I express an interest in mountain sheep. He runs the tip of a pink tongue all the way around his lips, pausing to watch an oystercatcher pass on quivering wings. He calls his dog, Shep, to his side.

He knows the mountains well, the farmers better, and the sheep best of all. Michael spent a large part of his life working for the Agricultural Institute in Ireland, mostly in research in the hill sheep division. He became a renowned expert on sheep and grassland. A regular attender at international meetings all over the world, you could find him at a peat congress in Russia one month, a grass seminar in Italy the next, and a gathering of sheep shearers in New Zealand a month later. He attended conferences in the United States, Canada and Scandinavia, and compared notes at numerous meetings with his counterparts in Wales and Scotland.

Wherever sheep were discussed on the world circuit, Michael O'Toole was there, offering his knowledge, experience and skills. He has written papers for specialist journals in Ireland and Britain. He tells me the black-faced mountain sheep were brought into Galway and west Mayo from Scotland in the 1850s.

'They are probably the hardiest sheep anywhere in Ireland,' he says. 'They started originally as hill sheep and had to survive all year round on the hill. The Scots developed the system of bringing the sheep down in the winter and it softened up the animals.'

Michael talks about the differences between the Scottish sheep and those in the west of Ireland.

'They had more wool on them in Scotland. They had a strong Roman nose and their horns lie a certain way on the side of their head. Generally they have a better bone structure. But there is a contradiction between hardiness and wool. Wool is a biological commodity and sheep need to be well fed to produce good wool.'

When Michael farmed, he had 500 head of sheep. It is not an easy life, but not a difficult life either, he insists.

'There is not that much to do with the sheep but let them roam. Sometimes, like climbers and walkers, they fall off cliffs or get stuck in bog pools but that's all part of the job.'

Walking over Irish hills has been a dominant theme in his life. Michael believes they are undervalued.

'The mountains are among the least appreciated of our natural assets. They yield little, while aesthetically they strike most people as desolate, barren and useless expanses.'

After our coffee I wander around the exhibits, housed in a long, low white building. The museum is crammed with all the mechanised tools that kept the homespun weavers of the west of Ireland busy. A collection of antique looms – single and fly-shuttle – as well as spinning wheels, occupies the floor space. Wrought-iron hand-shearing machines, improvised 'bicycle' machines for threading and bobbing, and machines for making sashes or belts of the type worn by women in the Aran Islands stand as silent reminders of a noisy 250-year-old industry.

The romantic side of life is captured with pictures of hand-spinners at work, sitting on wooden stools outside lime-washed thatched cottages. Information is also provided on the various production processes including dyeing, weaving, felting, fulling, napping, shearing the sheep, carding and spinning the wool.

As I leave, I make a mental note to keep an eye out for those sheep with large Roman noses the next time I am up close and personal.

Two days later, on the road back to Rosroe Pier, I need my sunglasses to protect my eyes from the bright glare as I make my attempt on Mweelrea. The mountain is in full view but dark clouds hang high overhead. It is half-seven and already there is a scrum of activity at the Killary Salmon Farm. Cages are being towed around the yard, vans come and go, several men are preparing to set off in a boat, and two others in diving gear get ready to check on the dead fish. Abdon introduces me to a tall, quiet fisherman called Barney Coyne. He has agreed to take me across and pick me up in the afternoon. We arrange a collection time of three o'clock, giving me six hours to scale and descend Mweelrea.

We cross the calm Killary waters in a fifteen-foot plastic Norwegian boat with an outboard motor. Barney calls it a polar boat. He has worked for six years at the fish farm. His job is feeding the salmon and making sure they have enough to make them grow. They eat a mixture of fish meal, fish oil and grains with added vitamins. We cruise past lines of floats securing five 100-metre circular salmon pens bobbing in the harbour. Barney operates a computer. He has a monitor on his boat and, through a video camera, ensures that the fish are eating the food they are given which is fed to them through pipes. Each of the cages contains up to 40,000 fish. The two biggest cages house about 130,000.

We cross swiftly in an easterly wind. Less than ten minutes later he cuts the throttle, drops me on Mayo soil and wishes me good luck. I walk up through rocky outcrops. Wild violets press close to the rocks. Five dark black faces stare at the stranger in their hills, exchanging glances before cantering off. I have seen them long enough to work out they are not the Roman-nosed breed. After half an hour of steady plodding, I reach a plateau. The now familiar cloud cap is moving slowly across the top. I sit on a rock for twenty minutes to see if it clears, but it is getting worse. A pair of ravens, with their long wedge-shaped tails, dart above me, honking their throaty 'pruc pruc' welcome call. The easterly wind gathers momentum. The sun reappears, disappears and then reappears. As I move around the side of the mountain, the Maumturks and Twelve Bens, all boiling with cloud-toppedness, come into sight.

On the other side of the mountain I look out across the sunlit fields of south-west Mayo. I check the map to orient myself, conjuring with the names of townlands in front of me: Sixnoggins, Thallabawn, Kinnadoohy, Roonkeel, Barnabaun. At the halfway mark the clouds are worsening. I am determined to get to the top, but need to consider my safety; a tense stand-off is developing between the clouds and me. The sun has filtered out again. I decide to push on, hoping that by the time I reach the summit it will have cleared. I am a Capricorn after all. We are not quitters, but stayers: stubborn, obtuse, contrary – and that's just the agreeable side. My resolve is steadfast.

In an instant I hit the cloud cover. I shelter in a ravine and put on my woolly hat and gloves for the first time since leaving home nearly three weeks earlier. I listen to the music of the wind whistling in crags before finding a narrow track. By now the rawness of the gale has reached whirlwind proportions. I am almost lifted off my feet, held down by the weight of my rucksack. Every pore of my skin is penetrated by the wind. It is energising. I relish every moment of it. Visibility is about five yards. Several times I lose my footing in the mist. The wind howls in all directions. I find a shelter belt. The mist swirls round the corner, determined to get me, even following me into a crevice where I am cowering. There is a feeling of being marooned amongst the clouds. If ever a cliché were true, then 'head in the clouds' is particularly apt.

I am surrounded by pure fluffy whiteness, just like the sheep's wool, only not as soft. Struggling with the compass and map, I arrive at the summit runny-nosed, wind-lashed, mist-sodden, energy-sapped and boggy-footed. The mountain goat has made it. Proudly, I sit alone on the top of Mayo's Mweelrea, a mighty, misty mountain massif – the highest point at 2,688 feet, with Connaught laid out before me – except I can see none of it. I remember Abdon calling it 'cloudland' and reflect on Thoreau's description of being in the clouds on Mount Greylock:

> All around beneath me was spread for a hundred miles on every side, as far as the eye could reach, an undulating country of clouds, answering in the varied swell of its surface to the terrestrial world it veiled. It was such a country as we might see in dreams, with all the delights of paradise.

The mist is not unfriendly. I do not think it is getting any worse, but I worry about losing my way. I retrace my steps along the track, stepping carefully in the wind. On the ascent I had had no opportunity to concentrate on what was behind me and once I get out of the cloud cover, County Galway opens up in front of my eyes. A third of the way downhill I stop for lunch. Panning the binoculars across the Killaries, I work around the coast following the road with cottages aligned to it the whole way to Renvyle and Tully Mountain. Killary Harbour is serene. A couple of small craft lie hugger-mugger at the pier. A boat crosses to the salmon cages and returns to the pier. Killary is the only fjord in Ireland and is nine miles long. I lie back and understand vertigo; it is a precipitous slope.

I make my way down a different ravine, coming across the remains of a famine village in a hollow in the townland of Derry. Stone walls belonging to five houses are all that are left of this deserted village. Those that remain are solid. One of the best preserved has a lintel over the doorway and small square spaces representing windows. Rushes, grass and dandelions cover the ground. A stream runs through the remains. It is a stark reminder of a dark episode in Irish history.

Returning to my pick-up point at the water's edge, I wait for Barney. It is 2.30 p.m. and I am ahead of schedule. I disturb a grey heron that lifts off with a tremendous flapping commotion. Four herring gulls sail low across the water to a rock. The all-white *Connemara Lady* glides past at a sedate pace. Half a dozen people lean on the rail at the front, observing the work of the fish farm. I watch it head up the Killary, past the small island of Gubderrynasliggan, continuing its afternoon excursion into the Atlantic. Barney is three-quarters of the way across before I see him, as I have been absorbed in the Killary wildlife show.

'How was the walk?'

'Great. I made it to the top and I know that I've climbed a mountain today.'

We speed across in rough conditions in a fantail of foam. The boat tips and turns; I wonder if it is going to cope. Barney laughs. 'It is getting fresh,' he says, 'and the cruiser always upsets the waters.' It laps round my legs, boots and rucksack. I step ashore wet and tired, but with a triumphal air, having at last overcome *Cnoc Maol Réidh*, 'the grey bald one'.

6

Mountain Ears and Cramponed Sheep

The mountains are the ultimate realm of wild nature.

Jim Crumley, *Among Mountains*

Mountains, large and small, rise on every side in Galway. The vast expanse of Lough Corrib divides the county into two contrasting halves. Maam Cross to Killary Harbour is only fifteen miles but it takes me four hours to drive it. I stop often, switch off the engine, and get out to watch the evening light, listening to the emptiness.

I had gone for a wet afternoon drive over to Roundstone and returned to my cottage via one of Galway's GMRs. The Maam Cross road is quintessential Connemara: lonely country, tough country. A couple of Roman-nosed friends wander across my path. The only sign of any habitation in this Celtic tundra is the wind on the telephone wires. I park beside a fence-post where someone has left an upturned green wellington boot. Two cars and a White Van Man (WVM) pass. The scent of mountains – as far as they have their own smell – is all around. To the left and right they rise, ahead and astern – an all-consuming presence. I count 30 peaks. Mountains rushing up into the clouds frame every view. It is the most exciting road I have travelled so far. Between six and ten o'clock the light changes from grey to red to pink. O'Faoláin says that in Connemara there are no destinations – only pauses. 'Pause as you feel inclined', he writes, adding philosophically, 'You never get anywhere by going on. There is nowhere to get to!'

My destination does exist: Keane's pub near Maam, where I had been tipped off about a music session. Keane's is a substantial two-storey, ivy-covered building. The glow of a welcoming light shines over the front door but there is not a trusty bodhrán, bones, fiddle or squeeze-box to be seen. I ask the barman about music. It turns out I have got the wrong night. Come back on Saturday, he says, and there might be some music, although it is not really a big music pub.

I order a beer and a sandwich and he tells me about the bar. The stones used to build it are carboniferous limestone. The engineer, Alexander Nimmo, built the original house in the early 1800s while he supervised the building of bridges and roads in the area. The barman wipes the counter, folding his tea towel into a neat square. Every so often he feels the sides of his moustache. He agrees with me that in terms of locations for pubs with mountain views Keane's must rank as one of the greatest. The Maumturk Mountains fill the pub's front windows.

'There's an annual walk over them in May, if you're around,' he says hitching up his cords. 'I've never done it myself but I know it's a pretty tough hike.'

He rushes off to pull a couple of pints of stout for two red-faced farmers. I read the label on an empty bottle of Irish spring water which claims it was filtered for 2,000 years through the misty mountains of Ireland. On the screw cap the sell-by date is January 2004.

Sitting outside in the cool April air, I watch the sky break up and the mood swings of the mountains. In his ramblings, the Irish naturalist Robert Lloyd Praeger tramped over the Maumturks in a day without a second thought. A full traverse of them would take fifteen hours. He wandered everywhere, visiting each county, climbing the mountains and exploring rivers, lakes, caves and islands. He loved Ireland and wrote about it passionately in *The Way That I Went*. As well as being a botanical trail-blazer, Praeger was really a pre-mountaineer since he was walking the hills long before it became fashionable. His passion for the mountains shines through:

> Whether they are hung with crags or buried under great blankets of peat, for they represent freedom, and the full use of limbs, and the clear air and wide inspiring prospect: the only pity is that most of us have to leave them so soon, to return to the plains and cities, and to the uninspiring daily round.

I think of Praeger's boots striding across these hills a century ago, and the freedom they represented for him. By nightfall, under a quarter moon, the Maumturks glow in a luminous light. The bar has filled with a few more locals, some in the back lounge, which could pass for a cosy Connemara sitting room, minus the television. I remark on the silence to a craggy farmer with a big paunch sitting outside on his own cosy windowsill.

'Don't you believe it's all that quiet,' he says thumbing at the Maumturks. 'Let me tell you, they're listening to ya.'

'What do you mean?'

He gives me a wide grin. 'Sure don't they all have mountain ears.'

With my own finely-tuned 'mountain ears' I had heard some alarming reports about Galway's highest mountain, Benbaun. One man told me I must have permission from the national park to walk there; another said I need insurance to climb, and a woman warned me to look out for a local farmer who watches over it with a shotgun because he does not like walkers. He calls them the 'scum of the earth'.

What is not in dispute is that Benbaun is the hub of the Twelve Bens and the highest summit in County Galway. Driving around Connemara, I had not stopped long enough to identify the Bens individually. They are a confusing jumble of mountains with sharp peaks rising uncompromisingly. I reckon the man who had warned me about permission had mistaken it for Diamond Hill where access is banned owing to erosion of the bog caused by trampling feet.

A Connemara mountain hare, its ears swivelling, darts across the road in front of me into a lane, remains still for a few seconds on its haunches, then lollops out of sight. A watery sun, struggling to break between the clouds, filters through the white sky and lights up Kylemore Lough. I cruise around its shoreline. With barely a ripple across its silver surface, the lake reflects the replica image of the mountains in perfect evenness. I stop to take a photograph. Two French tourists, struggling with a tripod, are also trying to capture this Connemara spectacle.

After I turn off the main road to Recess, a cloth-capped farmer wearing a jumper full of holes gives me a nod: 'Grand day, sir.' A black-faced sheep provides a guided escort for the first stage of my walk along a soft and grassy riverside track; another acts as sweeper. They quickly lose interest in my company and head off for a drink in the Kylemore River. I survey the route ahead, looking up at the rounded massif of Luggatarriff, the invincible looking wall of overhangs and cliffs of Muckanaght and, dominating all, the ascending ridge of Benbaun. The summit seems tantalisingly close. I pass a forestry plantation running up the flank of Loughermore, an adjacent hillside. My left foot plunges into a boggy hollow and I suck out a wet sock and boot.

Leaving the boggy ground behind, I make my way breathlessly to the top. It is a strenuous, pathless ascent to the final foot of Benbaun's 2,395 feet. I gird my loins. For the last 100 yards of loose grey scree and grit I throw off my rucksack, and scramble up unencumbered. After an uncertain start the day is becoming hot. I feel exhausted and exhilarated. When I reach the rocky summit I am surprised how broad it is. From the car it looked as though a long narrow ridge led to the top.

There is no one around. I have the mountain to myself in the midst of a wide circle of twenty other mountains. The central location of Benbaun, *Beann ban*, 'white mountain', is an alluring all-round viewing point. I look across eleven other Bens and a wall of other mountains. With their quartzite glistening white and grey, they look bare and scrubbed, rock hard and dramatic. A bank of mist moves slowly across the Glencorbet Valley from the bulky Maumturks, the mountains I had seen the night before from Keane's Bar.

The air is clear and still. Visibility is good. The sun is high. The wide panorama of southern Connemara, with its fragmented coastline fringed by the Atlantic, spreads out below me. If it were a painting, the composition would be a masterpiece of symmetry made up of sky, earth, mountain and water. A multitude of small blue lakes sparkle in the lunch-time heat. The water is glassy calm. I pick out Roundstone and its hill – the lonely hump of Errisbeg – breaking the flat bogland. It is not hard to see how inspirational this scene has been for landscape painters. The view could be on loan from a Paul Henry canvas.

A squadron of about 40 wild duck turns and circles in formation directly overhead, then breaks into a figure of eight, turning again before disappearing at a call. Save for the birds, there is no noise. It is a deep quietness. I boulder down some rocks and join a grassy, slippery slope, just managing to keep my obsidian balance. It is thirsty work and I stop to refill my water flask. Nothing is more refreshing than cool water from a mountain spring on a hot day; one of the simple pleasures offered by the freedom of the Irish hills.

On my walk back to the car, Stephen Joyce greets me. He knows Benbaun 'inside out' and farms 1,647 acres of it. The 47 takes on greater significance than the 1,600. He has come to know all the subtle features of it while tending sheep, finding lost ones, and helping with the maintenance of the farm and general husbandry.

'I am familiar with all the hidden corners of it,' he says, amiably. 'I can tell where the foxes hide, where to find the rabbits and hares, and the areas where any awkward sheep stray. It is fairly steep all right; they say here that even the sheep need crampons to reach the top.'

With his stick in the air, he rattles through an inventory of mountain nomenclature without having to think of the names. His gaze travels evenly from peak to peak. A geography lesson follows as he points behind us: 'That's Doughruagh, which means "black stack", and Lemnaheltia behind Kylemore. That big one on the other side there is Letterbreckaun in the Maumturks. They're a bit like people, they all have their own names. Beside us here are Bencorrbeg, Bencorr, Bencollaghduff and Derryclare. Over that way in front of us – the one with the very green slopes – is Muckanaght which few people ever visit – and that's Benbrack, another of the Twelve Bens.'

He describes the views in all directions as 'magnificent',

but rarely has time to appreciate them.

'I've the sheep to look after and that's a full-time job in itself. It certainly keeps me outta devilment and outta the pub!'

Stephen has seen the nastier side of mountain walking at first hand. Nearly twenty years ago he came across a 28-year-old woman who had fallen to her death from the top of Benbaun.

'She fell off the steep southern side and ended face down in a stream. A helicopter and the mountain rescue services were quickly called but she was dead by that time. It was a terrible tragedy. A few years ago a Welshman was also killed on it, so Benbaun has had a sad history.'

7

Oiled in Boyle

To those men who are born for mountains, the struggle can never end, until their lives end – to them it holds the very quintessence of living – the fiery core, after the lesser parts have been burned away.

Elizabeth Knowlton, *The Naked Mountain*

From Leenaun a series of quiet roads skirting mountains and lakes take me to Roscommon; roads I have never travelled before, nor even knew existed like the one to Maumtrasna along the west side of Lough Nafooey. The Maumturks and Partry Mountains are shrouded in Saturday morning mist. On either side, the Devil's Mother and Bennaween rise steeply, hemming me in on a single-track road. A switchback brings me down to Lough

Nafooey where three cows greet my arrival. At a sandy beach, two boats, *Angler's Fancy* and *Forelle*, are tied up. A lake, Thoreau informs me on the cassette, 'is the landscape's most beautiful and expressive feature. It is the earth's eye, looking into which the beholder measures the depth of his own nature'.

A thin sheen of mist covers the lough. The sun is playing hide and seek. A bridge over the Owenbrin River marks the spot where I leave behind the mountains of Mayo and Galway. I follow the course of a thick white line in the middle of the road driving the Bluebird past hedges high with gorse. With the windows down, I catch brief snatches of birdsong.

To get a better view of the vastness of Lough Mask and its aquatic wildlife I turn into a lane, passing a sign listing the Angling Bye-Laws from the West Region Fisheries Board. A low wall with fence posts running out into the water teems with birds. Common gulls sit on each post at intervals of three feet. Shelduck swim around them and to one side a heron keeps a respectful distance. The bustling water traffic includes mallard, tufted duck, a flotilla of common terns and two taxiing moorhens. I watch the gulls closely. Some are still; others flap wings and scratch. Half a dozen suddenly lift off and two others follow suit. Their peace is disturbed with the arrival of two coots. The gulls' loud screeches reverberate across the lake, 'kee-ya, kee-ya', and 'gak-gak-gak'.

From the surrounding trees there is an accompanying cacophony of birdsong. A family of magpies chatters in the trees and undergrowth, flapping between the lakeshore and the small wooded islands. Back on the road a cyclist, clad in fluorescent pea-green Lycra, gives me a wave. In a field, four cows slumber in the sun which has at last decided to put in an extended appearance. For several miles I follow the bird-haunted shore.

I cross over to Roscommon via Bohola, Kiltamagh, Cloonfallagh, Kilmovee and Ballyglass. A man building a wall enclosing the front garden of his house throws the question back at me: 'The highest place in Roscommon? Y'know I don't think I know, that's the gospel truth. They're not high as mountains go; I suppose you'd call them hills.'

I had stopped at the side of the road to interrupt his DIY. 'Ballaghaderreen, where you are now, is not very high ground,' he says. I climb out of the car and he comes round to study the map with me. He rubs the back of his hand across his mouth, pointing with his trowel towards the north.

'There's hills up there towards Boyle and I think they might be where you want. But there's also a place across here called Fairymount which is on elevated land.'

He moves round the car. The trowel is raised again.

'See those trees there? Well that's it; it's easy to find. It's fairly high and I think that could be the highest place anywhere in the county. Mind you, I'm a Galway man myself, so perhaps I am not the best person to ask.' He looks me over. 'You from the North?'

'I am.'

'Usta know a fella called Tommy Chittick from up

there. I worked with him in Galway and we played football together many years ago. Do you know him?'

'Can't say I do.'

'Well, you're welcome to the South. I hope you like it.'

The architecture of the hills of Roscommon is confined to the Curlew Mountains and the Arigna Hills in the north. This part of Roscommon is flat, featureless countryside, undemonstrative and unexceptional, with only a few rises here and there. After a week in Connemara, it is relaxing and restful not to have to look up at high mountains and work out which one is which. Towards Boyle the land rises. The hands on the clock tower in the town read two minutes to six. There's a traffic jam. A garda directing traffic tells me there's been a funeral for which it seems the whole town and countryside has turned out.

McDonagh's newsagents sells eleven kinds of Cadbury's chocolate, the bar with eight squares and multi-coloured wrappers, including my own childhood/adult favourite, Tiffin. A bar a day, well aimed, I always believe, keeps the doctor (if not the dentist) away. My usual sources of information are cut off from me. The post office, tourist information office and library are all closed. The girl with oblique eyes in McDonagh's asks me to wait while she goes in search of Frank Feighan; instead of studying the map I had just bought, I study the chocolate counter. It's a feast that would delight Billy Bunter.

Frank is not sure where Roscommon's loftiest point lies, but thinks the answer is in the Arigna Hills.

'I should know,' he insists. 'I am a born, bred and buttered Boyle man after all.'

He whips a mobile from his back pocket. 'Kevin ... is that Kevin? It's Frank. Do you wanna be a millionaire? I've a question for you.'

He drops his voice. Unlike most mobile phone users, he does not want to share his conversation with the customers. I pretend not to listen.

'It's a bit of an odd, er, an unusual query, er, silly really, but there's a man here who's er, trying to find the highest point in County Roscommon. Can you help?'

There's a pause of twenty seconds. 'Yeah, yeah ... I thought it was somewhere up in Arigna. OK, bye.'

Frank clicks a grey button on his Nokia saying it confirms what he thought. The Arigna Hills, and in particular Corry Mountain, is where I need to go. He says he'll be in Kate Lavin's pub after nine o'clock and offers to introduce me to a few local people.

In the meantime I head off in search of dinner. My landlady in the Abbey B&B, situated within the grounds of the ruins of Boyle Abbey, had told me that Boyle is under-performing from a culinary point of view. The only choices are a carry-out from The Little Chick Takeaway or dinner at the Royal Hotel. Since it's Saturday night, I plump for the hotel. The dining room of the Royal is peopled with Saturday night couples relaxing over a meal.

A leaflet I picked up in the hotel lobby describes the county as 'The heart of undiscovered Ireland'. Roscommon gave ancient Ireland its last High King and modern Ireland its first President. Its nickname is the 'Cinderella' county. A third of it is under bog – most in the west around Castlerea and Ballaghaderreen. The 'Ros' in the county title means a 'wooded or pleasant gentle height'. Roscommon is entirely inland and the only land-locked county in Connaught.

Having refilled my 'little-known facts about Roscommon file', I turn to the papers. As a connoisseur of obituaries, I engross myself in the death notices. Within a couple of days two celebrated people have died: Thor Heyerdahl, the adventurer and explorer, and William Scholl, the man who invented the exercise sandal.

At the next table a discussion involving two sets of couples is turned from hushed tones into more animated ones. The men are in black suits and the women in sensible blouses and trousers. These are late middle-aged couples who have brought up their children and now spend their time complaining about them. A woman with several large chins, a face crowded with red freckles, and a turquoise top, says she has done all her mothering: 'I reared eight of them and I have tried to teach them right from wrong, but sometimes it's a lost cause. I don't make an issue of it but they have to know what they can and can't do.'

I delve into the life (and death) of Heyerdahl, whose main claims to fame were said to have been the notion of the sea as connector, not barrier, and the now indisputable fact of a link between South America and Polynesia.

It's hard not to overhear the social affairs discussion, now ranging over religious beliefs, car insurance, job-searching, drug abuse, crime and young love. A silver-haired man with a drawling voice says they brought up their five children by making sure they all went to mass and then when they were old enough, they could make up their own minds about whether or not they wanted to continue attending.

'That's a terrible approach,' one woman counters. 'Sure don't you have them indoctrinated from an early age, so their minds are closed to anything but the church.'

The freckle-faced, trebled-chinned, turquoise-topped woman butts in, returning with a vehement anti-children rant.

'If I had my life again, I would have only cats or dogs. It's the thanklessness with children that's the worst thing. I mean you don't expect gratitude in this day and age, but a little of it would be nice once in a while. But it's all give, give, give and what do you get in return?'

Her husband laughs through broken teeth. He is having a battle with his minted Roscommon lamb cutlets.

I return to the deaths: after the Second World War William Scholl was determined to liberate feet that at the time were seen as ugly, smelly and comic.

Kate Lavin's pub has a warm smell of turf. There is a buzz of friendliness and instant camaraderie. Frank introduces me to friends at the bar, then leaves for a family party. The pub is filling up with Saturday night regulars and revellers. It attracts young people and those happy to be classified as 'middle-youth'. When Frank explained my mission, the owner exclaimed, 'Omigod, wud you take me wid you?'

The word goes round of my exploits and within a matter of minutes I have half a dozen offers – not of the proposition-ing variety, but for the more mundane answer to the coun-ty's crowning glory:

1. McDonagh's shop because they have so much money that when they pile it all up it is the highest place (that was from Frank).

2. The top of Elphin Windmill (from Catherine).

3. The highest point is the point of the highest mountain (from Harry).

4. The flagpole of King House (from Jim Smith).

5. The top of the chimney in Arigna coal mine (from Christy, aka Columbus).

6. The giraffe in Roscommon zoo (from the barman).

A large number of conversations are going on simulta-neously. The glow of peat from the fire, the dark oak pan-elling and wooden benches, soft Dolores Keane on the CD, and the fact that the pub is devoid of natural light all help create the atmosphere. It exudes well-being. Its strength is its simplicity. It is free of antique agricultural ironmongery. No television, no pool table, no machines, no Formica table tops, and no framed photograph of a uniformed Michael Collins are to be seen.

Christy is the original barstool crackerbarrel philoso-pher and Roscommon polymath. He sinks pints of stout at the rate of one every fifteen minutes, drinking with regu-larity but without hurry. He can demolish a pint in four tilts. He is now on his ninth, or maybe tenth – I have lost count. Integrated into the nineteenth-century fabric of the pub, he's known as Columbus or 'Chippy' because he has a built-in memory chip of most events in history.

He discourses on many controversial issues. A Renaissance man, Christy is an authority on the ramifications of human nature; he spans the centuries, ranging chronologically from early Irish history, through the famine to the euro. He is both local and global. He likes a passive audience. He talks about *crannógs*, holy wells, sweathouses and other 'archaeological mysteries'; the differences between people in south and north Roscommon (they are not a 'common' people at all despite the name; in fact, he says, they are all sheep-stealers); he moves on – in no particular order – to discuss building in the countryside, An Taisce, football talk, Tiger talk, the roads, the politicians, the Internet, the ozone layer, the winner of the 2.30 at Uttoxeter, and his favourite topic – the quality of the Guinness which, in Lavin's pub, is the best in Ireland since it has a 'short run' because it comes from underneath the stairs.

Christy is an expert on the history of Boyle's pubs. From the days of the first inns in the early 1700s, when publicans sold home-made usquebaugh, through the years of illicit poteen-making, to the fair days of the 1940s and 1950s when some pubs had a special licence to open at six in the morning.

'It is a fascinating topic,' he says. 'There used to be 32 pubs here – one for each county in Ireland – but now there's only about twenty. In Patrick Street there were twelve pubs and they were known as the 'twelve Apostles'. One bar, called Devines, became famous for selling an extra large bottle of stout called a "Jumbo". In the 1950s Grehan's pub had a hiding place under the stairs. Every time the gardaí raided, the late night drinkers adjourned to their hidey-hole. But one night the gardaí stayed on the premises a bit longer and heard one of the drinkers asking aloud "Are they gone yet?" so the game was up.'

There is no hiding place in Lavin's, and no hiding place for Brendan the barman, who is under pressure: serving, washing glasses, clearing up, tending the fire, restocking the shelves, checking the taps, and providing a quick-fire counselling service to some Boyleian girls home for the weekend.

Through a drunken haze Christy tells me the story of the 'Boyle Froth-Blowers Association'. In the 1940s they protested about the price of a pint of porter being increased from sevenpence to eightpence. Their motto survives and is a local catch phrase: I'd rather be boiled in oil than oiled in Boyle.

Before anybody else can get oiled, Brendan ushers people out, bidding them sweet dreams. Through the Roscommon moonlight I walk back to the Abbey B&B. Two docile cats, Ginger and Marmalade, maintain a vigil from their snug position on a green mat at the side door. With four gimlet eyes, they keep a perpetual watch on the comings and goings of their visitors. On the way in I stumble over them, receiving an intimidating look that says they've seen it all before: another late night B&B arrival, 'boiling, babbling and bubbling in Boyle'.

The tolling bell of St Joseph's Church awakens me on Sunday morning. One look at the weather and I decide to skip breakfast and have a lie in. The overnight rain has stopped and a layer of thick white mist lies all around. I can't even make out the walls of the majestic Boyle Abbey twenty yards from me. The mist looks as if it's there for the day; it is an overcast morning with a leaden sky. My head boils and throbs from the night before. An extra hour in bed, I feel, will make all the difference.

Boyle is a quiet, humble town. It comes awake slowly on a Sunday. A house sparrow calls its chirrup from the finial of a rooftop. The road to Corry runs through a tunnel of trees skirting the southern section of Lough Key Forest. I pass woodlands of hazel, ash and oak, the ground around them covered with bluebells, wood anemone, ragged robin and wild garlic.

The mist thickens. The day is lost. Undaunted, I press on for Keadew, Ireland's Tidiest Town in 1993, so a notice says, and the centre of O'Carolan Country. The mountain behind it – Kilronan is cloaked in stubborn mist with only the lower forested foothills discernible. I have been intrigued by the map of the area which is sprinkled with numerous sweathouses. In the section enclosing Lough Allen and Lough Arrow I count more than 25 marked with small red dots. They are the dominant archaeological attraction, far outnumbering megalithic tombs, mounds, *crannógs* and holy wells.

Over a sandwich in the Harp and Shamrock Bar and grocery store, I ask about them. The barman says that people suffering from arthritis and rheumatism used them. He describes them as ancient saunas for sweating out illnesses.

There were dozens of them all over the area housed in small stone buildings. They date back to the sixth century.

'They used to light a big turf fire in them for hours. When it was hot enough, the patient crawled into the sweathouse and sat on a bundle of straw. When they'd sweated enough and could bear the intense heat no longer they came out and leapt into the nearest stream they could find to cool off.'

I drive along the south-west shore of Lough Allen. A wooden fingerpost points to the Miners' Way. According to my guidebook the mining communities here worked the iron ore and coal seams for more than 400 years. Initially iron ore was extracted but, later, coal mining became the main activity.

Small farms, some with scrapyards of abandoned cars, diggers, lorries and trailers, line the roadside. Scarcely a dog bothers to bark or even wag its tail at me. The rain is beating down in sheets. If this were a walking day then I would give up. My aerial takes a battering and the car radio goes fuzzy.

Turning off the Arigna Scenic Drive, I come to a gate saying 'No Trespassing'. I nudge the car at five mph along a rough stone track, more suited to all-wheel-drives than Bluebirds. Roscommon's summit is a bleak place with patches of bare ground, a legacy of the mining activity; the only noise, the 'thrum-thrum' of ten windmills, similar to the soft clicking of a bird's wings. In the post-industrial landscape, with the closure of the mines, wind farms have taken over as a source of renewable energy. The government is also promoting wind power to help it meet targets for the reduction of greenhouse gases. Wind farms in Ireland seem to be sited in what are regarded as 'non-scenic areas'. While they may (in the eyes of some) be desirable on economic and environmental grounds, they are visually obtrusive. I am surprised to find them here in a desolate area trying hard to promote its scenic charm. The silence and space that gives this area its special character is compromised by the noise of the giant churning blades. Roscommon could take a leaf out of Kerry's tourism book where wind farms are regarded less fondly as money-wasting blots on the landscape. Kerry has designated over half the county as a 'no-go area' for them. On the other hand, at least they don't cause damage to people's health and, unlike coal, there is no air pollution, just aural pollution.

The lower slopes of Corry were extensively mined in an area marked on the map as Spion Kop. The only views are of slanting rain and the low mist. The wonders of the scenic route are lost. In the absence of a sweathouse at the top offering a place in which to generate some heat, I return to the car for warmth. Corry Mountain overlaps with County Sligo. In fact, its highest point is in Sligo, but the highest point of Roscommon is the part of Corry at 1,358 feet.

On my way back to Arigna, the hillsides give way to hawthorn hedges. A tall chimney spews thick white smoke. It is strange to think of this landscape as having been industrialised with coal extraction. But Arigna was the main coal-mining village in Ireland over the past couple of centuries. The mines closed in 1990 and 250 men lost their jobs. Arigna continues the coal tradition by producing smokeless briquettes, using imported raw materials.

For two nights I had slept within the precincts of Boyle Abbey and on Monday morning I feel I should do justice to the imposing ruins. A woman with a plastic tag, who says her name is 'Valerie Dúchas', takes the history tour. Monks from Mellifont who arrived in 1148 founded the abbey. After three unsuccessful attempts to find a site, they settled at Boyle in 1161. Valerie describes it as the most impressive surviving example in Ireland of a Cistercian church of the late twelfth or early thirteenth centuries – even though the buildings were greatly damaged by later military occupation. The square tower formed part of the church from the beginning and was raised in height at a later date. Its chequered history has been a series of raids, sackings, plunderings and sieges. It was sacked by William de Burgo in 1202; more than 30 years later, in 1235, it was raided and plundered by the English; in 1595 it was besieged by Hugh O'Neill, and eight years later was given to Sir John King, in whose family it remained until the end of the nineteenth century.

Valerie points out the intricate carvings at the west end of the nave: capitals with trumpet-scallops, grotesque beasts and human figures. Her talk is updated to the twenty-first century. She explains about a recent hare-brained proposal to demolish the abbey and build a new one. Apparently some in the town felt that because the abbey was in such a poor state, it would be better to knock it down. Building a modern version would also create much-needed employment in the area.

'The buttresses are weak, and the local councillors felt it would be pointless spending money strengthening them. They suggested knocking down the remains and starting all over again.'

Happily the proposal was not accepted. Boyle Abbey is now a national monument. A team of craftsmen is repointing the walls, while a team of jackdaws exploits its cavities and crevices for nesting. It is a time capsule, and one that has a place in the consciousness of the people. Tourists come from all over the world to see this architecturally rewarding structure. Before leaving I leaf through the comments by the visiting literary exhibitionists. There are the usual offerings of 'groovy', 'fab', 'a treasure', 'spiritual' and 'inspirational'. I note down others that amuse me:

'I hope the monks' peace will be forever with us.' US tourist.
'It's a pity the English came.' Spanish visitor.
'Has anyone seen Abbey?' Anonymous.

It is a sunless morning and I am on a rough track to nowhere. A new week is beginning and I am not sure where I'll be spending it. There is a word for this condition – 'gandermooning', which is said to derive from the aimless meandering of the gander when the goose is sitting. I pull in at the Coffee Nook in Drumshanbo. The waitress thinks I'm waiting for someone else to arrive. I browse the tourism literature: 'Leitrim: A guide to it's [*sic*] beauty, activities and history.' I decide to carry out to the letter of the law the wishes of the Leitrim tourist authorities: 'Relax and let Leitrim happen to you. Leitrim is just the place to chill out and combat stressful living. A holiday here is a recipe for relaxation and renewal – immerse yourself in Leitrim.' Today's sugar quote is a simple offering: 'The people will meet but the hills and mountains never.'

The mountains that I am going to meet – the Slieve Anierins – surrounding the town, are still covered in a wreath of opalescent cloud. On closer inspection I detect a slight thinning and traces of blue emerging in the sky.

The elderly woman behind the desk in the Slieve Anierin Visitor Centre is in a mid-morning catatonic slumber. She uncoils from a chair and jumps when I open the door. Her eyes and mouth open in synchronicity when I pose my tricky Leitrim question. Her face wears a look of horror that anyone should have the temerity to ask such a question. She has just returned from living in Australia for 50 years, so how should she know?

'I'll phone Patricia. She'll know.' She phones Patricia: no reply. 'I'll phone Maureen': no reply. 'I'll try Anne, she should be in or her husband might be.'

Anne's husband is in. 'Slieve Anierin? 19,000 feet. OK thanks.'

'Nineteen thousand feet … in Leitrim? I don't think that's possible.'

'That's what he said. Here speak to him yourself.' She hands me the phone.

'Yes, yes, 1,900 feet. OK, thank you.'

The shelves promote Leitrim's poets, fiddlers and uilleann

pipers; there are books on the land war in the area, and pamphlets on rebels and Frenchmen. Videos, showing traditional farming methods and old Irish crafts, feature the blacksmith, the tinsmith, the wheelwright and the creel-maker. The woman tells me there's an audio-visual display upstairs. After I buy a couple of pamphlets, she says, 'thanks a ton'.

Leitrim is a long thin county. Its name, *Liath Droim*, means 'the grey hill ridge'. The composition of the county is divided by Lough Allen into two topographical areas. South of the lough, Slieve Anierin is the highest point and the natural visual focus. The mountains, which rise to nearly 2,000 feet, straddle the border with Cavan. Many travellers with their pens have passed through Leitrim expressing mixed opinions about the scenery. Hayward said the mountains were 'noble, table-topped and splendidly escarped', but Praeger was not so effusive, calling them 'stubborn hills' because of the unsuccessful attempts to extract good quality coal from them. Frank O'Connor in *Irish Miles* referred to the 'sunlit green rollers' of Leitrim. The county, he said, had a maze of mountains and hills.

Behind the rolling green hills lurk grim statistics. Leitrim has some of the worst land anywhere in Ireland. For all its beauty, the people do not want to stay here. Young people are not interested in farming the Leitrim soil. Every census report since the famine shows a decline in the county's population, although in the census for 2002 there is an optimistic trend. For the first time on record, the population of the county showed an increase. It went up by 758, rising to 25,815, and giving it a population density of just fifteen people per square kilometre. It remains the least populous county in Ireland and has the highest rate of decline. The entire population of the county could be a good crowd at an important gaelic football fixture. In fact, it is said that Leitrim has more trees than people.

From Drumshanbo my GMR ('gandermooning mountain road') takes me to Aghacashel. Road signs advertise dog kennels, wooden fences and the Kingfisher Cycle Trail. I stop to check on access roads into the hills. Jackie Lee is Aghacashel's garrulous postmaster. He also runs a supermarket and a petrol pump selling BP tractor diesel. Outside the shop a cat prowls, sniffing around five kilogram bags of Arigna Cosy-glo and Ecobrite, moving on to empty gas cylinders before settling, with its tail neatly curled round its body, at piles of wooden pallets.

Jackie's grandfather, John Lee, was the National Schoolteacher and opened the shop and post office in 1875.

'There was a lot of emigration from here right along the mountain in those days,' he says. 'He decided to start a shipping agency and was the agent of United States Lines, Cunard White Star and the Greek Shipping Line. My father carried on from him and then I took over, although there's not so much need for a shipping agency nowadays.'

Slieve Anierin, *Sliabh an Iarainn*, translates as 'Mountain of Iron' and takes its name from the fact that iron and coal were smelted from it. Like Roscommon next door, the double world of mountain and mine has come to an end. According to Jackie, the rock is millstone grit with narrow seams of coal running through it in places. It was mined and used to fire the electrical power generating station on Lough Allen. Nowadays, coal is imported from Poland and America. The pits at Aghacashel and the station at Arigna are closed.

'During the Second World War the Aghacashel and Arigna coal pits supplied the home fires. There was also clay found on the mountains for making pipes but it wasn't viable. They made clay pipes for a while but it fizzled away as a business proposition. The Ha'Penny Bridge in Dublin, which was erected in 1816, was made from the iron that was smelted here.

'Some years ago a few of us started a hillwalking club and we hold festivals in June and September. People sitting at desks in cities love to come here and shake a leg at the weekends. We get a fair amount of rain but that doesn't seem to deter them. The Leitrim soil is supposed to be exceptionally retentive of water. With so many lakes, there's an old joke that land in the county is sold by the gallon rather than by the acre.

'The proper mountain climber would only call them hills but we call them mountains, or at least mini-mountains, because they're the highest we have. The big thing to look for is the Brevega Stone. According to legend, Finn MacCool threw this rock across Lough Allen at his girl-friend Deirdre and her lover Diarmuid as they fled his wrath. They say if you put your fingers in Finn's hand-prints on top of the stone, you'll have the gift of stamina.'

The cat has slithered its way up on to the pallets and

eyes my departure carefully. He bids a soft parting miaow. The cloud has lifted over the long, smooth outline of Slieve Anierin. A stiff breeze blows when I pull up at a farm track, part way up the mountain. A 45-minute walk across tinder-dry terrain and along a grassy track used by coal lorries, and now overgrown with tussocks, takes me to the summit concrete plinth standing at 1,922 feet.

Apart from a curve, which from down below seems much more pronounced, the top is almost flat. The sun is hidden again behind clouds. I count more than 30 lakes and watch the River Shannon wending its way southwards. My views to the northwest end with the mountains of Sligo. I make out windmills on Corry. Lough Allen, forming part of the Shannon, rests between the mountains, its waters remarkably calm and free of any rock- or stone-throwing warriors. Interludes of bright sunshine magnify a country-side of miniature fields, tracts of shrubbery and forests. Long, thin strips of sunlight stretching for miles light up sections of land. It is as if certain fields, trees, houses and farms have been selected to have transient light while the rest are without electricity. I watch the course of a yellow school bus weaving along the country roads and dropping off pupils.

A song thrush interrupts my thoughts and serenades my descent with an early evening dusk chorus. Birdsong gives a dimension to the landscape. I have always been intrigued by it and wonder how birds manage such melo-dious sounds. For a few minutes I study it, trilling on a fence post. The song thrush is one of the more common countryside birds in Ireland, although there has been a significant decline in their numbers. At the beginning of the millennium up to eighteen species were nearing extinction in Ireland; the list of endangered birds includes yellowhammer, grey partridge, barn owl and corn bunting. They are on the so-called 'red' list and need immediate action by conservation bodies to ensure their survival. More than 100 are on the 'green' list, meaning they are safe for the present, while up to 70 are on the 'amber' list requiring continuing vigilance by everyone concerned about their future.

Henry's Haven, conveniently a few doors from my guest house in Drumshanbo, has a long bar counter at the back that you come to after walking through a lounge at the front. The walls carry framed photographs of the victorious Allen Gaels football team. There are individual pictures of some players. A CD plays hits from the 1980s. I have just ordered a pint and am hoping for some quiet conversation when a gaggle of five women breezes noisily in. The waitress had been telling me about a new drink, black sambuca, which they are promoting with a black felt-tip notice that urges: Try out our latest – One shot of Black Sambuca.

'There's a flame on it and you have to knock it back in one,' she explains. 'It's very popular with the young ones and women also like it.'

The five potential black sambuca drinkers are members of an aerobics class on their annual night out. They are in a merry mood. I reckon they have exceeded, in one night, the maximum weekly limit of fourteen units of alcohol that medical experts recommend for women. The last pub they were in was Monica's, 100 yards down the street. I classify them as being 'middle-youth', i.e. the age-bracket between mid-thirties and 50. On the floor they deposit handbags and plastic carrier bags containing bottles of beer and cider. One of the problems of drinking on your own is that people feel sorry for you and want to involve you in their conversation. After the 'Allen Aerobics' girls order what can be best described as 'family size' vodkas (or 'vogkas' as they pronounce it) they turn their focus on me, asking what I am drinking. One of their cast, Moya, who has parked an entire bottle of white wine in an ice-bucket on the counter, can barely stand up. She latches on to my arm for support. Another sidles up, introducing herself.

'Hiya, I am Bernie McHardie, but my friends call me Bernie Bacardi.' Living up to her nickname, she lifts a glass, draining the contents in one go. She smiles. 'That's what we call an aerobics energiser.'

A third, Babs, a tall dark woman with enormous arms who could pass for a champion weight-lifter or corner-forward for the Allen Gaels, asks, through a drunken haze, what I am up to. Her friends call her 'two burgers Babs'. By this stage the two other members of the party – Mary and Emma – have gone off to shimmy with each other under the strobe lights and fine-tune their skills. Hands clapping above their heads to 'Dancing Queen' and 'Brown Girl in the Ring', they lift their knees in unison. I never thought aerobics classes could be such fun; they seem to be putting some of their 'hips, bums and tums' skills into practice until Mary falls flat with an almighty crash on her face and returns to the bar with a bloody nose.

The evening is degenerating into a drunken spree. Any form of sensible conversation is a non-runner. Bernie perches on a bar stool, orders a black sambuca, and informs me, between a bout of harsh coughing, that they don't get out often with kids and the constraints of family life. Moya has gone to lie in the corner and stretches out on the floor, groaning about drink and attempting to push buttons on a mobile phone. Within minutes she's dead to the world. Emma and Mary are holding a scatological conversation and then jointly turn on me. Emma has a penchant for earrings. She has four dangling from her ears, a small one in her nose, and another on her navel. They can't understand why I don't want to join in the dance or at least have a drink. Am I odd … a poofter … a priest … a transvestite … a transsexual … and what's wrong with having a good time with the Leitrim lasses …? And why am I travelling alone? I feel a Thoreauesque moment: I find it wholesome to be alone the greater part of the time.

Ironically, in Henry's Haven, one of the best lines of nineteenth-century literature is missed on Mary. She staggers up close, staring me in the eye. There's a strong, petrolly smell from her breath. With full metal-jacketed lips she plants a cidrous kiss on my cheek.

'I am footloose and fiancé free. Are you married or what?'

The pressure is on to join in the fun. I laugh heartily, or at least half-heartily. Persisting with my solo beer, I tell Bernie that I only drink to make other people interesting or to stop me doing aerobics. She doesn't seem to get the joke. But the jeu d'esprit wanes when the bar owner pulls down the shutters and signals a siren call at the lateness of the hour.

'For the love of God, would youse all go home,' he pleads. 'C'mon girls, you've had more than enough for one night.'

Taking this as my cue, I exit unobtrusively by a side door, stretching, toning and spinning the whole way back to the Allendale Guest House. The midnight town is silent and empty. Ten minutes later the peace is shattered. It is the legless ladettes stepping – or perhaps spinning – aerobically homeward and singing uncharacteristically quietly, but off-key, their very own Leitrim love songs.

8

The Benwiskin Bull

Yet often the mountain gives itself most completely when I have no destination, when I reach nowhere in particular, but have gone out merely to be with the mountain as one visits a friend with no intention but to be with him.

Nan Shepherd, *The Living Mountain*

I wake up and turn on the radio news. I half expect to hear the police have arrested the entire Leitrim ladies aerobics team for breach of the peace, or at least for being drunk and disorderly. The world hasn't ended overnight, which is the main reason why most people listen to the news – just to make sure. The headlines provide a snapshot of world events: Osama bin Laden is reported to be alive in the hills of central Afghanistan; Pakistan has announced that it is to crack down on militants; and there is concern about an invasion of Argentine ants reportedly conquering Europe. The invading ants are in millions of nests in a super colony stretching from northern Italy, through the south of France, to the Atlantic coast of Spain. There is no mention of them arriving in either Ireland or the lakeland region – my destination for the day.

The people who live in the Fermanagh and Cavan drumlins are a hardy lot. They could probably cope well with an invasion of ants. In Cavan, one of those mysteriously neglected counties, they are more used to dealing with pigs. It is pig-production country. But as mountaineering country, it is singularly lacking in visual drama and eminences. Bumps in County Cavan are something people drive over, or what pregnant women talk about when fondling their tummies. Fermanagh, on the other hand, is tourism country. It is better known for its lakes but has its fair share of prominent hills.

It should be a short hop from Leitrim to my mountain goal straddling the Cavan-Fermanagh border. As I drive to Ballyconnell, the landscape grows more watery. The whole rippling drumlin belt is an area of grass, lakes, overgrown hedges, modest farms and winding lanes. The owner of Bannon's newsagents in Ballyconnell talks about the weather.

'It's what we call the wet season here,' he smiles. 'That is to say spring, summer, autumn and winter.'

He says he is no geographer but tells me they have 'bits of hills' in the county. I spread my newly-purchased map over his counter. If I am looking for high places, he says, I should try the top of the pre-blending tower at Quinn's cement factory on the outskirts of the village.

I'd noticed the tower on my way in. It is several hundred feet tall and stands beside the foothills of Slieve Rushen. It is used for heating the stones that go into the kiln to make cement – one of the big industries of the area. Lorries from the Seán Quinn cement works predominate on the roads. In their distinctive green livery, they rattle along the narrow byways of west Cavan. In the fifteen miles to Ballyconnell I encounter a herd of fifteen of Quinn's trucks – an average of one per mile: sand lorries, cement lorries, tipper trucks, lorries carrying glass, plying to and from the quarries.

The Quinn group employs more than 1,000 people from the town and surrounding border hinterland. A new cement plant has just opened. The net result of this investment means Ballyconnell has become one of the nouveau riche villages of Ireland. It used to be a pit stop on the way to the west but is now a destination in its own right.

As I set out to tackle Cuilcagh, the highest point of the area, I reflect that many others have travelled this way before me. Praeger remarked that Cavan was 'rather grim and lonely' towards the northwest of the county. Hayward was kinder, referring to its 'opulent lacustrine loveliness'.

Everything has a grey, stark and forbidding appearance. The colour is drained from the sky and that 'lacustrine loveliness' is not apparent. I sense a considerable ring of truth in the saying that, after heavy winter flooding, for half the year Lough Erne is in Fermanagh, while in the other half, Fermanagh is in Lough Erne. All the guidebooks say it is a wet place. The day starts off with persistent heavy showers and looks as though it is going to be a soaker.

My approach to the mountain is along the back roads that criss-cross the barren border country leading to Swanlinbar. A leaflet 'Explore Cuilcagh' informs me that the Irish name for Swanlinbar, *Muileann an Iarainn*, means 'Iron Mill'. The English name has a different origin. It stems from the seventeenth century when four entrepreneurs set up a mill using iron ore from the Slieve Anierin Mountains. The men's names were **SW**ift, **SAN**ders, Dar**LIN**g and **BAR**ry from which Swanlinbar originated.

Each hill in this area is often a tiny townland in its own right, linked by sinewy roads, bumping along from one to the next. From Swanlinbar I follow a narrow road that turns on to the Gortalughany scenic route – a twisty, steeply rising road that ends in a grassy tracked cul-de-sac. Signs urge drivers to engage a low gear. It's my lucky day. The rain stops at precisely the same time as the Bluebird.

Cuilcagh, in Irish, *Cailceach* meaning 'chalky' and pronounced 'Kulk-yach' or 'Kullkie', lies in the south-west corner of the county. It is what might be termed the only true mountain in Fermanagh. On the map it looks as if a large dollop of ink has been splodged by cartographers and has spread its way out over a wavy circle of up to ten miles. The entire ridge stretches for two and a half miles. Today, most of its steep summit massif of shales and eroding sandstones is smothered in low cloud and grey bundles of mist. At 2,188 feet, Cuilcagh outstrips its nearest rival by well over 1,000 feet. In fact, it is the highest summit in the lakeland region covering Fermanagh, Cavan and Leitrim. The mountain is shared by Fermanagh and Cavan, so one walk will account for two county summits. Links between the two counties are close. Not only does Cuilcagh's spine conjoin them but their river systems also flow into each other and are an important tourism venture for both counties.

Like so much of the Northern countryside, Cuilcagh has many environmental labels. The whole area is designated as a Mountain Park lying within the West Fermanagh and Erne Lakeland Environmentally Sensitive Area (ESA) – a scheme aimed at promoting less intensive methods of farming and encouraging good conservation practices. Cuilcagh sags under a weight of important titles. It is an Area of Special Scientific Interest (ASSI), a candidate for Special Area of Conservation (SAC), a Ramsar site of international importance, and has been given a Geopark designation.

I have often wondered about this bureaucratic, acronymic, armour-cladding protection for the countryside. In recent years there has been a proliferation of these labels with European Union directives coming into force. Northern Ireland, the smallest of the four countries of the UK, represents the highest area in percentage terms of Areas of Outstanding Natural Beauty (AONBs). Twenty per cent of the countryside is AONB (compared with four per cent in Wales, thirteen per cent in Scotland and sixteen per cent in England). For good measure, 70 per cent of the coastline is classified as AONB. What I have never understood is, if there are so many imposing and protective labels attached to the countryside, then why isn't it secure for future generations? These areas, which include mountain ranges in each of the five other Northern counties, are all specially protected. I am all in favour of conservation and am not arguing against these sites, but if they continue to highlight the countryside in this way, then what will be special about the bits that have been given a designation? It appears to me that this policy reflects an eclectic involvement with some elements rather than the whole. The entire Northern landscape, it seems, is in danger of becoming one huge area of special protection. The worry is that parts of the countryside will become compartmentalised or fragmented and the landscape will be treated as a series of disparate parts rather than a unified system.

As I plod through hallowed turf I mull this over. The very peatland is now globally a scarce habitat. It has suffered serious damage owing to pressures from mechanised peat extraction and the heavy drainage work that goes with it, plus overgrazing and an indiscriminate use of All Terrain Vehicles. Every sodden step I take is probably causing untold damage. Having said that, the track marks left by tyres show evidence of Land Rovers and 4WDs having recently used some sections.

For all this, on my visit there doesn't seem to be much pressure on Cuilcagh. Scarcely a telegraph pole, electricity cable, wind turbine, mobile phone mast, or even a crippled tree, is to be seen. There are no farms – even deserted ones, no outstanding features to look out for, and there are no people. South of my route a fence runs east-west, marking the county boundary as well as the border between North and South. It is shown on the map by a thick broken black line that swings north through Cuilcagh Gap up to Blacklion. Consulting the map, I had been puzzled by the mention of Swallow Holes marked in half a dozen areas. A closer reading of it also throws up some intriguing names including Cats Hole, Cradle Hole, and Ratting Hole, all appearing to be linked to the Marble Arch caves system.

My approach is from the northeastern side. Via a series of widely spaced yellow wooden posts, marking the route of the Ulster Way, I am transported through a time warp; except for the birds – and there are only a few of them – it is a curiously deep silence. I frighten a golden plover into a frantic burst for safety, carrying its loud cry into the distance. The Cuilcagh terrain is suitable for plovers which like to nest on mountain tops, wet blanket bogs and cut-over bogs, although their numbers too have been declining. Halfway along I take my bearings. Three ravens croak their harsh chorus. I look across a huge expanse of upland blanket bog which turns the area into an unexpected wilderness unchanged by human hand. My map had given me no idea of the scale of the territory. To some, it is an ecosystem of fascination and beauty. To me, the bogland feels featureless and boring: a dull monochromatic place, hard work, a wet slog and a million miles from the local tourist board's description of it as 'a world of inspiration'.

Two significant Fermanagh rivers – the Owenbrean and the poetically named Sruh Croppa – have their sources in Cuilcagh. They both flow from the north-facing slopes and disappear into sink holes. I scrunch across a mattress of water-laden vegetation, an intermingling of heather, cotton grass, sphagnum moss, stag's horn moss and the upright spikes of club moss. My footsteps require careful selection. The guidebook says the flora of the area includes creeping willow, sundew, crowberry, starry saxifrage, milkwort, thyme and a plant called purging flax. In olden days it was used as a remedy for constipation and was known as 'mil-mountain'. The guidebook quotes the words of one herbalist:

> Take a hand full of this mil-mountain, using the whole plant, leaves, seeds, floures and all, bruise it and put in a small tunne or pipkin of a pinte filled with white wine, and set it on the embers to infuse all night, and drinke that wine in the morning fasting.

After two hours of slow, squelchy slogging, dodging bog pools and sludgy tussocks, slipping into hidden swampy sink holes, slithering across small streams and negotiating my way around dark peat stacks, I could use a handful of 'mil-mountain'. It would taste even sweeter if it were accompanied by a large Cuilcagh cupful of wine to infuse my embers.

The broad flat summit is topped by coarse sandstone and shale, forming a gritstone edge exposed in some places as dramatic cliffs, sweeping down to the middle slopes. By the time I get there the weather has calmed, although damp mist swirls in waves. Some hills poke their heads above the mostly flat countryside. Northwards I make out Skea Hill, Trien and Benaughlin. Like so many vistas on my travels, farming has shaped the countryside. Agriculture is more important here than anywhere else in the UK, with 30 per cent of the workforce engaged in some type of farming. From this vantage-point it is not hard to appreciate why Cuilcagh was central to the triangulation of Ireland by Captain Portlock in the 1830s. It was an important station for the original Ordnance Survey of Ireland when the sappers camped for months on the summit, plotting the bearings of distant mountains, including Keeper Hill near Limerick, more than 200 miles to the south.

With a raven's-eye view I can just see the chaotic jigsaw of interlaced wooded islands that make up Lough Erne. In its own way it is an astonishing aspect full of surprises, as if a vast secret landscape has opened up. I focus the binoculars on the lakes, studying the tricks of light. The colour of the water changes from pale silver to dark grey. Hayward's 'lacustrine loveliness' is now easier to understand. I remove my wet leggings and damp fleece. I wish I had brought a spare pair of dry socks, but my boots and feet are so wet, I am past caring. This has been my wettest conquest so far, in one of the wettest parts of Ireland. I watch a couple of tiny ants crawl their damp way across a rocky outcrop. Could they, I wonder, be part of the invading South American super colony, newly arrived like me, to conquer craggy old Cuilcagh?

D-day has come. After crossing a GMR known as the Bellavally Gap, a series of 'D' towns and villages – Dowra, Drumkeeran, Drumduffy, Drumkeel and Dromahair in the

'Wild Rose County Scenic Tour' – are my passage across mountain and lake country to the far-famed hills and mountain roads of County Sligo.

I have come to love GMRs, which is just as well since I have spent many days driving across them. Nearing the end of the first section of my quest, I have covered more than 2,000 miles, a large proportion of it on high mountain road country. Driving towards Sligo, I reflect on their appeal. I love the fact that they are all different: their width, their layout, their undulations, their curvaceousness, their crests and twists, and the fact that they contain more history than any traveller could possibly exhaust. Many have a venerable lineage, still remaining important and fundamental components of the landscape. I like the space and the different perspectives the mountain roads offer, and the small towns they take me to, each with its own distinctive character and self-containedness.

What a contrast twenty-first-century Ireland is with the time of the early roads, which were mainly paths connecting small pockets of civilisation. They were known as *sliadgh* and existed for more than 4,000 years. Made of timber, they provided roads on soft ground for light traffic. At the time when Tara was the heart of Ireland, five arteries radiated from it: the *Slighe Cualann*, the south road, ran towards the south of Dublin; the *Slighe Mor*, the great western road or midwest road, was via Dublin to Galway; the *Slighe Asail*, the northwest road, ran near the present Mullingar; the *Slighe Dala* ran southwest; and the *Slighe Midluachra* was the northern road.

Today the main road network of Ireland is far removed from that time of Celtic songlines. By the turn of the century one million pounds a day was being spent on the development of motorways and major roads. The National Roads Authority allocates certain amounts to each county for improvements and maintenance. A large amount is co-financed by the European Union. The familiar EU logo trumpeting major road projects is hard to avoid. The main purpose of this investment is to offset the impact of Ireland's peripheral location and to improve the competitiveness of the economy by reducing transport costs. All this means that Ireland is a country of non-stop road works: teams of workers with road rollers build relief roads, roundabouts, bypasses and new junctions. Two of the towns I have passed through – Dowra and Dromahair – both smell of burning asphalt.

Ireland has become obsessed with roads and their condition. Whole swathes of countryside are being gobbled up with developments. Robust debate has taken place about the location of new bypasses, toll roads, motorways and superhighways. There has been trouble over the compulsory acquisition of farmland by the State: farmers have called it unjust and inequitable, and claim that their livelihood has been damaged. Day in and day out the newspapers are filled with articles reporting the agitation, consternation and near hysteria of those opposed to more road building.

But it is the GMRs where my heart lies. I make an inventory in my head of their best-loved qualities and what qualifies them to be classified as GMRs. Some of the prerequisites are obstinate sheep, obtuse goats, obdurate ducks, obstreperous magpies and obnoxious geese.

There shall also be the obligatory, obsessive and objectionable white van man, travelling at high speed and occupying three-quarters of the single-track road.

The slow, uphill climb shall last at least three miles and employ second gear.

There shall be spectacular views of wind farms, all of which shall be missed because of concentration on driving or mobile phoning.

Their flanks shall be draped by brown, grey, purple or green hills, with the waterfalls dressing their slopes, flooding the road.

There shall be a lay-by, or stopping place, where an optimistic notice reads 'Panoramic views'.

The landlady in my B&B at Ballintrillick is envious of my trip. She would like to have more time to climb mountains and travel the mountain roads.

She sighs. 'To tell you the truth at the moment the only mountain I see is the mountain of ironing sitting on the kitchen floor.'

After breakfast I turn into the Ballintrillick road. A man is wearing a baseball cap that tells me he supports 'Magnum HiTec'. He gives a wave and I pull over. He talks about the mountains, advising me to look out for the man they call 'the Benwiskin Bull'. He warns me not to wear anything red just in case. He laughs and tips his cap, saying I'll discover what he means soon enough.

Sligo has a varied and generously endowed hill and mountain combination. It possesses towering mountains with steep rugged sides, and some much humbler ones. Several high mountains compete for my attention. The highest ground lies in the range of the limestone Dartry Mountains. Benbulbin, at 1,722 feet, is known as Ireland's table mountain, but Truskmore or *Trosc Mór* (*trosc* means a codfish) is far and away the highest point at 2,113 feet, easily outpacing the Benbulbin showpiece in terms of footage. Like some of the other mountains in this area, Truskmore is a table shape – a characteristic profile that also applies to Cuilcagh and Slieve Anierin – all in an area known as West Bríefne.

A morning of bright sun greets me as I set out for Truskmore. A thin veneer of cloud sits on top of Benbulbin but a confident sun is rising high. The road to Ballintrillick is straight and narrow and is overshadowed by the Benwiskin Ridge. Four gulls have come inland several hundred yards to field-forage beside recently felled trees. Road signs say: No Dumping, Celtic Seaweed Baths, Holiday Cottage Toilet (someone has added the extra 'i').

The road takes me around the north side of the sublime outline of Benwiskin with its forested hillside. At Keelogues a black and white collie sits in the centre of the road, basking in the sun. It refuses to budge for any traffic. A cocker spaniel runs round it in circles, then repeats the action anticlockwise. I stop to watch; the milkman is first on the scene and slows his van, swerving delicately and setting his milk on the wall at the side of the farm. An Eircom van drives past, just managing to squeeze through on the left side; a tractor arrives performing another squeeze-past trick without the collie as much as flinching. His number is up when a flame red Opel Corsa driver puts a stop to all the fun. Despite his blaring horn, the collie sleeps through it all. He gets out, shouting 'hup dog, hup, ye brute'. Drowsily and lethargically, the collie shifts itself, rising and pottering towards the farmyard.

At the Benwiskin Centre the woman in charge describes the area as 'unpredictable country'.

'If you're going up Truskmore, you're OK,' she says. 'It's owned by the Rooneys and Gilmartins. Just stick to what we call the "TV road" and don't wander too far away. There is a problem getting on to Benwiskin and we don't advise people to go there. You'll see all the notices when you're up there – you can't miss them.'

'So what exactly is the problem?'

'We're, er, not in a position to say very much more about it. It's really nothing to do with us anyway.'

'Even though you are called the Benwiskin Centre?'

'We cater for groups and parties who want to stay here and sort out their accommodation. We also run classes and workshops. I think you'd be better concentrating on the romantic aspect of the hills. There's the cliffs of Annacoona, the cave where Dairmuid and Gráinne spent their last night, and the Creevykeel megalithic tombs.'

She plies me with leaflets: 'Sligo, Land of Heart's Desire', and 'A Glimpse of Ballintrillick'.

For some years controversy over access rights has

plagued this scenic part of Sligo. Hillwalkers have been at loggerheads with a local farmer, Andy McSharry, who owns land close to Benwiskin. He has been waging a campaign to keep walkers off land near his farm at Gleniff horseshoe. An old miners' road has attracted walkers because of the scenery but they have been advised to avoid the area. Mr McSharry has been taken to court and fined for his actions. He has been convicted of assaulting walkers who trespassed on his land. The judge said a landowner's right to protect his property did not extend to physical violence or the use of threatening and foul language. Mr McSharry has objected to walkers going on his land. He has been known to throw stones at people and once produced a gun.

I follow the signs for the Gleniff horseshoe. When I reach the gates for the tarred road to Truskmore, a Telecom engineer is about to lace a chunky blue chain around them. I ask about going up and he says there is another van man at the top so it should be OK to drive up. I pass the red capital-lettered standard PRIVATE ROAD sign. A narrow serpentine road uncoils into the mountain. I have no idea what will happen if I meet another vehicle, let alone a raging bull. The views across to Benwiskin and Benbulbin are spectacular, but I can't appreciate them because it is hard to take my eyes off the road. Cattle grids and potholes every so often along its three-mile stretch slow my progress as it twists and spirals dangerously around the side of the mountain.

A strong wind brews at the top. The area around the mast is 'hard-hat' territory. My woolly purple hat doesn't qualify. Other signs warn: 'Staff only, keep out', and 'No unauthorised personnel beyond this point'.

The summit is sprinkled with large boulders. I look across a bowl of mountains into the quilted, sunlit interior of Benwiskin and Benbulbin, both with long ridges across their tops. Sligo sits in a hollow. Across the bay, high above the Hill of Knocknarea, I watch the contrails of a 747 set off across the Atlantic flying in and out of the clouds.

On the return leg, my foot rests on the brake for the long descent until I reach the gate. It is a hairy drive, one of the most difficult of all GMRs I have travelled so far. I continue round the six-mile circular horseshoe and come to 'McSharry country'. His bungalow at the foot of Benwiskin is a white house with a strong wooden front door. Net curtains hang in the windows. Fence posts with blue rope strung between them stand around the front of the house. The house and precincts are plastered with warnings. White signs attached to wooden boards in fields caution:

Private Property – No Trespassing
As Yeats himself might say – 'maybe you should arise and go now'
No Entry – You have been warned

A signed notice reads:

I the undersigned wish to state that my lands at Gortnadrung and Oughtagorey are strictly private. Hillwalkers, ramblers, etc are strictly prohibited due to false information published

On the back of a trailer at the front of his house a sign reads:

Strictly no right of way on Upper Mine Road
Beware of the Bull McSharry
There are no walks available on these lands

Other signs, with bad marks for spelling, ask people to please note:

Those with good [*sic*] books and maps with rouths [*sic*] marked through this land you have been mislead [*sic*]. This is a special notice to the North Leitrim Glens and Hillwalkers to stay off route 33 as it interferes with private property. Tourists and hillwalkers strictly prohibited

The McSharry house is one of the few in the entire horseshoe. It is in a bowl surrounded on all sides by mountains. From his front door you look across to Truskmore and Tievebaun Mountain. Behind is Benwiskin, with Benbulbin stretching away into Kings Mountain. It is a deserted road; apart from the white van men, I have met no other traffic in two hours.

I try the front door. No reply. I get the distinct impression that I will be persona non grata although I would like to talk to him. He seems to be a selfish man who wants to keep the mountains, the views and scenery to himself and not allow others to use this tremendous natural resource. The Sligo County Tourism Committee has produced a brochure that does not feature Mr McSharry – *Sligo: A*

County for Infatuation.

Sligo marks the end of the first section of my trip. With eleven county tops conquered, I contemplate my own infatuation with the mountains and those I have yet to climb. The challenge of the highest peaks in Ireland, in the southwest, waits to be tackled; before then, the hills of home are calling.

PART II

9

Spinning Yarns in Oldcastle

Ulster sits in the middle of five thousand hills,
But the county of Meath lies level as a board.

Old Ulster proverb

The unseasonably warm April sunshine has spilled over into May. Newspaper reports say March and April have been the warmest for 1,000 years, although how this is worked out is not explained. Early May finds me on the road again, on a cross-country route over to the Burren in County Clare. This leg of my journey – through the verdant midlands – begins in the Meath countryside, which has undergone a spring clean. On the way into Nobber the road is lined with newly shaven hedges; hemlock grows wildly along the roadside; fields are full of large herds of fat Angus cattle. It's an area of small hummocky fields. 'A country of bubbles' is how the writer T.H. White described the hills of Meath. Most of the high points are on the east side – Tara, Slane, Newgrange are all symbolic places in the landscape.

Long runs of trees and high hedges divide the fields into multi-shaped sizes. I watch a wood pigeon fly into the top of an ash tree. The map throws up solid but curiously respectable names: Trim, Yellow Furze, Black Bull, Pike Corner, and Summerhill. I am looking for a café. It's bank holiday Monday, and Nobber, Drumcondra and Thomastown are all shut. In Moynalty the green blinds are drawn on the post office windows. The only sign of life is a house sparrow flitting around the windows, determined to get inside, but fighting a losing battle.

I order a toasted sandwich in O'Shaughnessy's Lounge in Kells. It seems to be the only place open in County Meath. A blackboard demonstrates to good effect some of the finest examples of the aberrant apostrophe 's': lunche's, light bar snack's, stir-fry's, steak's, and sandwich's, plus live sport on three screen's.

The woman serving wears a black T-shirt saying 'The beer, the food, the craic'. I ask about high places. She says there's a 90-foot tower in Kells, but she's not sure if it is possible to climb to the top. It seems most of the town is having a holiday lie-in. I try in vain to buy a phonecard and film for my camera. The man in the heritage centre, which had opened at lunch time, points me in the direction of the Loughcrew Hills near Oldcastle in the western tip of the county. The highest point is Carnbane East.

'We call them small mountains or big hills,' he says. He gives me a leaflet that outlines a ridge of hills as *Sliabh na Callighe*, meaning the 'Hag's Mountain', or the 'Hill of the Witch'.

'You'll not get near them though,' he warns, 'because of the foot-and-mouth from last year. Local farmers closed them to the public because they didn't want people walking over them.'

Legends surround the hills of Meath, especially the Loughcrew Hills. One of the main ones relates to the name of the Hill of the Witch, where the witch is said to have jumped from one hill to the next, dropping stones from her apron to form the cairns. After she had jumped on to three hills, she still had to get to another and make a fourth group of cairns in order to attain great power. As she tried to reach the last one she fell to her death.

A few miles after Kells, the dramatic outline of the rounded humps emerges against the sky. The range extends about two miles in an east-west direction. The cairns on these four limestone hills are the remains of one of Ireland's largest neolithic cemeteries dating to around 3000 BC.

I am pleased to find that place-mythology still lives on. The mythical side to the county is exploited for every ounce of its worth by Meath Tourism. A booklet, funded by the EU Initiative for Rural Development, testifies to the seductive quality of the land and its people. Aerial photographs, shot on hazy days with dawn breaking over the stones and cairns, are accompanied by the purple prose of the marketing people:

Meath's past is full of mystery and excitement, tragedy and humour. There are High Kings and scholarly monks, Vikings and Normans, castles and crosses, winged horses, wise fish – rumour has it that some even talk – singing stones, magical sagas and fabulous fairytales … the mysterious imagination and sharp-witted humour of medieval monks still resonate in towns like Kells … Tara is imbued with a magical, mythical atmosphere.

The literature urges me to 'Listen carefully for the cries of Lia Fáil – the Stone of Destiny'. There is a reference to hens in Newgrange that lay coloured eggs and a little-known snail, *theba pisana*, unique to the sand dunes along Meath's short stretch of coastline. The syrupy words bowl me over: wise fish that talk, winged horses, singing stones, humorous monks, coloured eggs, and, to cap it all, *theba pisana* – all within a few miles in one small county.

At Ballinlough, twelve trees drip with cherry blossom. A country road, with signs warning of steep gradients, leads into the heart of the Loughcrew Hills. Two orange-tipped butterflies flirt in the bright sun at the car park. A coach party of 30 Germans has just beaten me to the prominent mound along a short path. Despite the mini heatwave they are not taking any chances, carrying anoraks, heavy duffel coats, hats, gloves and umbrellas.

A cairn, about 40 yards in diameter with a cross-shaped chamber covered by a mound of stones, marks the top. There is a great commotion as the gate into the chamber is opened. The Germans queue, video-toting, in restless fashion, ducking their heads to file in and study the stones. I catch a few words of a loud discussion. One woman, Ingrid, is doubly noisy.

'Gut, gut … yah, yah … nien, nien … bitte, bitte …'

At five feet tall, the man marshalling the entry into the chamber is a perfect height for the job. He wears a tweed hat, glasses and a grey jacket. He tells me they are from Hanover.

'We calm from Newgrange and Dub-ling and Kilkenny and we stay at hotel in Dub-ling tonight and are leaving for Dusseldorf tomorrow. We haf a party of 29 persons.'

He motions me inside with four others. We shuffle through a slender chamber, ducking into an inner room where we can just about stand to full height. It is a dark, circular cramped chamber about five metres in length, with three side recesses. Another man, with a grey moustache and matching grey torch, shows off the stones. Waving his beam across the rocks, he explains in broken English, how they have been oriented carefully to catch the rising sun on certain days.

'Links to richts, in Marsh and Ziptembre, on ze days of ze equinox, ze light from ze rizing zun comes in here and illuminates ze line patterns. Ze beam lights up ze mysterious zines and zcribings carved on ze stones in ze tomb.'

Patches of torchlight illuminate the back stones. They are profusely decorated with unique engraved carvings and radial line patterns that could be suns or flower motifs. There are also circles, arcs, zigzags and spirals. It is understood that they mark the expected variations of the sunbeam with the drifting of the equinoctial rising sun. It is believed that this was used to track the behaviour of the sun around the equinox, although why this was done is a mystery. Carvings are also found on the sills, lintels and roof stones.

'It is a ferry important site vitch catches ze interplay of light, stones and shadows.'

Several other women are anxious to get inside. The space is limited to five people. They triplicate their speech for effect to make sure they are heard above the general hubbub.

'Jah, jah, jah; moment, moment, moment; bitte, bitte bitte …'

After the Germans leave, things quieten down. Order is restored and birdsong resumes across the stone ritual landscape. Two skylarks indulge in a high-pitched sustained glissando lasting more than a minute. They repeat their song, perhaps an influence from the German visitors. A man with a Dalmatian arrives and two other couples lie in the sun sipping lemonade.

I am surrounded on all sides by traces of the past. Many periods of Irish history are represented. In the immediate foreground are a number of small hills, two circular ones and clusters of cairns with stones. They were each given a letter of the alphabet in the 1860s. Carnbane East is known as Cairn T and is the dominant and central mound of the complex; two others are labelled Cairn S and Cairn D, while Cairn L is situated on Carnbane West, a smaller hill on which I watch two people make sluggish progress. Boulders sit in open fields. Scattered all around are ring forts, standing stones, souterrains, holy wells, stone crosses and the remains of castles. The heavily forested Patrickstown Hill directly across from me has a tomb but looks difficult to access.

The flat plains are a patchwork of velvet green fields, some of which are divided by long stone walls curving at angles. A few villages pockmark the countryside. Small details of country life catch my eye: a tractor moves evenly up and down a field, spreading slurry with a steady rhythm; three men burn bracken, brambles and branches in an adjoining field beside a barn with a rust-red roof; a silver car stops at a stone bridge over a river; clothes dance on a washing line outside a white farmhouse; two bikers build up the throttle along a ruler-straight stretch of road before banking into a corner. Oldcastle appears to be a single street, hemmed in at either end by tall church spires poking like stalagmites through the trees. I pick out the colours on the façades of some doors and buildings: salmon-pink, sienna, buff, fire-engine red, and the pale yellow of Wimbledon tennis balls.

On this sun-kissed day the views are all-encompassing. A hundred miles away the hills of Sligo delimit the horizon to the northwest; to the northeast the Mournes and Cooley Hills crowd the skyline. Away to the southeast the line of the mountains of Wicklow are on display, and two large cooling towers stand out in the direction of Offaly. A man from Drogheda and his girlfriend tell me that on a good day, without too much hazy sunshine, you can see eighteen counties. It is, he proclaims, the best view from any mountaintop in Ireland.

I have spent three hours basking in the sunshine and exploring the inscrutable stones. It is a numinous place. For such a short climb, the views are outstanding. An information board, erected in a corner of the field, informs me that Loughcrew comes from *Loch Craobh*, which translates as the 'Lake of the Branches'. The tombs are thought likely to have been a focal point for a group or tribe, perhaps territorial markers. The symbolic carving and the orientation of some of the tombs to the sun reinforce the ritual nature of the monuments.

Traces of about 25 tombs survive on these venerated hillsides. Examination and excavation of the site has produced objects such as beads, ornaments of glass and amber, pieces of pottery, bronze and iron objects, and bones. Over the years, particularly at Patrickstown, some destruction has taken place. But today the Loughcrew Hills, with their carefully arranged system of mounds, offer one of the best-preserved examples of a neolithic landscape calendar.

Looming larger in historical terms than its height of 911 feet warrants, Carnbane East (*Carn Bane*, 'the white cairn') is one of the shortest, but most striking of any of the county summits on my itinerary. I call up the words of Daphne Pochin Mould who wrote: 'In a country like Ireland the smallest hill may take upon itself an importance that it could never have in more mountainous terrain.'

Few Irish hills can boast such an impressive connection with an older world and one that links the language of ancient art and archaeoastronomy. With its complex and mysterious stone engravings, its symbols and signs, Loughcrew is a captivating and enigmatic site, a rich repository of archaeology, history and mythology, and a touchstone of Ireland's megalithic cultural heritage. The decorative prehistoric rock art has a mesmerising and bewitching quality of mana; this legendary hilltop leaves an indelible impression and reminds me that the past is both long and deep.

The man running the Boolies B&B near Oldcastle gives me a couple of names of people who know Loughcrew well.

'Old Mr Connolly would be good,' he suggests. 'He lives up near Loughcrew. He's well into his eighties and cycles every day in his suit and hat. You'll see him cycling round the roads, head down and backside up in the air. He bought a new bike recently and thinks it's a racer. The other man you want to get your hands on is Bernard Heaney. You'll find him in some of the pubs in town tonight. Try Farrelley's or the Mountain Dew. If you've no luck there, then ask at the Bunker and if he's not there then he could be in the Fincourt, or possibly the Naper Arms. You'll definitely find him if you ask around.'

Oldcastle in County Meath is twinned, so a sign tells me, with its Canadian namesake in Tecumseh, Ontario. Another sign reads: 'Welcome to Oldcastle. Home of Respa bedding. Please keep our town tidy.'

The County Meath Oldcastle is a resolutely old-fashioned Irish town. A historic place, it developed in the eighteenth century as the largest yarn market in the country. In those days the town and surrounding lands were the property of the Naper family whose name lives on in the Naper Arms Hotel. The town has a Georgian character, with elegant three-storey houses. In the irregular central 'square' a large map lists places of interest, most of which appear no longer to exist. The El Dorado Ballroom, the Castle cinema, the railway station, and the St Vincent de Paul Hall are all closed.

I while away half an hour in Paula's Food Hall, an old-style café specialising in a mouthwatering display of coffee diamonds, chocolate caramel squares, strawberry creams, fudge cakes, traybakes, apple tarts and fresh cream éclairs. The sugar bowl offers some homespun wisdom with a thought for the day which rekindles the witchy atmosphere on the summit of the Loughcrew Hills and makes me reflect on the mystery of history: 'What is strange is wonderful.'

When I ask for Bernard Heaney, the barman wiping glasses with a blue and white tea-towel in Farrelley's says, 'He was here and has just left. You might see him in later but he's unpredictable; he likes to move around the different bars.'

At the Bunker a woman with a waxy face says she hasn't seen him and suggests I try the Mountain Dew. The barman there says to try the Fincourt. My pub-crawl of Oldcastle ends at the bar of the Naper Arms Hotel where, after a whispered consultation with a waiter, I am directed to a man having a drink with a friend.

Bernard Heaney greets me convivially with a wide grin. A tall man with broad shoulders, he has a healthy crimson complexion. With his blue, animated eyes and fresh face he could pass for a 50-year-old rather than a man of 70. His teeth have rotted and the ones that are left on the bottom row sit at eccentric angles. He is well dressed, with a brown sports jacket complemented by an open-neck, light brown shirt. He wears black trousers with shining black shoes. A retired gentleman farmer, Bernard walks with a limp and uses a stick to aid him around the streets. He is having a drink with Dan Madden. Bernard needs a little encouragement to start his reminiscing about farming on Loughcrew. He gives me an anticipatory look, smacking his lips: 'Some birdseed always helps make me sing.'

I order three bottles of Smithwicks. Bernard raises a glass in salutation, saying *sláinte*. He orders a Hamlet. He likes a cigar each night, he says. He lights it and draws slowly on it, leaning back. His parents were from Cavan and he was born there but they came to live in Meath when he was a boy. He was the eldest in the family and was brought up in Meath. Bernard remembers working in the fields from a young age and helping out on the farm with horses. He looks back with affection on those days.

'I did National School and from the age of fifteen I worked up in Loughcrew. I grew up with those hills and worked on land underneath the mountain.'

He spits out some words; several times splatters hit my arm and hand.

'We had about 50 acres in Summerbank in the foothills of the Loughcrews. You have to remember times were different then. There are far too many grants, schemes and subsidies nowadays. It wasn't as hard to live back in those days as it is now. I know young farmers and they're not dependent on the land because they have jobs elsewhere. It would be hard to live now without a weekly pay packet.'

Bernard takes a long drag on his cigar. He thinks carefully, looking down the length of the empty bar into the middle distance; then the floodgates open and the words flow spontaneously.

'I ploughed with horses, I planted potatoes with horses, and I mowed hay with them during the war years in the 1940s. When the war broke out in '39 there was compulsory tillage and any man with land had to do a certain amount to it. The tillage inspectors went around with their book and maps and every farmer was told he had to plough so much ground because of the war. They would come around and say "you haven't enough ploughed" and tell you to plough more. People were poor in those days but they were happy – they didn't have all the material things people own today.'

He stubs out his cigar. Talk of horses seems to fire him with excitement. His eyes light up as he recalls the days of the Irish draught and the Clydesdales.

'It's sad when I look back to my earlier days in Loughcrew. There was nothing as nice as a pair of horses in a plough or a mowing machine. The Clydesdale was a heavy horse in the legs, but the draught was a lightish type of horse, although it was a good, durable working animal but very hot-tempered. If you hit the draught she might break all on her. Let her cool, let her settle and pick the grass, and once you got her going, you could work her round that meadow ploughing and harvesting till the sun'd go down. There wouldn't be a drop of sweat on her. You'd have to know your animal. The Clydesdale was a quiet animal but when you yoked her she was fresh and frisky. But it all changed when the tractor came in, and there is no horse work being done now.'

Bernard has a good recollection of farming times, but on a couple of occasions his memory bank – his internal search engine – stalls fleetingly. He drains his drink and places his hand on my thigh, looking me square in the eyes.

'I know every inch of that mountain. I farmed up there until I was in my mid-sixties and I am a little bit older than that now. When I was a young fella, I walked all those hills. I am using a walking stick and mightn't be so able to do it now.'

'Why did you never get married?'

'I suppose I wasn't lucky in that line. Y'know, it's hard to know. I certainly had a lot of opportunities in my early days but was so busy I hadn't time for it. I've heard other men say there's only one thing in the world better than a good wife – no wife.'

Bernard talks to his friend about Oldcastle. Dan says it is famed for its bedding and that is why they call it a sleepy town.

'The beauty of this town is that it is off the beaten track and on the road to nowhere. It is an agricultural community with the least amount of unemployment of any town in Ireland. Bedding is the booming business. A local man started making mattresses after the war for the want of something else to do, and they're all at it now, with small satellite factories. It's a great little business town. We're very old Oldcastlers. We call ourselves the Oldcastle Oldies, but we were going to call ourselves the Oldcastle Youngies, because we don't feel like geriatrics.'

His yarns all spun, Bernard shakes hands with me, struggles down from the barstool and shuffles off cheerfully around the streets in search of some more wool.

10

The Lowest Highest

I am a hill: where poets walk. Mountain surrounded by dancing signs, words, lines of dreams unspoken in daily happening, past and future intertwined, wild ranks of evergrowing green reaching outward, down and upward seeking the sound of birds singing in the cold of winter's night.

Amergin, The Song of Amergin

On Lyric FM's 'Quiet Corner', the first movement of Mozart's horn concerto in E flat is playing with terrific verve, brightening a murky morning. I nibble my way through a pound of seedless grapes bought at the outdoor fruit market in Oldcastle, from where a short cross-county hop will take me to the northern corner of County Westmeath. Mullaghmeen is not as famous as its easterly

Meath neighbour, Loughcrew. It is uncelebrated, unsung, unheralded, unsignposted, and unknown to German visitors. For a while on my Wednesday morning search, it also remains unsighted.

With exquisite warmth of feeling, the second movement, the romanza, is reaching its end while I have made little progress to my Westmeath finale. For 30 minutes I lose myself in a complex web of small country roads with antique, white cast-iron signs at crossroads. I am not sure if I am in Meath or Westmeath. I stop to ask directions of two men in stonewashed jeans mortaring a wall.

'I am looking for Mullaghmeen. Can you help me?'

'Is that Mullaghmeen Hardware?'

'No, the mountain. It's somewhere round these parts.'

'Oh Jeez, the mountain. Jump up here, I'll show you it.'

He pulls me on to the top of the wall. 'See that ridge of coloured trees which is light green, mid-green and dark green? Well the bit with dark green trees in the middle is where you wanna go. It used to be called white hill years ago when there were no trees on it. It was old grass that had turned white in the way that people's hair often turns grey when they get old. I was told that as a child. Now I suppose it's called green hill.'

Discreetly camouflaged with a blanket of dense mixed forest, Mullaghmeen is no more than a bland blip on the landscape and doesn't look anything like its 894 feet. It does look as though it is living up to its claim to fame as the smallest of all the Irish county tops. I follow a third-class road, its hedges thronged with the white flowers of stitchwort. Just as the third and final movement, the rondo, reaches its rousing conclusion, I come to a forestry sign announcing Mullaghmeen. The signage at the entrance gate bans pony trekking, hunting and shooting; it doesn't mention the use of a hunting horn that has been keeping me entertained on the radio. A public information notice boasts that Mullaghmeen Wood has the largest planted block of broadleaves in Western Europe. It is strangely quiet. A mile along the forest track, two men pause from their labours in a small wooden hut. They are making walking sticks and are surprised to have a visitor.

The men are working beside a wooden shed with a cream Stanley Eight range. Tommy Kane puts down his rasp and tells me about the skills involved in the craft of making walking sticks. When the best blackthorn, hazel and ash bundles have been selected, he shapes the ends, takes off the knots and pares them down, removing the bark. Ash and hazel make the best sticks because they are strong wood. After cutting them and peeling the skin, they are left for several weeks, then smoothed with sandpaper. Using a blowtorch, he blackens the wood. The sticks are given three coats of varnish, including an exterior long-life yacht varnish. On an average day, with the help of two other men, Tommy makes 40 sticks.

'I like the blackthorn best. You only sandpaper the knots on them. To get them dead straight is a hard job. People use them as souvenirs and they keep blackthorn sticks for a long time.'

I ask about the skills involved in his job: 'It seems to be

an art in its own right – perfecting the work. You really are a craftsman?'

Tommy coughs with laughter; the other man doubles up at his workbench.

'I dunno about the craftsman end of it; crafty man maybe. The best thing about this job is being out in the fresh air. I worked in a sawmill in Tipperary. My whole life has been tied up with woods and working with timber, so I suppose it is my first love.'

Tommy introduces me to Martin Smyth who has a grandiose title in the Mullaghmeen Forest Park Group. He is manager of the social economy project, funded by the National Development Plan.

Martin pours out historical facts and figures about Mullaghmeen: it covers 1,000 acres spread over five townlands; 200 acres are in the townland of Half Carton in County Meath; it is threaded by fourteen miles of forest track; originally the land was part of Lord Buckinghamshire's Irish estate and later became an outfarm belonging to Lord Gradwell of Dowth Hall in County Meath. The Department of Agriculture bought it in the 1930s and decided the land was suitable for planting deciduous trees. The geology of the area is brown earth on top of limestone rock which is ideal for growing beech. The forest has thousands of beech trees.

'Beech is a scarce timber worldwide and a mature beech tree is a very valuable asset, fetching a lot of money,' says Martin. 'It is predominantly used in furniture manufacturing. Most of the top quality fitted kitchens are made from beech.'

In the 1920s and 1930s the area around Mullaghmeen was famous for flax growing.

'There were four flax mills in the locality, now it's quarrying and concrete that's the main business here.'

Until a few years ago, Martin tells me, most people in Westmeath thought the highest point was the hill of Knockine, south of Tullamore.

'But a recent survey showed that Mullaghmeen is 52 feet higher. We are seventeen feet lower than Loughcrew in Meath and that makes us the lowest highest point in Ireland, which is a bit of a tongue twister.'

Martin gives me a stick. 'It's the finest Westmeath hazel,' he gushes, running his fingers along the newly varnished dark wood.

'Some young lads used to make fishing rods out of the hazel. They were long and fine and suited their needs. It's a lucky stick to carry. It's strong, sturdy and will keep bulls and dogs at bay. If you're travelling at night it'll protect you from the fairies.'

I decide to test its sturdiness immediately with a walk to the top. I follow a forest path, passing acres of beech trees and blue marker signs. The forest floor is dry enough for trainers. A circular cairn with stones about fifteen feet in diameter marks the top. From my vantage-point on a simple larch bench, through a break in recently felled spruce trees, I look down on Lough Sheelin. I count 30 sheep in a spit of land running out into Church Island. It's siesta time on the lake – not a duck, moorhen or swan moves across its placid surface. By contrast, the forest is seething with life.

Munching my remaining grapes, I listen to a song contest featuring the collective vernal voices of a dozen different birds: a couple of wood pigeons and their muffled 'cooo-cooo'; the cheerful, repetitive two-note 'tink-tank' call of the chiffchaff; the loud bursts like a musical pile-driver from a wren; some unidentified birds – one with a regular rhythmic 'chirrup chirrup chirrup', another trilling its elongated delivery, and a medley of whistling, chattering, gurgling, wheezing and clicking, producing a mid-afternoon concerto reminiscent of all the spontaneity and purity of spirit of a full orchestral performance. A friendly company of flies lands on my seat, and crawls over my grapes and stick. A Thoreau moment; he knew the woods well having lived two years in Walden Pond:

> We need the tonic of wildness – to wade sometimes in marshes where the bittern and the meadow-hen lurk, and hear the booming of snipe; to smell the whispering sedge where only some wilder and more solitary fowl builds her nest, and the mink crawls with its belly close to the ground … we can never have enough of Nature.

Thoreau had so much respect for wildness, he even gave nature a capital N.

The woodland floor is a rich tableau of wildflowers: white wood sorrel, bluebells, wild violets, daisies, primroses and dandelions. A watery sun filters in, lighting up my seat. The path down has contrasting shades. It takes me through a darkened wood and suddenly into bright sunlight. Three butterflies cavort in front of me. I pass piles of tree-trunks waiting to be turned into sticks. I follow the flight of a mistle thrush into a tree and stop for a close-up view of its pot-bellied, darkly-spotted throat. Apart from the venerable beech, towering sycamore, and thin Scots pine, recently planted ash, fir and oak also grow here. My eye catches a diminutive, mouse-like bird moving on a beech tree; it is a treecreeper scurrying stealthily up the bole, pointing its curved bill into holes and crevices in its search for morsels. I crunch my way over a canopy of fresh, tinder-dry yellow leaf-litter, cracking branches and twigs. The woods are bursting with spring freshness; the cacophonous birds are my only company in this place of elevated Westmeathian tranquillity.

The dictates of the geography of the road determine that the logical route for heading to Offaly is through Mullingar and on to Tullamore. Logic does not always feature on my internal map. The next morning, for no particular reason other than I like its comic name and I wish to avoid large towns, I decide on a detour to look for a place called Crazy Corner. It is marked on my Michelin road map as being halfway between Monilea and Cloughan. Clumps of sweet woodruff and cowslip line the roadside verges of this part of central Westmeath. There are no signposts to Crazy Corner; it is not marked on my Ordnance Survey map. My curiosity grows. Why would a place appear on some maps, yet have no signs anywhere indicating how to get to it or in which direction it lies? I ask half a dozen people for directions and information about Crazy Corner before I find it.

Woman at the Wood Bar & Lounge in Crooked Wood: there is only a filling station near there; I dunno why it was so called, maybe they are all crazy people there. Are you looking for anyone in particular?

Two men tidying up a cemetery: you are looking for the Crazy Corner? There's nothing there, just a meeting of the roads, a wonky offset crossroads with some wonky people. They're all rogues and chancers.

Woman weeding at Cloughan Inn: there are a lot of funny names in this area. There is Crooked Wood above that way, Mount Robert over there, Castlelost and The Downs over this way. Crazy Corner is only a couple of houses with a school and a hurling pitch.

Woman walking with a bicycle: it was always called Crazy Corner since I was a young girl. In fact, we called it the Crazy Road. I think it is to do with the fact that the cars drive like crazy along it.

Woman in Texaco garage: I dunno how it got its name, but this is Lee's Corner. If you ask for Paddy or Johnny Nooney, they should be able to help you.

Man cutting garden hedge: Crazy Corner? Haven't a notion. I never heard of it but then I have only been living here sixteen years.

When I find it, Crazy Corner consists of a crossroads with a newly-built stone house and what I believe at first sight to be a derelict two-storey house on the corner. It is a dangerous, staggered junction with an uneven road surface. The main road is a long half-mile stretch bisecting a minor road where it rises into a crest. Crazy Corner Kennels is 50 yards down the road and a primary school with a hurling pitch is on the other minor road. I sit at the crossroads for twenty minutes. Cars come and go in all directions. On the main road they reach up to 60 while on the minor one they approach it slowly observing a rusted 'Yield Right of Way' sign.

Something alerts me to the fact that the house I had assumed to be deserted is in fact occupied. A jackdaw struts across the road at the front gate and a melodious blackbird sits on the roof. Overgrown bushes of laurel and ivy surround it along with sycamore trees. Four empty tins of cat food (Cat Club with chicken) and a chair with a yellow plastic seat stand in a corner of the garden. The grass has not been cut for at least a month. I knock on the door. A man of about 65 introduces himself as Paddy Nooney. I ask if he knows anything about Crazy Corner and how it came to be so named.

He comes outside to chat at the front hedge. Paddy is wearing a Prussian blue shirt and a dark blue speckled jumper. He is holding a pair of small spectacles. Paddy lives in the house with his cats. He searches me with wary eyes. They roam the car's back seat littered with maps, books, newspapers, binoculars, clothes, Tiffin wrappers, a half-finished plastic bottle of 7-Up, boots and a hazel walking stick. The schools have just got out. I get the impression he thinks I am a child abductor. He silently examines his tan shoes for five seconds. His tongue moves slowly over his lips.

'Why do you want to know about Crazy Corner?'
'Just curious, I like the name.'

'What part of London are you from?'

'I am not from London. I am from Belfast.'

'Crazy Corner has existed for a long time. There used to be a blacksmith's forge at the corner that is now a derelict stone building. The blacksmith's name was Gracey and over the years it was corrupted and became "Crazy". So that is how it got the name Crazy Corner. It was an old school-teacher, who's dead now, who told me that. The blacksmith died during the last war and the place has been empty since then.'

'So it has nothing to do with the bad junction or bad people?'

'I don't think so, but you should have been here about fifteen years ago – that's when all the old people died off. They're all dead now, bar myself. My father was 89 when he died and he knew all about the name.'

I ask why there are no signposts anywhere in the area nor any indication that the place even exists. Paddy takes me by the arm to the side of his house. He goes down on his knees, and pulls away grass and ivy growing at the bottom of the wall. He reveals a stone made of granite with the letters CRAZY CORNEr neatly engraved on it and just about legible. The 'r' did not fit and is slotted in as a lower case letter. This tiny unknown piece of Westmeath architectural roadside heritage turned up out of the blue many years ago in his father's time.

'It was done by a skilled stonemason more than 200 years ago. It's a spud stone, which is the bottom stone for holding a gate. Years ago they used to put the bottom leg of the gate on to that stone.'

'Do local people know about this?'

'Not really. A few of them might, but most aren't that interested.'

'Why is it hidden?'

'I think it was just forgotten about down the years and became overgrown.'

With a black felt-tip marker, Paddy circles the letters, highlighting them to bring them out clearly. He says his house used to be a thatched coaching inn and was a stabling place for horses.

'What's it like living in Crazy Corner?'

'It's a quiet place but there have been lots of changes. The old ways are going fast. The farmers are doing well with EEC subsidies that account for more than half their income.'

'Are you happy here?'

'You can't be happy all the time. I am miserable half the time and happy the other half. I suppose 50-50 isn't too bad. I have two tomcats to keep me company. I used to have eight cats but six of them got killed on that road.'

'Will Crazy Corner live on?'

'I think so. It would be a shame if it died out. You'll not find it on the new land maps nowadays, but its name will certainly live on.'

There is another five-second pause. Paddy asks if I am heading back home tonight.

'No, not tonight. I'm travelling around the country, looking at mountains and wildlife … talking to people.'

He is astounded that anyone could be doing this. He questions me on the financial details of my trip.

'How are you managing for food, shelter and money? Where do you stay?'

'I get by, live cheaply, stay in hostels and B&Bs, eat in pubs. I always carry a little roughness of money for a sandwich and a drink. Remember what the poet said?'

'What's that?'

'Decant your wine and live every day as if it's your last.'

'Well that's all very well, but I think I would prefer to decant my wine in San Francisco or Las Vegas, rather than Westmeath.'

'Depends on how you look at things, I suppose.'

'S'pose so, but this is a great country too. We've no snakes and no quakes.'

He scrutinises the Bluebird, touching a few rust spots.

'It's a lotta drivin' you're doing. Do you never get tired?'

'I don't drive long distances every day. I drive slowly because I'm not in a hurry to get anywhere.'

'I would invite you into the house for a drink but I have to tend to a calf with meningitis. The vet's coming in about ten minutes, but you'd be welcome to come for something to eat later if you like. How long will your trip take?'

'Forever maybe.'

11

Coming Round the Mountain

Men go out to wonder at the mountain heights.

St Augustine, 'Confessions'

Like Siamese siblings, Laois and Offaly are always together. Sometimes they appear hyphenated, sometimes a slash separates them, and occasionally an ampersand links them; but whatever punctuation is used, the names of the two counties jointly trip off the tongue in the same way as salt and pepper, sugar and spice, bacon and eggs. They have commonalities of interest: they are treated as one electoral constituency, they share Map 54 in the OS Discovery Series, they appear together on postcards, and are linked by business, farming, rural development and tourism partnership organisations.

For me the main interest in this umbilical conjoining is a topographical one. Between them they share a mountain range, the Slieve Blooms. My objective, Arderin, cuts across the Laois-Offaly border, meaning that climbing one peak knocks off two counties. The Slieve Blooms are a long frieze of low hills made up of a staggering 60,000 acres. Appropriately, my first glimpse of them comes just after passing the Mountain View Tavern in Mountbolus. They look in harmony with the undersides of sombre clouds lingering over their blue-green domes. The writer Hubert Butler described the Slieve Blooms as 'a low, demure-looking range of hills, very suitable for middle-aged, unadventurous mountaineers with children and picnic-baskets'.

Via a series of unsignposted crossroads, post office hamlets, a railway bridge, an ivy-covered stone bridge over the Grand Canal, and several T-junctions, I arrive in Cadamstown.

My Little Tea and Craft Shop is a natural refuelling stop. The café is a shrine to the Slieve Blooms and the gentle art of hillwalking. Joan Roche manages the business from her house – the hub of the village. She offers home-baked scones, sandwiches, cakes and muffins as well as a one-woman personalised cottage industry. The walls are devoted to photographs of hillwalkers and groups posing for pictures. There are detailed maps of the area and a satellite map. Bits of typewritten white paper with slogans are sellotaped to walking sticks costing €12: 'The Year of the Hiker', 'Me, my dog and a good stout mountain stick', 'Ridge of Capard', 'The Hiker's Reward', 'Clonaslee Your Beauty for Me' and 'The

Bull McCabe'.

Joan joins me at the table. We sip our cappuccinos sharing a sugar teaspoonful of enlightenment: 'A good word in court is better than a pound in your purse.'

When I explain my trip, she says, 'You'd be better off to stay with one peak covering the two counties ... unless your conscience is so troubled that you feel you have to do one for each'.

Originally from Connemara, Joan was born in the fishing village of Cleggan. She was living in London when an aunt became ill and she inherited the house from her. Pensively, she pours a rich, milky refill.

'As you can imagine it was a huge culture shock moving from Highgate in north London to Cadamstown in north Offaly. My aunt had a post office and shop and I took over the office until the phones went automatic. My husband works on the lighthouses and is away a lot of the time, so sitting here on my own I thought I should start a tea shop for people passing through or walking around the area. I opened it ten years ago. First of all, I started in a corner of my kitchen but the business grew and I ended up having people all over the house – in the sitting room, kitchen and everywhere.'

'It seems to be a unique set-up you are offering – a place where hill and café culture meet?'

'A lot of people say it's like coming across an oasis in the desert. English and European people are not used to going into pubs for tea or coffee whereas the Irish know you get both in a pub, and many families don't like bringing children into pubs.'

'So what sparked your interest in the hills?'

'There are 27 glens and I got interested in the variety of walking routes. I'm the coordinator of the Ardara walking club. We have 140 members from all over Ireland. There are close links between Laois and Offaly, but it's a shame the Slieve Blooms are split between the two counties. If one body or association owned it, then it would be better looked after. The bigger portion – about three-quarters of it – is in Laois, and a quarter is in Offaly. For marketing purposes it would be better handled as one united area and promoted properly. There are so many people who have never heard of the Slieve Blooms. Mind you, some people come to the mountains simply because they are the way they are. If you market it like Wicklow for example you'll have hundreds of people on the hills and you'll find others won't come. Living here is magic and the mountains are a haven from the outside world.'

In Kinnitty the man in Peavoy's grocery shop is more than happy to make me a ham and cheese sandwich to take into the hills. He disappears for a few minutes into his kitchen in search of bread and butter. My eyes scan the old-world names on the shelves behind the counter:

Odlums 100% Irish Self-Raising Flour (in a new stronger bag)

Gem's Traditional Irish Custard (minus the quotations)

Sweet Afton Cigarettes

Tins of Homestead Processed Peas

Chivers Sliced Carrots (in salted water)

Hanley's Corned Beef

Campbell's Meat Balls (in onion gravy)

A raffle ticket for St Finan's Church Renovation fund-raising draw is propped up between tins of Green Giant Niblets Sweet Corn and jars of Hellmann's Mayonnaise.

'There y'are; that'll be €2. I hope you enjoy your walk and don't get lost in the hills.'

Never mind getting lost in the hills – finding a path to take me to them is the first obstacle to surmount. A labyrinth of mountain roads crosses the Slieve Blooms. There are few signposts, apart from one pointing to the Glendine Valley and Glendine Gap. There is no one around to ask. I call at several houses; all are empty. I am uncertain of the best approach to Arderin. From the map it looks possible to access it from the northern side, although there is dense woodland. In places large chunks at the sides of the roads are worn away, leaving dangerously exposed gaps beside the hedges. Several times I take wrong turnings, getting hopelessly lost. I am mildly distraught; I could be driving into a dead end for all I know.

I look across to what I believe is Arderin. It is impenetrable from this side. Farther along, a sign welcomes me to County Laois. Three miles of hairpin bends lead to a crossroads where I swing right in the search for another approach into Arderin. A sign: EXTREMELY HAZARDOUS ROAD IN WINTER. Another GMR, probably an eight on my ometer, but I'm too concerned about finding the right road to think about it. I drive round to the southern side, cross a narrow bridge and turn at three brown fingerposts pointing to Srahan Castle, Srahan Moat and Glenkitt. A bumpy track takes me as far as a farmyard and barn.

Under a bright late afternoon sun, I climb over a barbed wire fence, passing cattle with dandelion yellow identity tags hanging from their ears. Clumps of ling heather, not yet in bloom, starting shin-high and quickly becoming chest-high are my introduction to the lower slopes of Arderin, 'the height of Ireland', standing at 1,734 feet. My Westmeath hazel stick proves its worth. At the small summit cairn someone has tied a white and orange flag to a stick. The views from here were once regarded as the most extensive in Ireland. In his *Statistical Survey of the King's County*, published in 1801, Sir Charles Coote, described the expanse as 'equal to one-third of Ireland and comprising some ten or eleven counties'.

A heat haze is obscuring long-range views, preventing me from seeing a third of Ireland. To my north and west the views embody large parcels of mountains, many with forested ridges. County Laois lies south and east. There is nothing to indicate a county boundary. I pick out a couple of villages and isolated farms with outbuildings. I identify Carroll's Hill, Stillbrook Hill, and Wolftrap and Knockachoora Mountains.

I reflect on my quota of luck with the weather. This is my fourteenth county top and another day of uninterrupted sunshine which improves as the afternoon progresses. A whisper of a breeze murmurs. Several wasps buzz around. The pure white fluffy wool of the bobbing heads of bog cotton surrounds me. Every field purrs in the sunshine. I count more than twenty hilltops of varying width and length. I now appreciate why people who walk in the scarcely-known Slieve Blooms say it's easy to lose yourself. A man could easily lose himself here and still be happy basking in the silence. It is somnolently serene. Apart from a brief visit from a skylark, there is no sound. The hills are also remarkably free of the ugly phone masts that blight so many parts of the Irish countryside. These towering antennae have crept into many areas, causing visual intrusion as well as fear and apprehension in local communities – and all to accommodate the mobile phone menace.

To distract me from another rant, I demolish a bar of Tiffin stashed away in a side pocket of my rucksack, and finish off with an apple. Back at the car a team of indignant Laois-Offaly heifers has assembled at a fence. Standing like statues, they fix me with challenging stares and watch me change my clothes.

I have booked myself into the Glendine Inn B&B in Kinnitty. In such a small place it is an unlikely find, especially with an attached bistro. Dinner is a noisy affair. A party of twenty women is enjoying an end of term celebration. They have just finished a spring course in food hygiene and preparation, serving skills and catering management. Glasses tinkle every so often with a variety of toasts, including one to the skilled art of opening and tasting a bottle of wine. The evening ends in Giltraps Bar across the road. The women arrive fairly well oiled (as they would say in Boyle) and occupy a long table. Cigarettes cocked behind their ears, they launch into a repertoire of songs that includes 'Red River Valley', 'Galway Bay', 'Molly Malone', 'The Rose of Tralee' and 'Will Ye Go Lassie Go'.

One of their number, Sinead, takes on the role of coryphaeus. During a break, she chats to me at the bar as she orders a large round of drinks. She has a loud boisterous laugh.

'What do you think of that crowd?' she asks. 'They are grandmothers and granddaughters and they're all now fully trained in the art of cooking, serving, dining and ...'

'And singing?'

'Well, although you might not think it from the noise, we're really all very well behaved. Offaly is called the Faithful County, that's cos we are all faithful to our husbands. I'm not sure how faithful they are to their wives as there are so many women in Kinnitty – we outnumber the men by four to one in this area.'

Sinead returns to the table with a request from me for some mountain songs. They let loose with 'The Mountains of Mourne' and 'Come Down from the Mountain, Katie Daly'. A robustly built forty-something called Nuala stands up and, to a roar of whoops and ribald applause, launches into a rendition of 'He'll be comin' round the mountain when he comes'.

Very soon, Sinead is back for another round of drinks. By the time the last orders are called, it feels like the middle of the night, but the clock says 12.30 a.m.

'It's half past and we're half pissed,' she laughs.

As the dregs of the glasses are being drunk, the awfully

devoted Offaly husbands arrive to pick up their spouses and keep their half of the faith.

Paddy Heaney shifts his baseball cap decorated with IRELAND in small green capitals. He greets me with a welcoming and friendly smile.

'I am more than delighted to see people like yourself coming here, enjoying the mountains and asking questions about them. In ancient times people thought Arderin was the highest point in Ireland.'

On Joan Roche's recommendation, I made an arrangement to see Paddy in Cadamstown. He's an easy-going man with a glint of merriment in his eye. Paddy's incandescent enthusiasm for the area shines like a beacon. A bachelor in his early seventies, he lives with his sister. In the spirit of the retired local historian, he has plenty of time on his hands and loves talking about his parish. He uses his time to look after the interests of the village. A man in tune with the history of the area and the grammar of the landscape, Paddy speaks with a soft Offaly burr, patient and considerate. It may be a cliché but in his case it is historically true: he is rooted to the soil; his rootedness is epic, bred of an ancestral longevity stretching back 400 years. His grandfather lived to 105 and his father died at 95. This lineage is inextricably linked to the mountains.

'The old oral tradition was handed down from generation to generation,' Paddy says. 'My grandfather farmed in a place called Glenletter Valley three miles south of Cadamstown. The land wasn't that good. It was mostly mountain grazing with sheep and cattle and a few fields for potatoes, vegetables and corn. But they were self-sufficient and they had a great custom of storytelling. When I was a young lad I used to visit houses all over the Slieve Blooms. I would sit on the hearth under the chimney and listen to the stories, the songs and the music.

'The old generation loved the mountains. That's where they lived, where they brought up their families and eked out an existence. When the younger generation grew up, they went to England and America and saw a different lifestyle. When they came back they didn't want to live here. They didn't have the profound interest in the mountains that the old people had. They wouldn't know that they are full of Bronze Age burial mounds, ring forts, standing stones, hill forts, ruins of monastic sites and castles; but the most important thing of all is the Gaelic place-names, which are fascinating.

'Sir William Petty did the first survey of Ireland for the Cromwellian confiscations in 1647, '48 and '49. He trained 100 British army officers to do the survey over a period of thirteen months. He emphasised to each of them to write down the Gaelic names as the natives pronounced them, and only for that we would have lost those beautiful names. They all tell a story: Borlaghan means "the broad summit"; Glenletter means "the valley of the marshy hillside"; Barnascairt means "the tops of the thickets".'

I ask about Arderin and pagan assemblies attached to it. Paddy says a Lughnasa festival used to be celebrated on it. The last Sunday in July was an important one because it was fraughan Sunday, when they picked bilberries.

'People used to go up and pick the berries and each person carried a stone in their hand or their pocket. The tradition of placing them up there goes back to druidic times. About twenty years ago, at the foot of Arderin, there used to be a timber dancing board. Crowds came at the beginning and I used to lead the walks up Arderin from Srahanboy. We'd all come back and have tea, sandwiches and dancing until dark. Sometimes the conditions were a bit blustery but it didn't stop people doing their set-dances, *sean-nós* and waltzes. When we put up our first dancing board, I formed a group and played the banjo. We got accordions and singers and then we would have a dance in the local hall in Kinnitty. Around that time the Offaly hurling team began to gain prominence and unfortunately the Leinster final fell on the last Sunday in July and people started to drift away to Croke Park instead of climbing the mountains. They must have found it more stimulating than the hills.'

'What are your earliest memories of Arderin?'

'I remember when I was two or three, everybody used to leave the village and walk up from all over. I had five sisters and they would carry me in turn on their shoulders until we arrived at Lettercross. They came over the border from Laois, they came up from Kinnitty, they came over from Clonaslee and from Kilcormac, and there would be hundreds there.'

In the 1890s walking up Arderin was particularly popular and people came from all over Laois and Offaly. They danced on the west side of the mountain in an area now known as Glendine West. Paddy is a living repository of information and anecdote. Pausing briefly during his impassioned monologue, he squints into the far distance as he recollects a story that he heard many years ago about a celebrated incident.

'They used to elect a girl known as the Maid of the Mountain. She was crowned with a wreath or garland of heather and that's how "garland" Sunday came about. The girl, who was about sixteen, would sit on a chair and people would dance around her. That was also a pagan custom. But on the last occasion that happened, one of the Laois men passed an insulting remark about the Maid, who was an Offaly girl, and a faction fight started. Two men were killed.'

'What was the remark that was passed?'

'We don't know, but the walk up the mountain was disbanded for about twenty years. It must've been something serious. There was always a bit of spleen between Laois and Offaly – King's County and Queen's County, as they were once called. Apart from faction fights in those days, there was also bitter rivalry over the hurling.'

'You know the mountains intimately – what do they mean to you?'

'Put it like this, if I'd a choice of living somewhere else, I would not go. I love the stories of the fairies and the banshees and how people came here. A lot of Northern families settled in the Slieve Blooms after O'Neill passed through in 1601. There were Donnellys, Heaneys, Duffys, Corrigans, Breslins, Danaghers, Mullins, McMurraghs,

Mulveys, O'Neills. They all brought their own particular talent from the North – the great heritage of singing and dancing. My grandmother was the last speaker of Irish in the mountains and spoke nothing but Gaelic. She died in 1912. She was called Daly and came from a Northern family as well.'

Paddy's affection for the past is not based on sentimentality; it is based on his knowledge, long memory, and sensitivity to history, archaeology, geology, topography, folklore, half-forgotten legend, and especially to the people who live in these little-known hills. He talks with special fascination about the pre-Christian legacy.

'The mountains were never really opened up to people, so they're something of a mystery. Over the last 30 years people began to realise there was something there and so we started the walks. Visitors asked questions about what the names meant and who lived there. It unlocked a whole new vista of imagination. You walk up a road and see a gate, a tree or rock and then you see a stream or waterfall or the ruins of a house or a castle, so the whole thing is different each time and it is a place of great variety. The tops of the hills are special places and it is great for your soul to be up there. But to this day there are parts of the mountain that people know nothing at all about. When I go into the mountains I can sense the presence of the druids. They were terrific people and much more advanced than we are.'

'In what way?'

'Scientifically, they could forecast the weather long before a storm or rain came along. They were ancient soothsayers and placed emphasis on the five elements of sky, earth, sea, sun and moon.'

'What are the secrets of these mountains?'

'As far as I'm concerned my idea of their secrets is to try to work out what the druids were about – what they did, how they lived and how they carried on. But that will always remain a secret and I doubt if we will ever work out why and how they built the burial mounds, the standing stones, the hut sites. The other mystery is about its name. The anglicised form of *Sliabh Bladhma* is Slieve Bloom (Bladma's Mountain) but the meaning of Bladhma is not known. It has been lost for hundreds of years and we will never know who he was. Some old people know the secrets these mountains hold and they will take them to the grave.'

'Will you be taking yours with you?'

'I will.'

A coloured leaflet selling the county grabs my attention: 'Offaly is a county devoid of highways, and its byways reveal a new surprise around every corner'. One thing it is not devoid of is bogs. It has many large tracts of flat bog-land. There is even a bog train. On the map I pick out All Saints Bog, Boora Bog and Clara Bog.

Apart from a man drinking a half-pint of Guinness and reading *The Farmers' Journal*, the Gracelands Bar in Kilcormac is empty. I ask the owner about the bogs.

'Do y'know I cycle past Boora Bog twice a day,' she laughs, 'but I've never explored it properly. About two years ago students came from Limerick to set off some sort of experimental rocket from the bog but it didn't go very well for them.'

She rummages in a drawer under the bar counter for a newspaper clipping which she hands to me. Over a toasted chicken sandwich I read of an attempt to launch a liquid-fuelled rocket from Boora Bog. Students brought a rocket to the area and were granted permission by air traffic control to divert all planes. The rocket contained crushed ice that created pressure to compress a hydrogen peroxide and kerosene mix. Theoretically this should have been ignited by a flare which would have sent the rocket 5,000 feet into the sky, but the ice failed to deliver the pressure necessary for blast-off and the first attempt was aborted just before ignition. It had been a brave effort but the rocket failed to even lift off the ground. The newspaper reported one of the students quoting the Russian aeronautical engineer, Tsiolkovsky: What is impossible today becomes possible tomorrow; a quote worthy of the Gem sugar company.

This part of north-west Offaly, along with southern Westmeath, is a journey through esker country. Eskers are mounds of sand or gravel left by streams of melted ice. They were formed at a point where a hill, a lake or the sea halted a glacier. Hundreds of these small steep-sided biscuit-coloured hillocks straddle the midland counties forming a great ridge through the heart of the country. I had seen them in southern Westmeath and Longford. The presence of eskers is reflected in place-names: Eskerroe, Eskerboy, Eskerkeel, Eskershamore, Eskerbeg, Eskerbaun, Eskerhill,

Eskermurray, Eskerballycahill and Moylisker. They provided Ireland's first settlers with important high roads between the boggy lowlands. Eskers still determine the line of the roads over the central plain. In Celtic times the most important was *Eiscir Ríada* (Riding Ridge), the royal esker or esker of the chariots, which carried the main east-west road from Dublin to the west coast. It ran along a series of eskers known as the Arden Hills and it crossed the Shannon at Clonmacnoise, a main junction of the land and water communication system and a sacred crossroads. The best-known esker route is 'The Pilgrim's Road' running east from Clonmacnoise, skirting Mongan Bog and which can be traced as far as Doon. It may have been part of the *Eiscir Ríada*.

From Boora I pass through a cluster of towns – Ballycumber, Grogan, Ferbane, Doon and over to Clonmacnoise – at moderately illegal speed. Along parts of the route are long lines of low eskers. At Ferbane the girl on the till in the Centra is not much help about eskers. She thinks I want the Esker Hills Golf Club.

'You'll not find too many mountains here,' she sniggers. I repeat my question about eskers and in return she gives me a blank look, saying she has never heard of them.

'Mind you, there is the Esker Riada Céili Band over in Killeigh which I often heard my father talk about.'

It's getting late. I need to make some ground because I've dallied too long in Offaly. The Chariot Way Coffee Shop in Doon does not detain me as it's closed. To the right of my road, on an elevation, lies the *Eiscir Ríada*. It's not a very high ridge, rising to only about 30 feet. The area is composed of sand hills. This is big concrete country. A convoy of four sand lorries from Nally's Quarry rattles past, throwing up long trails of white dust. Small stones of gravel and dirt litter the roads.

Running parallel with the main road are several miles of low hills speckled with gorse and cows. Isolated eskers pop up suddenly through the trees over the crests of the road. Near Clonmacnoise I stop to study the countryside. The clear, early evening call of the local cuckoo resonates across the eskers. The road turns sharply south through Shannonbridge and on to Banagher where I cross the Shannon into the flatlands of southeast Galway. Friday evening rain has arrived with a vengeance as I drive through Rooaun, Eyrecourt, Fahy and Ballycrossaun – all unknown villages and all destined to remain so, before arriving at Portumna for a bed at the Shannon Bridge Hostel.

In the Portumna Diner the waitress has the endearing but wearying habit of referring to everyone and everything with the appendage 'my dear', viz … hello, my dear; the menu, my dear; the wine list, my dear; mayonnaise and ketchup, my dear; sweet, my dear; the bill, my dear; have a great weekend, my dear.

Portumna is an outdoors town. It attracts people for boating, fishing and golfing. Five Germans on a fishing expedition from Munich at the next table tuck into a meal the size of a small horse. One eats his salmon and chips as if there is no tomorrow. We discuss the golf, fishing, climbing and the weather. They have some fun at my expense, laugh at the rain and shrug. I bamboozle them with the quote from Tsiolkovsky: 'What is impossible today becomes possible tomorrow'. They smile benignly, splutter a few Teutonic *sláintes*, and raise five glasses of red wine to sunnier days.

The man behind the counter in Starr's newsagents takes a great interest in my route when I ask about driving across the Slieve Aughty Mountains. The easiest way to go, he says, is via Loughrea. I tell him I don't want the easy way – that would be too easy; I want the mountain road.

'Gawd, that is a lonely road, I am telling you sir. You wouldn't need to break down. You'd need a reliable motor car with a good spare wheel and a jack. And make sure you've a tow rope just in case. All the same it'll be a grand spin.'

'I am driving a reliable car. She flies like a bird and hasn't let me down yet.'

'Are you flying solo?'

'I am.'

'I would come wid you if I wasn't stuck in here all day. It's exactly 28 miles to Gort. I've travelled it a few times myself and it's a great road. You want to head straight for Abbey, then Derrybrien, veer right three miles out that road and keep straight as a die after that until you come to Gort. You'll have to take it easy. It's rough and narrow in places, and there are horses up there.'

'Is it horsey country?'

'No, not really, just wild horses, roaming the roads. Have you a full tank of petrol?'

It feels like I am embarking on a journey into the Australian outback: perhaps I should call it the Aughtback road; petrol, provisions, water, emergency supplies – and all for less than 30 miles. In the event, the road turns out to be an anti-climax. It has many of the characteristics of a GMR: traffic-free, some tree-covered hills which fail to make the mountain league, and longer-range views over to the limestone hills of the Burren. Not a single dingo, Aborigine, or kangaroo jumps out at me; the only animal road-traffic is two elderly but well-behaved horses on the way into Gort.

The Burren is reached through an indefinable border; there is only one main road in from the north and one going south. I wrestle with three maps to complete my cross-boreen journey from Gort to Ballyvaghan, negotiating a series of back roads through the townlands of Tirneevin, Cappaghmore, Funshin More, Corcomroe and Bell Harbour. High hedges running along narrow flat roads – just wide enough for one car – give way to stone walls. Soon I cross over into the Baroney of the Burren. Two yellow but-terflies flit past in front of the car, a sure sign that I have entered Burren territory. The limestone gleams in the lunchtime sun. The bright hills look their grey sunlit best; it's as if someone is holding a spotlight and shining it across the top of Cappanawalla Mountain.

12

Galloping Through Turbulent Tipperary

Last night I had a curious dream about Kanchenjunga. I was looking at the mountain and it was pure white, absolutely pure, especially the peaks that lie to the west. And I saw the pure beauty of their shape and outline, all in white. It is beautiful, chastely white in the morning sun and right in view of the bungalow window. There is another side to Kanchenjunga and to every mountain; the side that has never been photographed and turned into postcards. That is the only side worth seeing.

Thomas Merton, *The Other Side of the Mountain (Journal VII)*

Following the admirable motto of the *Clare Champion*, 'I arise to complete my task', and set out to tackle the county top. Clare's highest point, Moylussa, is not to be found within the limestone hills of the Burren but much farther south in the Slieve Bearnagh range near Killaloe.

Galway Bay FM weather forecast promises a day 'littered with heavy showers'. True to form ten minutes of sun on the limestone is closely followed by grey clouds pouring out thin sheets of light rain. I set the wipers to intermittent.

The Burren is a digression but gives me the chance to rest, catch up on some laundry and reading, and the opportunity to write up my journal. It also allows me to work out the next stage. Having got the western part of Ulster, Connaught and the Midlands under my belt, I now have to tackle Munster, which boasts Ireland's biggest mountains.

The east Clare landscape is 460 million years old, according to some walking cards I have picked up. As I drive south along rain-drenched roads, my mind grapples with what sort of era this was. The road takes me through Spancelhill, Clooney and Tulla, which a sign says means 'the windswept hill'. At O'Callaghan's Mills the barely discernible tops of the Slieve Bearnagh Hills melt into a slate-grey sky hanging ominously over them. It is turning into one of those wet/dry/wet/dry days. The postmaster in Broadford directs me to the cross-mountain road through Kilbane and over to Killaloe.

'You'll need to take it handy on that road,' he warns. 'It's very high and narrow but it is tarmacadam all the way to Killaloe. I've travelled it a few times and it is a great drive.'

A Fiat tractor squeezes past me on the road. Its yellow windscreen sticker reads:

Crime doesn't pay. Neither does farming

Climbing steadily for two miles, I see signs for the East Clare Way. Glenvagalliagh Mountain is enveloped in cloud. A couple of farmers are searching for stray cattle that have escaped from a field. I arouse suspicion on these back roads that get little traffic. They look over my car.

'Are you the fella about the wind farms?' one asks.

When I explain I am looking for Moylussa, he says I would be better tackling it from the other side of Killaloe.

'It's a day's work, and probably most of the night, going up there from this end. On the other side there's a forest track right up into the mountains.'

I head round through Killaloe, a boating town that is suffering from a bad affliction of the walking disease known as 'Waymarkitis'. I've seen a plethora of finger posts and signs pointing the walker in the direction of waymarked routes. The tourist authorities have created a network of walking paths for visitors, cashing in on local legend and folklore, as well as religion and literary history. Hardly can a county in Ireland have escaped the hand of the colour-coded waymarkers and their furnishings, which includes not only signposts, yellow or red finger arrows, but also information notices, maps and stiles.

At Killaloe the chosen colour is brown. Walking man signs urge me to take the Glen Way, the Lackaveagh Way, the Garraunboy Way, the East Clare Way, the Mid-Clare Way, the Lough Derg Way, and if that's not enough, then there are Killaloe country walks. Along the side of Lough Derg I turn off on to a minor road that soon becomes a mud-puddled track. My first obstacle is a closed barrier. As I puzzle over the map, two white Coillte van men arrive to open it. I ask about Moylussa – they've never heard of it. I wonder for a moment if I'm in the correct range of hills. Another three miles along forest tracks, the second obstacle involves removing the top end of a spruce tree that is partially blocking the way.

Eventually I come to a turning circle and for the first time see my quarry close up through the trees. Moylussa is a rounded mountain with a broad-topped hill above thick forests. Thousands of trees, standing in regimented rows, encircle me. A grassy track beside Feenlea Mountain passes a characterless young spruce plantation. With my Westmeath hazel stick I beat my way vigorously through the dense growth, battling with sticky green needles and the bluer, pricklier needles of sitka spruces, on to a pleasanter velvet carpet of mountain grass and bog cotton.

The morning of cloud is exchanged for an afternoon of sun. Notwithstanding the fact that I have made good inroads, it is still a moderately steep climb. Moylussa's two tops are about 30 yards apart. The summit furniture is unremarkable. To my east the huge expanse of Lough Derg is guarded by hills. The Arra Mountains rise on the other side of the lough. At the Derg Marina more than 50 boats sit hugger-mugger at the water's edge. I make out a few of the names with my binoculars: *The Lady Patricia, Miss Molly, Pooka, Tyreless, Why Knot?, Chantal, Ghost Rider, Harmony.* A couple of men potter around with ropes, while the owner of *Sea Urchin* touches up the blue lettering.

A breeze cools the hot air. Like a cormorant drying itself with arms outstretched, I stand in open communion at the top and feel the wind around me. I roar a 'hello' to see if anyone hears or can be bothered to answer but succeed only in frightening the life out of a skylark. A revving chainsaw replies, piercing the silence. Lying immediately to my west is the summit of Cragnamurragh, just 18 feet shorter than Moylussa. I look across the valley dividing Ballykildea and Glenvagalliagh Mountains. After the limestone country of the Burren, the hills, fields and hedges of east Clare are an exuberant blaze of green. It is a riotous foliage. I savour the scene and reflect on the galaxy of green – the colour that permeates the landscape is much more than an expressive backdrop. The song says there are at least 40 shades. I wonder about the degrees of green and their names: emerald, lime, sage, mint, British racing, celadon, olive, jade, bottle, khaki, teal, chartreuse, Winsor ... and a new one on the list, Eddie Stobart green, named after the road haulage magnet who runs lorries. I think about the ubiquitous nature of green and the variety of its usage: Greenpeace, Greensleeves, Green belt, Green pound, Greenhouse gases, Green vote, Green Paper, Green Beret, Greenland, a Greenhorn, the Green room, greengrocers, mushy green peas, and green-fingered gardeners. It's strange the things that come into your head on the top of green mountains in an ultra-green land.

A tense Saturday evening standoff is underway in Oola.

The elderly, grey-haired woman behind the counter in Meagher's foodstore is questioning a twelve-year-old boy who is trying to buy cigarettes.

'They're for a man in the pub,' he says.

'Who is he?'

'Seamie.'

'Seamie who?'

'I dunno, er, he just ast me to come up and get him ten Marlboro.'

'Well, you go and tell him to come up here and get them for himself. Now run along wid you.'

She shakes her head in disgust, looks at me, world weary eyebrows uplifted. 'Yessir, how are you?'

'A bar of Tiffin please and it's all for myself.'

She cackles with laughter. 'You couldn't watch those youngsters these days.'

I ask if she knows what Oola's name means. She believes it comes from the Irish word for apples, *ubhla*. There used to be lots of orchards in the area many years ago.

'It is a funny name,' she says. 'We have to repeat it for people all the time. Many moons ago I lived in England and when I phoned the homeplace here the telephone number in those days was Oola 2. I had great fun with the English operator. He got to know me quite well. Each time I came on and asked to be connected through the exchange he'd sing down the phone to me 'Ooh La La! … Ooh La La!'

I ask about a hostel in Cahir, but she either doesn't hear me or ignores my question. I have unlocked an anecdotal key. She's on an Oola roll. About twenty years ago, she recalls, tidying a pile of papers on the counter, some Americans came to town.

'They were looking for their roots and information about the area. They asked Tim at the petrol pumps if he knew of a place called Zero Zero LA.'

Without as much as a pause for a laughter break, or the bat of an eyelid, she launches into her next party piece, a short local jingle.

> Oola town, a hungry town,
> A church without a steeple
> Heaps of gawks at the half-doors
> Criticising all the people.

Gawks, she explains, are inquisitive people. All I wanted was chocolate, but I appear to have sparked off the hidden talents of a veteran Oola comedienne dispensing local lore free with each bar.

'We've an old saying,' the shopkeeper in The Heritage News and Deli in Cahir Square informs me with a bright smile; 'on the hills of Tipperary the visitor is a king'. As I drive through the South Riding of the county, I feel regal. My territory is the mountains and I am king for the next few days of all I survey. That means I am king of nothing because there is nothing to survey. The rain and mist has closed off even a hint of a view of the Galty Mountains. They may as well not be there. Admittedly, I am not quite the same pedigree as King Donal Mór, the King of Thomond, who ruled this part of the world in the twelfth century. I quickly slip out of my regal reverie to read black-lettered signs on white boards at the side of the road urging 'No Incinerator', 'Incinerator will poison our children' and 'Keep the Golden Vale clean and green'.

Tipperary is known as 'The Premier County'. During the eighteenth century it was the scene of many faction fights and was nicknamed 'Turbulent Tipperary', a name that lingers to this day. It is Ireland's largest inland county and is unique in that it still retains, for administrative purposes, an old English land demarcation from the Domesday Book by dividing itself into two – the North Riding and South Riding. For my purposes I will not be treating it as two separate counties but am content to tackle Galtymore, the single highest pinnacle covering both ridings, and the adjoining county of Limerick. Over a consolatory cafetière moment in the Cahir House Hotel, I stir a Gem sugar quote into my cup pondering what to do: 'The man with boots doesn't have to worry about where he puts his feet.' That shouldn't be a problem for me today. I have three options:

1. A tour of Cahir Castle in the rain.

2. The Munster senior hurling championship first round match between Clare and Tipperary everyone is talking about; the only trouble is that it is in Cork, about 70 miles away.

3. A trip to the races. I overheard an American ask about Clonmel Races. An afternoon race meeting starts at 2.15 and won't be affected by the rain.

A couple of men standing at the bar ask where I am from. When they discover I am 'chasing' mountains, they tell me that the man I need to speak to is Tom Dalton. The taller of the two, dressed in Sunday best and wearing a tweed jacket and sharply creased black trousers, says Tom runs a tyre business.

'He is de boss man of de walks, de head honcho, and he knows dem hills better than anyone else round here, but you'll not get him until tomorrow.'

Tipp FM is playing 'Oldies and Irish'. My musical accompaniment on the short drive over to Clonmel includes 'Johnny I Hardly Knew Ye', 'If You're Irish come into the Parlour' and 'Let Him Go, Let Him Tarry'.

By the time I reach the racetrack the 2.15 Kilsheelan Handicap is over. It has just been declared a photo finish. A man standing beside me describes the official going as 'yielding to soft'. It is a compact race ground with a crowd of about 500, outnumbering the bookies ten to one. I study my race card and invest €5 on Minamaia in the 2.45 Roscrea European Breeders Fund Fillies Maiden. Minamaia does not feature until the final furlong but by that stage it is too late.

My attention is drawn to the reclining hill of Slievenamon rising from the plains a few miles to the north-east. It towers over the course. The next race is the 3.45 Slievenamon Handicap Hurdle. The weather is improving and the mountain has reappeared from under a cloud top. I feel guilty that I hadn't climbed Galtymore, but the sport of kings has me gripped. Several wooden picnic tables are provided and I am joined at one by two well-dressed men who look as if they know the form. We discuss the prospects for the 4.15 Comeragh Novice Hurdle. One man suggests either Aye Aye Popeye or Penny Farthing. I plump for the latter. It comes in last while Aye Aye wins at 5-1. I squander a further €10 without any success and decide to cut my losses. King of Ireland is running in the last race. I have an inexplicable feel-good factor about him.

A flamboyant-looking man with a dirty black beard and large white overcoat shuffles over and stands beside me at the parade ring. His fleshy face, like an unmade bed, is suffused with the violet colour of heavy drinkers. His hair is greying at the side, like his bushy moustache and is in need of a trim. His fingers have a yellowish colouring. He is a tall man, wearing what might best be described as a 'coat of many odours'. I guess he is in his mid-sixties. In a voice marinated in nicotine, he mumbles something incoherent, introducing himself as Mick 'the horse' O'Brien. Everyone knows him as 'Micko' throughout Munster. He deals in horses: buying them, selling them, racing them, spending money on them. He loves talking about them. Each year he visits Buttevant and Ballinasloe, both famous for their horse fairs.

'I regard myself as an observer of people,' he explains. 'I like watching them and seeing them trade. The fairs are great places to meet friends you haven't seen for ages. You'll also get a great range of coloured horses there, as well as brood mares, foals, cobs and hunters.'

Micko says King of Ireland is not one of the fancied horses. 'Someone must have named him for romantic reasons after Brian Boru I suppose, but you never know, he could be the one for you.'

He checks the paper. The odds are 25-1. He explains that the jockeys are all apprentices. As King of Ireland snorts and shudders his way around the parade ring, Micko tells me about the qualities to look for in a horse.

'You need them broad-chested and narrow-legged. You want them to be fairly lively but at the same time calm, if you follow me. The jockeys have to have a good racing brain too and good hands.'

He asks where I am from. When I mention Belfast, he launches into a rhapsodic eulogy on Van Morrison, questioning me closely about his music.

'His early stuff was de best. "Madame George" … "Cyprus Avenue" … "Moondance" … they're all classics, but I've seen him performing and he's not very communicative in concert. I suppose he communicates through his songs.'

Micko's wife, Maureen, introduced him to Morrison's music. Without prompting, at the mention of her name, he pours out the story of his sad marriage. His powder-blue eyes take on an intense look. Quickly he's in full thunderous gallop. He'd got into brawls and was often drunk. He spent money he didn't have on horses and was seldom at home.

'It just wasn't gonna work out, so she left me.' Micko emphasises his words with a large gesture of his hand. 'Can't say I blame her. One Friday mornin' she just said she'd had enough and that was it. I loved her and was married for 25 years. But the hardest thing to take was that she left me for her boss in the factory where she worked.'

I ask if he is lonely. 'I'll tell ye the plain truth now, no lie – loneliness can be a problem, but it's not half as bad as having to live with someone else. I like my own company – sure life's lonely anyway.'

Micko is a warm-hearted and knowledgeable horsey man. I enjoy talking to him, but his smell is overpowering. I make my excuses, rush to the terraces and watch the last race. It is a slow start for 'the King' and gets even slower as the race progresses. Through my binoculars I watch a closely bunched field of galloping horses, with Slievenamon, now a well-defined outline, framed as a perfect backdrop. King of Ireland's jockey, with his royal blue and gold stars, stands out distinctively for his colours but not for his horse racing skills. He finishes third from last in a field of twenty.

I am in dire need of a caffeine kick. Never a truer word was penned on my Gem sugar sachet in the snack bar: 'The world can't make a racehorse out of a donkey.'

I tear up my beaten dockets, €30 poorer. I have had a clean sweep of losers. As I walk back to the car, the commentator's haunting refrain rings in my ears: 'winner all right … winner all right …'

When I arrive at Dalton Tyres on Monday morning, Tom Dalton's head is buried deep under a car bonnet. He lifts it to explain to a woman with an ancient BMW the intricacies of wheel-bearing loads. He points out the details on a stained white sheet of paper. I approach the car unobtrusively and mention Galtymore. He motions me to wait by the reception desk. I think he says I am a 'lunatic'; maybe

I've got the wrong man.

Tom's business is housed in a cavernous workshop. A wooden roadside sign in red letters reads DTS: Dalton Tyre Services. His name is painted over the main entrance in red and green capital letters. A white van parked outside carries the slogan 'Dalton Tyres Serving You'. The workshop is littered with smooth tyres, used tyres, remoulds, tractor tyres and tyres with punctures. Tom makes his way over to his office, rubbing his hands on a tea towel. We sit on easy chairs beside a low circular table sprinkled with tyre leaflets and a telephone. He puts on the kettle. I explain that I have been directed to come and see him as 'the boss man' of the hills. The phone rings. 'Dalton Towers ...' (his answer reminds me of an English fun-park) '... yes we'll have the Bridgestone by Wednesday at the latest.'

Tom is a well-built, fit-looking man in his early fifties. He has been selling tyres for 31 years. He has gentian blue eyes. His padded navy jerkin says 'World Championship Ten Years, Sparco'. When not selling tyres, his spare time is saturated with the mountains, particularly those in Tipperary and Waterford. He has also walked in other parts of Ireland and abroad. North to south, east to west, he has crossed the Galtees hundreds of times, an aficionado of the hills on his doorstep. He has an extraordinary force of attachment – bordering on summit love – with Galtymore. In the past ten years he has climbed it 1,500 times and has walked the length of the range more than 60 times.

He pours two cups of tea. 'Where do you want me to start?' he asks, not giving me an opportunity to answer.

'The first thing you have to remember about Galtymore is that it is a nunatak' (at least that's one mystery solved). 'That is to say it protruded through the ice. On the northern side of Galtymore there are four lakes and in each one there is still Arctic char to be caught today which are remnants of the ice age. They were the first freshwater fish to colonise Ireland more than 10,000 years ago and live only in the purest of waters. On the westernmost lake, Lough Curra, the glaciation marks are still visible to this day …'

'Hello Dalton Towers … Kevin's away for lunch, could you call back at 2.15 …'

Tom walks the hills every week and feels at a loss when he visits parts of Ireland that are bereft of mountains.

'When you go up you'll see a Celtic cross at the top that was put there by people from the Glen of Aherlow. But a lot of people misrepresent where the top is. The cross is not actually on the top; you pass it on the way to the top and I often wonder about the numbers of people who walk straight to the cross and have not been on the top of Galtymore. I would say 99 people out of 100 have never reached the real summit …

'Dalton Towers … yes, Goodyear Radials, we've any amount of them – how many do you want …?'

He continues as though we have not been interrupted.

'You have to remember only a small number ever visit Galtymore. Everybody will tell you that they must climb it before they die, but only a few ever get round to it. Years ago people were afraid to venture up it because they thought they would get lost – there always was some fear attached to it.'

'Was that because of the sheer height of it?'

'It may partly have been a form of acrophobia. People felt that it was a far steeper conical hill than it actually is. They worry about getting lost, about a fog coming down or bad weather closing in, but it is not really difficult to climb. In the famine times there were many difficulties. There were a lot of mud huts in one area, so the people had a very hard life. There was an old man of 97 I met a few years ago, he has since died – Henaghan was his name; he recalled his parents speaking about the famine but he said all he remembered was the stench of the potatoes coming up the valleys. To some people it was a kind place to live, but for others it was nothing but hardship …

'Dalton Towers … well we should have them in by tomorrow morning, gimme a call first before you come …

'The mountains also have a personal memory for me. Seven years ago I got a heart attack on Sugarloaf in the Knockmealdowns. In fact I had three: one hidden, and then two others in hospital. It was six months before I went for a walk. The first place I went was up the Black Road. It took me about six weeks, and for two or three days every week I would walk a bit farther each time. This particular day I walked to the top and there were about six people on the summit. It was a beautiful day and I turned to them and said I'm on the top of Galtymore and I am the happiest man in the world. They looked at me as if there was something wrong with me, but I had my own hidden agenda.'

'So they'll always have a special affection in your heart?'

'It's my second home when I go outdoors. The unique thing is the views. If you are lucky, you can even see the Aran Islands on a clear day. I have been there in all conditions: on the warmest days of the year, on days of snow with severe hoarfrost and spindrift on the rock. I am also one of the few people to have seen the Brocken Spectre on Galtymore. You'll often see a halo around your head similar to a mini-rainbow and that is the heat coming off your head. It's like Our Lord walking on the water.'

'Which county owns it?'

'I think you should treat it as being owned by both Tipperary and Limerick. I don't think anybody can define the boundaries of any counties in Ireland by inches or feet. It is just a general borderline that crosses between them.'

Tyre sales in Cahir are plummeting. Half a dozen people form a disjointed queue outside Tom's office. They're starting to get impatient. I can't get him stopped. He has a living to make from tyres but his passion is the mountains. He drips with love for them. If Galtymore has a guardian spirit, then it lives in the lithe frame of Tom Dalton. I walk backwards to the car. He's still talking to me. I stumble over an airline. He bowls a final jocular wobbly warning at me.

'… And another thing, just before you go, look out for the winds up there – they've been known to tear people apart.'

By the time I reach the Cahir to Mitchelstown road, the clouds have turned from grey to cotton wool white. The Knockmealdowns, a striking chain of hills running into Waterford, rise in an impressive procession to the south. A fingerpost saying 'Galtymore Climb' is my cue to turn off the fast main road five miles from Cahir. My first proper sight of Galtymore from the southern approaches is through a gap in a hedge along Black Road. It looks do-able in a couple of hours. Away from the roaring traffic, Black Road is an immediate contrast. About two-thirds of the way along I come to an abrupt halt. A herd of cows and calves driven at a snail's pace by a farmer with a yellow woolly hat fills the road with their lazy saunter. Thoreau would have approved of these cattle. He decreed that the best walking was a slow saunter – emulating the camel, the only beast he thought that could ruminate and walk at the same time.

'Welcome to Skeheenaranky,' the farmer beams through cracked teeth. 'They say the name means "The Dancing Bush" and this road you're on is called Black Road. In the late 1800s it was thick with people, so that's how it got its name. They came down on Sunday morning to go to mass in Ballyporeen even though there was a church nearer to them.'

More than twenty houses line the road, spanning three centuries of architecture. Nineteenth-century thatched cottages sit adjacent to twentieth-century two-storey farmhouses, while twenty-first-century villas with pillars, entrance gates and satellite dishes are perched back from the road on heights. On one of the pillars a pied wagtail warms itself in the sunshine. Black Road is a two-mile long tarred road ending in a car park with space for fifteen cars. Mine is the only one in it. A rutted bog track, a continuation of Black Road, with water instead of tar trickling down its centre, marks the starting point. I clamber over a couple of steel gates, passing the carcass of a dead sheep lying in the ditch. The stone path coalesces into a grassy path and immediately climbs into the hills. Quickly I gain height, watching the mist come down in swirls high above me. It now covers the main peak of Galtymore but the smaller neighbouring Galtybeg is clear. I pass the foothills of Knockeenatoung and, after an hour's steady walking, pause to admire the views, conscious that this opportunity may be denied me higher up. The Knockmealdowns are immersed in sunlight.

The path leads to the col between the two hills. An obstacle course of high bog hags means it is a 30-minute amble to the top. Tom Dalton told me that 99 people out of 100 believe the cross marks the top of the mountain but in fact the true top on Ireland's highest inland point at 3,018 feet is a cairn farther on. I have worn binoculars around my neck for the whole walk but to no avail. It is too cold for birds. Their songs would be blown away unheard. A wind is whipping up. I reach a tall metal cross firmly embedded in the ground and struggle another 100 yards over to the cairn.

A fierce battle against the elements develops to allow me to join that elite band of a minority of one per cent that makes it to the cairn. Little wonder the others ever venture beyond the cross. Lying sideways into the wind at an acute angle, I hold my hat firmly in place and with the other hand clutch my obsidian stone for balance. The mist swirls in circles. It is the most turbulent wind I have encountered so far, raging somewhere between storm and violent storm force. I have difficulty standing as well as breathing.

The cairn – perhaps fifteen feet high – provides partial protection. I wait for ten minutes. Huge conglomerate boulders stand along the narrow summit ridge. I shelter behind them. Gradually the mist uncoils and my spirits lift. It disappears to reveal a window showing off the valley glistening in a rainy after-glow. Roads criss-cross a mosaic of green fields over the Golden Vale. It is largely unforested and unfenced countryside – somewhat surprising as the name Galtymore translates as *Sliabh na gCoillteadh*, 'wooded mountain'. Steep ground lies on all sides, especially north west where Carrignabinnia and Slievecushnabinnia dominate the foreground. Southwards, the summits of the South Riding and Waterford are strung out before me.

On the other side of Galtymore the Glen of Aherlow sweeps away to the north. I look down on isolated farms and lakes. The views are short lived. The wind is reaching gale force. It cuts through the air like a razor slashing at my ears, roaring round my head. Mist returns; the only way for me is down, or remain at the top and risk being gusted into oblivion.

Over dinner in Cahir, the Tipperary wine – which has come a long way – tastes divine. It has been a tough day's walk and it is a relief to escape the buffeting from the wind. I allow myself a bottle of the Italian Barolo, 'the wine of kings and the king of wines'. I truly feel like a king who has conquered all he has seen: a latter-day king of Munster experiencing, not for the first time, a little bit of that famous 'Tipperary turbulence'.

Like pilgrims doing penance around the Stations of the Cross, the six women ignore me. In plodding circles, with heads bowed, their walk continues all day outside the gates of Mount Saint Joseph Abbey near Roscrea. I have booked myself in for a two-night full-board stay in the guest house at the Cistercian Monastery. Incongruously, it is caught up in the middle of an industrial relations crisis. The workers attached to the college beside the monastery are not liberating their hearts with prayer or a liturgy; they are picketing the main entrance gates as part of a strike.

A bearded man called Lionel, a lay worker who is not on strike and who helps run the guest house, greets me. He says I have come at a difficult time because of the industrial action but he assures me it is not affecting their guests. They can accommodate twenty visitors. At the moment just three are staying.

'You have arrived amidst a sea of troubles,' he says. 'About 30 catering and cleaning staff from the college are involved in the strike and, although the Labour Court ruled against them, they will continue to strike. The monks are upset by it and it is causing big problems.'

Although it is a detour in my mountain travels, I wish to find out how a modern community of Cistercians lives and works. Having seen the abbey at Boyle I am intrigued by their lifestyle. Mount Saint Joseph has a 'lights out' curfew by 9.30 p.m. My room is basic, clean and comfortable, with a well-sprung single bed, a table, two chairs and a wardrobe.

The bells ringing for 4.00 a.m. vigils waken me with an ungodly (or more correctly, godly) racket. I roll over and quickly fall back to sleep. At 8.30 a.m. mass in the public church the priest prays for a 'fair and just resolution' to the strike and for an end to conflicts.

Breakfast is a boiled egg with tea and toast served by a smiling Lionel. A long-serving monk, Father Ciaran Savage, offers to show me around. Since taking a vow of stability to live and remain with the Order in 1948, Father Ciaran has spent 54 years as a monk at Mount Saint Joseph. We walk over to the monastery where he points out some highlights. It is oriented east-west, a design which goes back long before Christ.

He grins. 'If you want to find the south and look up at the roof, you'll always see the spiders on the south aisle of the church because they like the warmth and the sun.'

The abbey was founded in 1878 and 34 monks now live in it. They bake their own bread, but apart from looking after a dairy herd they don't work on the farm. Their potatoes, vegetables and fruit are bought locally. For the most part, the cows and beef cattle provide their living and are the main source of income for the upkeep of the monastery.

Slight of build, standing just over five feet tall, Father Ciaran is a nimble and quietly spoken, plain-faced man with thin lips. He has a kind face and alert eyes for a 76-year-old. We walk through a well-stocked library of anti-quarian tomes on the way to his office where we sit surrounded by shelves groaning with Bibles, reference works, directories and dictionaries.

Father Ciaran's desk has a Toshiba laptop computer running Windows 98 with a screen-saver that says 'Jesus

Christ'. He wears a religious habit, the typical dress of the monk, dating to the Middle Ages. Underneath the hood is a cream robe tied around his waist with a leather belt. He has large round glasses. Father Ciaran speaks candidly and frankly about becoming a monk and why he chose the calling.

'We still follow the rules laid out by St Benedict in the year 500. It is a fine document and many lay people read it too. It states that if a young man comes to a monastery, he has to find out if he is truly seeking God. If he is, then he will make a monk. We gather together to sing the word of God seven times a day and read the Bible; singing psalms for 50 years you find extraordinary depths in them. Chanting psalms in Latin or in the vernacular has a very soothing and pacifying effect.'

If he senses an awkward question his eyelids flicker fast behind his Dennis Taylor-style spectacles and his voice drops to a whisper.

'So you don't cut yourselves off totally from the outside world because you buy produce from local shops?'

'If you're going to have a peaceful life, you have to, to some extent. Benedict legislates for that. The Cistercians are a branch of the Benedictines and went back to the Benedictine rule to have more solitude. But we have computers here with the Internet.'

'You have obviously embraced technology. Do you have e-mail?'

'We have, but we have to be careful that it doesn't take over, so we use the Internet sparingly.'

'Do you think a computer can enrich spiritual life?'

'Certainly we can get books more easily on the Internet and through websites than in libraries. We are not anti-technology, but on the whole we do have to be wary about being sucked into the whole modern world.'

'So you spend much more time reading the Bible than surfing the net?'

'Well, that's true, but we have a college website and many other monasteries throughout the world have their own.'

'Do you think old religion can be compatible with modern technology?'

'It can, there is no doubt about that, but it depends how you use it. You have to remember that we spend as much time as we can reading the Bible. We call this *Lectio divina* and we have to spend a lot of time on that.'

'What exactly is that?'

'*Lectio divina* is a way of reading the scriptures which has developed in western monasticism over more than 1,500 years. It is more than spiritual reading. "*Divina*" means divine, and shows that it is not any kind of reading; it is a prayer in itself.'

'Do you have any hobbies?'

'My hobby is Celtic spirituality. I've spent much time reading about High Crosses and have seen most of them. There is a lot to be learnt from the Celtic monks about contemplation. It is a great help to us in this modern world, especially their love of symbolism and the depths they saw in nature.'

'You have spent 54 years here – have you any regrets?'

'It's a great life, there is no life to compare with it at all. I could have led an even more secluded life. If I'd been with the Carthusians, they are more cut off and spend even more time in prayer than we do.'

'Is there anything you miss about outside life? For example, do you ever go into Roscrea?'

'I go in as little as possible. I am a bit of an introvert, so a silent life has been the ideal life for me.'

'Are you allowed to drink wine or beer?'

'Benedict said wine is not a drink for monks, but he allowed it. We do have wine on big feast days but there was a strong strain of alcoholism in our family so I believe in the Pioneers.'

After we finish our chat, I wander through the library. I notice a shelf behind a glass-fronted case lined with books about Thomas Merton. Father Ciaran's eyes light up when I show an interest in his work.

'Merton had a tremendous ability with words,' he says, pulling down a book from the shelves. 'His most famous work is *The Seven Storey Mountain*. He became a Trappist Monk at the age of 26. I was introduced to his writing when I came here in 1948. The novice master read me some of his work and it had an immediate impact on me. He hit things right to a tee for me back then.

'Merton was very against the world, a bit like myself really,' he chuckles. 'After the Vietnam War he became a great man for peace. He began to communicate with all the big shots, like the Dalai Lama and others. Then he went to live in a hermitage in the woods.'

'A bit like Thoreau, who wanted to pluck the finer fruits of life by living in the woods?'

'Yes, like him. I suppose Merton was the twentieth-century Thoreau. He was a spiritual theologian, but he was always a bit of a showman and liked publicity. In a sense he was really the first modern Cistercian monk. He was a strange and enigmatic man, a radical in many ways.'

'What is so special about his writing?'

'His writing was crystal clear, penetrative and wise. It was profound and vivid. One of the great strengths of it is that his readers identified with him. He wrote popular books about the spiritual life, as well as poetry and literary essays. His writing is about his relentless search to know God but he also wrote about world literature, politics and culture. He was a compulsive writer and a prolific one, turning out two books a year. He campaigned for social justice and peace, and really was an extraordinary phenomenon.'

'What happened to him?'

'Near the end of his life he was leaning towards Buddhism and Zen. He met a tragic end in an accident in Asia. He went to Bangkok in 1968 and was electrocuted in the shower at the age of 53.'

Today Merton's name lives on in monastic libraries around the world. Many books have been published about his writing and hundreds of studies of his life written.

The midday bells are calling Father Ciaran to sext (noon prayers) and he leaves me alone in the library. After lunch I amble over to see the pickets, still circumambulating at a crawl around the front gate. As well as being cold and wet,

I reckon they must be dizzy. They regard me with suspicion and refuse to talk. On the way back my attention is drawn to a commotion involving schoolboys. A group of about twelve is carrying a boy on their shoulders across the front lawn over to a waterfall leading into a stream where he is unceremoniously dumped.

'It's the traditional treat for the house captain,' one of them tells me. 'It's one of the annual pleasures that goes with the exalted title.'

'It's OK,' a tall angular boy sniggers, 'he's a fairly good swimmer.'

I ask about the impact of the strike. One says it is difficult getting clothes washed and ready for sports. A spotty, earnest lad with a rubicund face complains that the food has not been up to the normal standard.

'Last night there was no soup and the banoffi pie fell apart which would never happen when the normal cooks are in the kitchen.'

A heavy downpour forces me inside. During what is known in the monks' day as the 'siesta', I sit in my room writing up my notes. Over six o'clock dinner I share the table with a nun and a German youth called Johannes who is studying theology and carrying out research into the history of the Cistercians. The nun, Sister Anne, comes from Athlone and is a regular visitor. She and Johannes sit opposite me, and in the manner of an interrogation, launch a burst of rapid-fire questions.

Sister: Have you seen any of the Tuatha Dé Danann yet?
Johannes: Who is zis dé Danann?

Sister: They were the gods of pre-Christian Ireland – the people of the Goddess Danu who was a female fertility goddess. They are said to have arrived here on a dark cloud and were important in the early invasions of Ireland. They were divine beings in Irish mythology and were believed to have magical powers, but they were defeated by the Milesians and banished under the raths, grave mounds and hills. I suppose they are the fairies of modern Irish folklore.

Johannes is well versed in the five 'w's of journalism, or in his case, the five 'v's:

Vat is ze difference between ze hills and ze mountains in Ireland? Vat is ze meaning of zis Brocken Spectre? Vie do so many people vish to climb ze hills? Ven vil you vinish your travails? Ver do you go next time?

(For the record the answers are: 1,000 feet. 2,000 feet is a hill, 3,000 feet is a mountain; the Brocken Spectre is your own profile, or shadow, cast on the hillside by the winter sun and moisture, and the name comes from Brocken in the Harz Mountains of Germany; because they are there; the end of the summer; Vaterford, oops, Waterford.)

More exhausted than if I had climbed several mountains, I retire to the sanctuary of my room. It has been a day of questions and talk. After compline (night prayers) the monks settle down for a few hours' sleep. Tonight I learn silence. Normally, I am accustomed to a working world of noise: mobile phones, stentorian voices, digital editing machines spewing out interviews, a bank of television and radio monitors blaring at once, raucous laughter, editors barking orders over tannoys, frenetic people working against deadlines. This is an alternate world, an unhurried world and one removed from anything previously known to me. It is a sacred silence – a perfect stillness, the stillness of mountains. People speak softly, and move slowly – especially the strikers at the front gate.

The next day, as I prepare to leave the monks to their silent activity, their endless prayers, their strict simplicity, and their contemplation, I reflect on monastic life. The monks at Mount Saint Joseph lead a disciplined and austere existence. Having spent some time in their company, I feel a sense of peace and quietism. There are handshakes all round. Lionel wishes me Godspeed and a clear path on my quest. He invites me to return. I tell him that if I have taken nothing else away from my visit, then it has made me want to search out the books of Thomas Merton.

Of course my time in the abbey has meant more to me than the writings of a twentieth-century monk. In climbing mountains, I had always seen them as places of vision; now for the first time my power of inner vision has been enhanced. Like my talismanic obsidian stone, my time has helped bring an experience and understanding of silence and detachment. I had come as part of an inner quest as much as an outer one. The two nights have been a window on a vanishing world. My stay may have interrupted my progress, but it has not impeded it. It has enriched me and awakened the existential spirit dwelling within my soul.

13

The Witch of the Knockmealdowns

The road had the merit of all savage trails, and of all the
tracks a man still makes who is a-foot and free and can make
the shortest line for his goal; it enjoyed the hill.

Hilaire Belloc, *The Old Road*

The Lismore postmistress is having a bad day. It is
approaching closing time and she has had a busy afternoon on the stamp and pension-dispensing factory floor.
She has lost her spectacles and hearing aid. For the second
time, I repeat my question, enunciating the words clearly
and deliberately.

'Mountains ... I am looking for information about mountains.'

'You want to know about Madden's ... the pub? ... well

206

it's there – across the street on de right hand side. You can't miss it. They do food too.'

'No, no the MOUNTAINS, the Knockmealdowns.'

'Knock-you-down? What on earth ARE you talking about?'

The woman standing behind her, leafing through a filing cabinet, collapses into coughing spasms of giggles, shoulders shuddering. When she brings herself under control she shouts to the postmistress.

'Maointains Mary. He's asking about hills.'

The euro cent finally droppeth with Mary.

'Aghhh,' she chortles, 'mountains, mountains, mountains.' She buries her face in the palms of her hands shaking with laughter. I join in the levity, pausing patiently for a respectable ten seconds, giving her time to recover her composure.

'Are there any old-timers in this area who would know anything about the Knockmealdowns and the history attached to them?'

'Ah, they're nearly all gone now,' she sighs wistfully. 'They just die and die and die, and keep on dying. I can't think of anyone in this town anyway. You could try the library or the heritage centre. In fact if you go over to Madden's pub and ask in there, they may know something. Owen Madden is a great walker and so is Mrs Madden.'

She smiles, 'Y'see I was right first time.'

The waitress in Madden's, a tall brunette, is perplexed when I express an interest in the hills and ask for Mrs Madden.

'I don't think she does a lot of walking these days,' she says; 'she's well into her seventies.'

'Is Owen around?'

'Who wants him?'

'He won't know me. I want to ask him about the mountains.'

'He's not here, but I'll phone him at home and see if he can help you.'

It's six o'clock and the pub is empty. The walls are adorned with framed black and white photographs of old Lismore from the 1920s showing three cars parked along the main street. A notice says Fred Astaire visited Madden's for a drink when he was a guest at Lismore Castle. The premises used to be an old shop with a grocery in front and a back bar. It was renovated in 1998. Until the 1970s Guinness was bottled and labelled on the premises. In 2001 Madden's won the national best shopfront award and a certificate of merit hangs at the door. The waitress returns with the hot news.

'He's not doing any walking in the hills any more. He's only playing five-a-side football to keep fit.'

Two hulking hill groups – the Knockmealdowns and the Comeraghs – dominate the mountain landscape of Waterford. The vee road, which was built in 1847 after the famine as part of a poor law relief scheme, climbs into the Knockmealdowns. It is a high quality GMR complete with hairpins and more sheep (including three dead ones lying in the middle) than cars. Mile after mile of wild rhododendron covers hillsides spilling deep into the valleys.

On a whim, outside Clogheen, I turn into the Parson's

Green Caravan and Camping Park. I have had my fill of B&Bs, guest houses, hostels and monasteries; I long for somewhere where I won't feel guilty if I don't eat the fourth egg and fifth rasher, and where I do not have to explain what I'm doing. Kathleen, who runs the site, shows me round a three-bedroom van called Phoenix King. I ask about the name Parson's Green. She says it is a townland marked on the old maps of the area but not on the newer ones.

'Some English people who come here think there is a connection between this and the Parsons Green tube station on the London Underground. It's just a name that has survived and we like to preserve it.'

The caravan meets my main criteria: it is enclosed by mountains on all sides – the Knockmealdowns lie to the south and the Galtees are north. I rustle up beans on toast and wash it all down with a generous pot of steaming tea. On a short hike around the site, I note that most vans seem to be variations of cream and beige: the colour of digestive biscuits, Irish cream liqueur, or the sand dunes of Tramore beach. The other guests are a Dutch couple in a camper van with stickers from European cities, three English-registered cars with towing caravans, and a young couple struggling in the wind to erect their two-person tent. The tents are mostly in shades of mellow sage green. I have nothing against caravanners or campers. I just don't often 'do' holidays in their midst. They have their own rules and rituals, their own equipment and furniture, their own quirks and caricatures and their own ways of doing things. Take the family of eight from Dublin, across from me in their mobile

Marauder. They have their own peculiar way of napalming steaks and sausages on barbecues with long skewers. The men especially seem to enjoy this task, while the women, generally wearing shorts that show off fat white legs, sit in deckchairs doing crosswords.

At first light my slumbers are disturbed by a clamour around the caravan. For a moment I panic and think someone is trying to break in; then I realise the noise is from above. It's a drumming patter that sounds like rain but isn't heavy enough. I listen for a few moments. The racket is coming from the van's aluminium roof – an attraction for the Parson's Green rooks. The scraping, scratching, tap-dancing and cawing lasts intermittently for the next ten minutes. This early-morning ritual is repeated at my neighbour's van. I pull back a flimsy curtain and across from me, on top of the Marauder, four overfed rooks hopscotch along, followed by a foxtrot, and their own pas de quatre.

Eventually I fall asleep again. Three hours later, under a blue-skied morning, a delight of dunnocks invites themselves to share my alfresco breakfast at the picnic tables. They bob and weave their way along the ground in grateful anticipation of scraps of soda bread, but reject the baked beans that accompany it. From the park, the Waterford apogee, Knockmealdown itself, is hidden behind Sugarloaf Hill. The mountain just sneaks into Waterford by a hair's-breadth. It lies in the extreme north-west of the county, part of a symmetrical group running into Tipperary. Probably the most pleasing view of Knockmealdown is from the Cappoquin road. The curves and contours give it an exemplary mountain shape. In *The Mountains of Ireland* Daphne Pochin Mould says the Knockmealdowns 'if not exciting to the climber, have the virtue of never looking tame'.

A tame chaffinch sings its heart out as I pull on my boots at the car park where the Lismore and Cappoquin roads diverge. After listening to its pleasant short twittery trill for five minutes, I lock the binoculars on to it, partly camouflaged in a vast commingling of trees and rhododendrons.

I classify the walk to the top of Knockmealdown as a mild slog – if that's not an oxymoron. After crossing the Glennandaree stream, I swing too far round to the west side, ending up in a tidal wave of leathery rhododendron thickets, ferns and tall heather which considerably slows my progress. Full of beans, I eventually pick up some well-trodden sheep paths. It's a surprise to find the last 30 yards covered with the most luxurious mattress of short heather on which it has ever been my privilege to place a pair of boots. It is a gloriously cushioned final assault to a forlorn trig point at 2,609 feet, the only indication that I have reached the summit.

The pastoral scenery of east Munster lies all around with extensive views of County Waterford. I follow the course of an orange and white Eircom van on the vee road as it wriggles and twists its way through forests and open land before falling into Lismore. On this Tuesday morning little traffic is moving; the countryside has a quiescent charm. A gust of wind arrives without warning. An enticing path and wall crosses the eastern Knockmealdowns over to the Sugarloaf. Small summit cairns are placed on several tops. A tangle of tracks, boreens and faint paths thread their way halfway up into the mountains. Many come to a dead end.

Other travellers have stood on this spot and described the scenery. Joseph Hansard created a moody word-picture in *The History, Topography and Antiquities of the County and City of Waterford*:

> From the summit there is a grand view extending in every direction: to the north, the celebrated Rock of Cashel and the cathedral are distinctly visible; to the south, the ocean, the old towns of Dungarvan and Youghal, with their harbors and a great extent of sea-coast may also be observed. What a place for the poet to take a peep at the 'dear old country' and behold its delightful scenery – sweet country of verdure and richness, variety and splendor – with her tall round towers – her oaks – her little old churchyards, with their mouldering ruins and their whitened tombstones, nettled with briers and ivy-roots – her holy wells – her lakes – place of woods and streams – of hills and valleys, and offering everything in its varied aspects to charm the eye and enchant the ear!

Kathleen had told me to ask for Mary Tuohy in Clogheen. She is one of the oldest people in the village and Kathleen thinks she may have a family connection to the mountains.

Mary, who is retired, lives with her son Brendan in the main street. She was a community welfare officer and has lived in Clogheen all her life. Her father, Jack, owned a pub at the other end of the street. Mary's maiden name was Moloney, a name under which the Knockmealdowns were known. The Moloneys were a group of families who came down the Shannon from Clare after Cromwell's time. Some settled in Dungarvan while others moved into the mountains. There were so many, she says, the name of the mountain was changed to *Cnoc Mhaoldomhnaigh*, the Hill of Moloney, or Moloney's Mountain.

'When I was about nine in the National School an inspector came one day. You could see the mountain from our classroom and he asked the pupils for its name. We were trained to say *Cnoc Maol-Dhoun*, the bare brown hill, although it was also called Slieve Gua. He asked if there was any other name for it and I was delighted. I put up my hand and said the "Hill of the Moloney's". He said that's right; you're a clever child. My father had told me all this and it had been handed down to him.'

'Does anybody else in Clogheen call it Moloney's Mountain?'

'There might be some but not many. I suppose it is our own special family name for it, but most people would know it as Knockmealdown.'

'How common is the name Moloney today?'

'It is quite plentiful around the Dungarvan area. There are some in Clogheen and Lismore. When I was young there used to be a John Moloney who had a drapery and boot shop where Shaw's is now.'

'Have you ever climbed Knockmealdown?'

'No I haven't and I won't be now since I'm 86. I was born on the first of May 1916 and my mother said I came at a very bad time because of the Easter Rising. I did once go up Galtymore – that was 1933 when I was well able to leg it, but 'twas no joke even in those days. The Knockmealdowns are full of stories. There's a Major Eeles – Henry Eeles – who's buried on the summit. He wasn't ever in the militia, but they called him Major. He was a fine cut of a man and was well dressed. He's supposed to be buried there with his horse, dog and gun because he wanted his last resting place to be nearer to heaven or, as others said, to be nearer the home of his beloved lightning. The day he was buried they pitched tents at the base of the mountain and had a wake with pipers, and drinking and dancing the whole night long.'

'What did he do?'

'In the 1730s Major Eeles was a land agent for the Lismore estate, and a talented person. He was the first man to discover the identity of lightning with electricity. He published papers dealing with the powers of electricity. There's also a corrie lake that is supposed to be haunted by a woman known as "Petticoat Loose". She wasn't a very good-living woman and apparently the priests denounced her at the altar. Some people say she was banished to the Red Sea.'

'What did she do that was so bad?'

'She was a bad-living person. Her husband was a carpenter and she lived with him near a small thatched church which people used after Cromwell had ransacked and burned their church. During the seventeenth century she had a shebeen in her house. She sold drink during mass and tried to stop people going to church.'

'What did she look like?'

'She was a very tall woman, about six feet in height and they say she weighed about two tons. That was supposed to be on account of the weight of her sins. She was at a dance one night and whatever way her skirt came loose, it fell off her and that's how she got the name "Petticoat Loose". Her real name was Hannigan and I think she killed her husband but I don't know how. I read a bit about her. Some of it may have been codology, although she did exist. In fact, she was known as the Witch of the Knockmealdowns. I remember when I was young hearing a poem about her:

> Petticoat Loose lived by a carpenter's shop,
> She had a shebeen and was fond of a drop
> She encouraged the neighbours on Sunday to stay
> Instead of going to mass, in the shebeen all day.'

I drive back to Lismore for an evening meal in Eamonn's Place, a snug pub in the centre of town. After a plate of chicken and bacon casserole, I scoop up my banoffi pie, its delicious crunchy toffee base topped with a liberal dollop of fresh whipped cream. A Gem sugar saying reminds me of the pupils and circling strikers at Mount Saint Joseph Abbey: 'The proof of the pudding is in the eating.'

14

Cafoodling around Cork

If you have dwelt in the secret heart of the mountains,
beholding the full glory of their revelation, as they unfold
their signs and wonders from the going down of the sun to
its uprising, nothing can efface the memory of such nights.

Julius Kugy, *Alpine Pilgrimage*

From Clogheen my path takes me into north Cork and a
series of 'M' towns: Mitchelstown, Mallow, Millstreet,
Macroom. Mountains in respectably high ranges – the
Ballyhouras, the Boggeraghs and the Derrynasaggarts – run
off in various directions, but the bigger mountains of west
Cork lie farther away, obscured by dismal rain and low
cloud. At a Tiffin recharge halt in O'Corocra's Foodmarket in
Ballingeary, the woman with eyes as big as saucers says

216

she's ashamed to admit that she doesn't know Cork's highest point. Another woman produces an old Ordnance Survey map and places it on top of copies of the *Examiner* and *Evening Echo*. They pore over it for five minutes before finding Priest's Leap and tracing their fingers over the contours to Knockboy.

'That's definitely it – Knockboy. Although it's on the border with Kerry, I think most of it is in Cork.'

High hedges, laden with fuchsia and flowers, including purple thistle, wood sorrel and buttercup, line the road into Glengarriff, a place invaded by several hundred cyclists. They're on an eight-day tour of Ireland as part of the annual FBD Rás – the Irish equivalent of the Tour de France. They have taken over every hostel, B&B and hotel room in the village. I manage to secure the last single room in the Seaview B&B. Through my bedroom window I watch a seal bob its dark head inquisitively above the water; a cormorant dries itself in the evening sun, its wings outstretched.

Some people in Glengarriff believe the hills on their doorstep – Hungry Hill and Sugarloaf Mountain in the Beara peninsula – are the highest in Cork. Knockboy is much less known, tucked away from the tourist traffic in a secluded corner. The word about music on the Glengarriff street is that Harrington's is the place to be. When I get there a mini concert is in full tilt. It's not so much a case of standing room only, more squeezing room only. The musical fame of Harrington's has spread to the cyclists. About twenty Lycra-clad bikers stand around the bar discussing front and rear derailleurs, chain rings, toe clips and helmets, ignoring the music.

The ensemble, gathered around window seats in a corner of the bar, is made up of seven musicians: two women in their thirties with long pony tails in the window seat play concert flute and accordion; four men variously play guitar, banjo, fiddle and harmonica while another woman is on the flute. Their music is a lively mixture of reels, polkas, jigs and eastern European folk songs. The mousy-haired man on harmonica is a mean player of that instrument – eyes closed, right index finger raised, and eyebrows doing all the work (apart from his mouth), he gives a virtuoso performance.

A couple of unappreciated tunes – 'Runaway Bicycle' and Mungo Jerry's 'Pushbike Song' – are played for the cyclists but they're too caught up in their route to Millstreet tomorrow to even notice. They leave after one drink. The musicians launch into a version of 'Norwegian Wood' which has the remaining tourists and locals humming the third verse in unison.

'Danny Boy', 'Arthur McBride', and 'The Wild Colonial Boy' never make it to Harrington's Bar; 'The Mountains of Mourne', 'Galway Bay' and 'Carrickfergus' tonight remain no more than unsung place-names on maps; there is no whiskey in the jar, the Salley gardens are shut, while the gate into the fields of Athenry remains resolutely closed … yet Irish eyes are smiling; the 'continental *ceilidh*' drips with pure musical joie de vivre.

Like Captain Farrell before him (best known for his walk over the Cork and Kerry mountains) Dennis Flynn is also counting out his money. He has just collected his weekly pension at Teddy O'Brien's Post Office and Foodstore in Ballylickey.

'When you go up that road there from Coomhola cross-roads,' he points outside, 'that'll bring you on to a very twisty mountainy track.'

He tucks eight crisp pink ten-euro notes into a faded brown leather wallet. A tall man, he holds himself erect and strong. He looks deep into my eyes.

'My advice is don't look around ye, or even look down, until ye get to the Priest's Lepp 'cos it's mighty steep. There is so much to distract ye, so drive careful and don't look to the left. Remember a good day in Coomhola or Ballylickey doesn't mean a good day up Knockboy.'

I ask how Priest's Leap, or 'Lepp', got its name. Dennis draws his sleeve across his forehead.

'There was once a priest, on his way by horse from Kerry to Bantry, to visit a sick man and he learnt on the summit that the man was dying. He feared he would arrive too late to give him his blessing so he knelt down, prayed and leapt from the summit of the mountain to his destination about five or six miles away. He's supposed to have landed on a rock in Bantry. Legend has it that you can see the print of his knees, his fingers and nose.'

Dennis speaks with a lively, energetic, fast-paced, sing-song Cork lilt. His voice falls in cadences with certain words and phrases being repeated diminuendo. Occasionally, as he stares at me, there is a dramatic Shakespearian pause for greater effect in his delivery.

During the 1950s he farmed on the slopes of Knockboy.

'In those days the sheep wool was eight pound a stone and there was big demand for it, very big demand. There wasn't the big numbers of mountain sheep that we have today because of the EEC grants.'

He is still the owner of the eastern side of Knockboy, although there is a dispute about it.

'We leased the land going very far back and prior to that we would have been the owners. The dispute arose because Brussels demanded maps for every perch of land within your folio so there could be no cafoodling with grants and everything would be above board. We were part of 2,220 acres divided between three. That's big, very big.'

He talks about the history of Knockboy. In the 1890s evictions on small farmsteads were carried out and his family was affected.

'My grand-aunt was evicted. It was very much a controversial affair, very controversial. She was Flynn – I can't remember her first name it's going back so far – but she was Flynn and she was thin, very thin.'

'Why was she evicted?'

'Money was almost non-existent, funds were low and rents were rising all the time. There was no earning up in that poor place, no earning at all. Times were bad and so the landlords evicted her. She had three children and one of them was later hanged in Cork jail. When one of the others grew up, he went to battle with the landlords over the eviction business.'

'What about the mountain today – do many people go

up there?'

'About 2,000 people went up to welcome in the millennium. There was every class and creed; they had medical people, teachers, youth clubs and mountaineers and they held a big bonfire. They landed tyres, hoisted in by helicopter to the top, and some people stayed on the peak all night.'

Before we end our chat Dennis tells me one other 'very special' thing about Knockboy.

'I'll tell ye something for nothing. When you go to the trouble of going up there as I have done many times there is a special spring. It is very difficult to find – it took me six hours. But I have taken water from it to patients in Bantry hospital and it has cured people. My daughter was there and had an operation for her appendix and it helped her. I told all the patients to use it sparingly as there is only a limited amount. At the end of the week there wasn't a one left inside in the ward; the whole lot were gone home, not a one was left.'

'So the Knockboy water cured them all. What is so special about it?'

'It's supposed to be genuine. Now I don't know whether 'tis or not. But somebody said it was certainly doing wonders for all the aches and pains of the people in the hospital. It is pure cold spring water coming right out of the north side of Knockboy and that is very hard to find these days, very hard. It's great for the kidneys and superior to tap water. It is very difficult to find, very difficult.'

'Could I find it?'

'Ah, you've no hope of finding it.' He gives a loud

guffaw. 'Other people have made exhaustive attempts to find it and failed. It comes from under a big rock. You'd want to get exact details.'

He gives me a final long hard look with a wag of a thick finger.

'I wouldn't recommend you start looking for it because we might never see you again. It's a great achievement to get up there, but don't look for the spring because you won't find it. Look around you when you get there – you can see Cork, Waterford, Kerry, everywhere. You'll not forget the trip when you get to the top of that road, and the scenery will last you for a lifetime, for a lifetime.'

The sinuous road north from Ballylickey loops around an inlet of the bay and has all the elements of a GMR. After two miles of kinks and blind summits it reconfigures itself by climbing into a series of hair-raising hairpins. In a couple of places the configuration of this high mountain pass is such that I can't see over the bonnet, and at one point I am not sure if I'll make it the seven miles to Priest's Leap. It is a triumph of engineering over sanity. Gripping the steering wheel, I follow Dennis's doubly good advice, not daring to take my eyes off this horrendously steep road. The last two miles are a first gear drive. Had there been a lower gear, I would have engaged it. Hanging precariously to the edge of Coomhola Mountain, the road rises and rises, swings higher and higher, and becomes sharper and sharper. There are no crash barriers.

When I arrive at Priest's Leap my hands are sweating and heart beating a little faster. I have gained a lot of height, but lost some driving confidence. I reverse into a layby, get out and peer over the top of the metal cross that looks down over the road. The precipitous nature of it is even more evident from this vantage-point. It is built into a middle portion of the mountain with a 1,000-foot drop on its western side. More birds fly below me than above. Even though I cursed it as I made my slow, white-knuckled progress, it is a GMR par excellence. I rate it nine out of ten on the ometer.

As I lace up my boots, Red FM, 'serving Cork city and county', is reporting a breaking news story from the World Cup in Japan. The Irish team captain Roy Keane has had a row with the manager Mick McCarthy. He has been dismissed and is to be sent home. The row is over what Keane sees as inadequate training facilities and having no training kits or footballs.

At the end of the news bulletin the reader warns of 'tundery showers'. This forecast is accurate. Three short thunderously heavy showers of hailstones mark the first half-hour of my Knockboy walk. Like a tap being turned on and off for a power shower, they stop as quickly as they started. Fortunately there are plenty of large boulders to hide behind and I arrive at the top, relatively dry after more than an hour's slog over boggy terrain. The reward is more than worth the effort. Peak piles upon distant peak as I advance towards the trig point. A brisk wind scuds the clouds across the sky. Blueness returns. From the top, a dramatic vista opens in front of me. Nothing, not even Dennis's 'views for a lifetime' iteration, had prepared me for this visual thrill.

Perched on a boulder, my legs dangling over the edge, I

try to make some topographical sense of it all. Range after range sweeps around from north Cork in a tumultuous confusing jumble. There are at least ten ranges. Some mountains are tightly bunched together; there are runs of three or four in alignment, all similar in height; others are spaced out separately at uniform intervals; with some there is no pattern or logical order; there are lolloping sprawls carelessly thrown together, strange bedfellows haphazardly juxtaposed, while a few stand on their own, detached, aloof, not part of the herd. No single peak dominates.

My eyes rove over the ranges on the three peninsulas – Beara, Iveragh and Dingle. I frame them, digest them, and move my binoculars along. The serrated tops of the Caha Mountains in Beara protrude clearly; on the Ring of Kerry the topmost peaks of the MacGillycuddy's Reeks are sheathed in mist, and behind them the Slieve Mish range in the Dingle peninsula thrusts upwards in a wispy haze. Moving across, my eyes are drawn to the distinctive twin peaklets of the Paps, perfectly rounded, modest molehills in comparison to the higher Kerry peaks, slumbering in the afternoon sun. The Paps, known as *Dha Choich Dhana*, are the two breasts of Dana (or Danu), the mother goddess of the Tuatha Dé Danann. It is a bewildering array. The Cork sky gods are good gods, clearing the clouds and presenting this kaleidoscopically awesome view. For some time I stand on top of the rock, my obsidian stone giving balance. There are mountains every way I look: a 360-degree mountainscape, an embarrassment of soaring riches.

I adjust my binoculars looking for small details: a

mountain road goes into a chicane; the sun brings out some wrinkles and fissures, and I focus on the white icing decorating one peak; no one else appears to be out walking. It is an unpeopled landscape. There is no sign of a modern-day Captain Farrell. The emptiness, the isolation, the timelessness, the spaciousness is intoxicating. I attune myself to the surroundings. It is a monumental silence: the silence of a Cistercian monastery without the strikers. Not a bird sings, not a sheep bleats, not a cow lows, nothing moves.

Never mind Dennis's mountain spring, if I could only bottle these views and capture the moment then it would last me a lifetime. A marketing executive could sell it as the 'genuine mountain sound of silence'. I linger on the top for more than two hours letting the stillness embrace me. Anyone who has never understood the magnetism of mountains and wishes to reach a transcendental level of calm should, on a day of limitless visibility, stand on the crown of County Cork at 2,321 feet above sea level. A Thoreau moment, writing about a Cape Cod beach, leaps to mind: 'A thousand men could not have seriously interrupted it, but would have been lost in the vastness of the scenery.'

The unrelenting spread of sitka spruce has not penetrated these rugged mountains. There is not a white Coillte van to be seen. Most of the bigger ranges are free of blanket afforestation although some trees carpet the slopes of hills in north Cork. I marvel at the range of shape and size, and at the variety of summitry: flat tops, serrated ridges, sawtoothed, ragged notches, conical, pyramidal, craggy, moderately contoured, bare and rounded, heather-covered, smooth or grassy-sided, shale or sandstone.

Daphne Pochin Mould's description of the hindquarters of an elephant comes into my head, but to me they look more whaleback than elephantine. A breeze brews up as I sip my tomato soup. The hills of Kerry are my next destination – specifically the MacGillycuddy's Reeks. Climbing Knockboy, *Cnoc buí*, 'yellow hill', has given me a fix of immensity and the perspective I sought to allow me to grasp the scale of the scenery.

I have never felt a desire to run up or down mountains, but descending Knockboy I adopt a gentle jog along a different downhill route. It seems to suit the terrain and my cheerful mood. Skipping like a mountain goat, I leap from rock to tussock, slipping in slime and several times landing ignominiously on my hindquarters. Panting and sweating, I delicately work my way round a quagmire in the valley. I could use some of the pure mountain spring water. Varying the downward route brings rewards. The large-flowered butterwort grows profusely in clumps. This flower, acknowledged as the jewel of the spring flora of the southwest of Ireland, is insectivorous. The ground throngs with milkwort, tormentil and staghorn moss, but the butterwort, known as the 'Kerry violet', lords over all. To avoid getting my feet, trousers, and hindquarters any more sodden, I make my way over to the road. Under a spitting sky, and with a sore derrière, I trudge uphill for a mile and prepare for a dizzying descent in the drizzle.

A leaden sky confronts me the next morning. From late the

previous afternoon – about an hour after I had knocked off Knockboy – a weather revolution hit the southwest. The Cork sky gods that were yesterday so benevolent have turned nasty, if not downright angry. I had phoned Pat Falvey in Kerry to ask about climbing Carrauntoohill with him. He organises guided tours of the MacGillycuddy's Reeks but says any thoughts of tackling it over the weekend are out of the question. He reminds me that four people have been killed on the mountain since Christmas. Throughout Cork the weather is playing havoc with the routine of daily life. The fast-ferry services have been cancelled, local crossings to Cape Clear, Sherkin and Hare Islands are suspended, and Cork Airport is closed until further notice owing to violent winds. Fishing boats are unable to leave the ports of Union Hall, Schull and Castletownbere. The lobster boats are tied up and the first West Cork Traditional Wooden Boat Festival to be held in Baltimore over the weekend is a washout.

The woman in charge of the Mermaids Café in Schull is despondent. From her elevated position, standing on a chair chalking up the blackboard prices for haddock, cod and plaice, she tells me the fishing boats have been tied up for four days; and what's worse, she has run out of fish.

'We had to import stocks from Cork city,' she sniffs at the very idea of it with a trace of malevolence in her voice. 'And because of that we've had to put up our prices.'

The twelve fishing vessels and four lobster boats that operate out of Schull are grounded.

'One of the lobstermen overturned in his boat two days

ago. It was Tony's boat. He rowed for Ireland once, so he's strong as an ox but it was a lucky escape. He lost all his gear – pots, nets, everything went down. I heard some of the older people say it's the worst May for more than 50 years.'

A Galway hooker was smashed off the coast after being caught in a storm. It broke its moorings in Glandore harbour and was swept on to rocks.

'Luckily no one was on board, but it was one of the most famous hookers. It was about 100 years old and had sailed across the Atlantic and to the Arctic. Everything is affected by the weather. It's a disaster.'

More rain falls, quickly becoming heavier and hammering on the windscreen, overwhelming the metronomic sweep of the wipers. Rain, cold and a damp depression; dankness and a doleful dismalness sum up my mood. I feel tired. An attack of the blues is coming on. I had a sleepless night in an uncomfortable and empty hostel in Bantry. Thunder rumbles, a lightning flash, ferocious rain – the whole symphonic west Cork works in fact. Thunder slams again, more lightning.

Feeling musically peckish, I fiddle with the car radio, browsing the wavelengths to cheer myself up: a snatch of Mozart, a Steve Earle song, a burst of Daniel O'Donnell, Bizet's 'Habañera'. Red FM issues a road danger alert from the motoring organisations; their message is simple: stay at home. Headlights are blazing on cars by midday. The demister is slow to clear the back window and I can't see anything through my rear view mirror. I get out to clean the window, anxious not to miss any sudden views of misty hills. Two cars swish past, soaking me. Several roads are badly flooded and half a dozen minor ones are closed. The deluge continues unabated. It is a supersaturated landscape. Fields are swamped; the banks of the River Ilen are dangerously swollen, threatening to submerge the road. On my way out of Skibbereen, three horses cower in a field behind a hedge, and cattle with dazed expressions wander aimlessly around. A group of Belgian tourists sits listlessly in two camper vans in a layby, looking at equally listless sheep nibbling waterlogged grass. When the stair-rodding rain relents I sniff the cool air. I muse over how the wild flowers survive. Curtains of red valerian blow on the top of roadside walls and the tall Mexican fleabane dances in the wind. Common ragwort and red clover shiver beside each other.

15

Waiting for Gheraun-tuel

This song of the waters is audible to every ear, but there is
other music in these hills, by no means audible to all. To
hear even a few notes of it you must first live here for a
long time, and you must know the speech of hills and
rivers. Then on a still night, when the campfire is low and
the Pleiades have climbed over rimrocks, sit quietly and
listen for a wolf to howl, and think hard of everything you
have seen and tried to understand.

Aldo Leopold, *A Sand County Almanac*

I set off for Kerry with a heart almost as heavy as the continuous rain. The county is entered via a gloomy road
tunnel north of Glengarriff, leading into a 90-degree bend.
Mountains are all around but the only ones I can see are

those on my map: Baurearagh, Killane, Esk. The roadside verges are covered with swathes of St Patrick's cabbage growing in abundance, adding splashes of colour along stretches of rocky walls; there is also ragged robin, dog violet and selfheal. Dense banks of rhododendrons and hawthorn add a pink and white flourish.

Kenmare is in a bowl of invisible mountains on all sides. An old-fashioned laconic yellow sign on the road northwards, partially hidden by hawthorn trees, reads 'Road Unsafe for Horse Caravans'. There may be no horse caravans, but it is a treeless, twisty, uninhabited road that zigzags over the Caha Pass to Moll's Gap. Kerry County Council has put up a danger sign warning of approaching coaches on the road at Moll's Gap. Two Far & Wide tour coaches, closely followed by the Tir na nÓg tour bus swing round the corner as I search for the turn off for the Gap of Dunloe. A tortuous single-track road lying ahead of me like a dead snake takes me down into the Black Valley. For three miles it twists and turns, allowing a maximum speed of twenty mph. When I reach the bottom the road plateaus out. I stop to look at a stonechat perched conspicuously on a fence post, its clear 'week tsack tsack' echoing across the valley.

The road follows the course of the Owenreagh River passing Dale Wood, a huge forested area. Water cascades from the lower visible regions of the mountains. The Reeks are ahead of me, their tops submerged in cloud that looks rooted to them as part of their natural attire. The Gap of Dunloe should receive the Blue Ribbon award for the best

GMR so far (although the use of the term 'road' is to be questioned). The fifteen miles between the Black Valley and Kate Kearney's Cottage are rich in zigs and zags, puddly potholes and cuddly crests. It is not a road for the faint-hearted, darkness or dodgy brakes. Its surface is badly broken and uneven. For a stretch of several miles the entire central section is gouged out, replaced with stones that are ineffective, leaving holes of up to ten inches in diameter. I am still determined to enjoy what I can of the scenery, and stop frequently. At Auger Lake a windswept pied wagtail trembles, its feathers ruffled after a bird bath, and hops and pecks amongst the sheep droppings.

When I arrive at Pat Falvey's house he offers me a heart-warming plateful of steaming lasagne, a smooth glass of Chardonnay and a hospitable house to recover from the weather, the roads and the driving. His mountain lodge is about a mile from Beaufort, the nearest hamlet to the MacGillycuddy's Reeks. Pat does not look the archetypal mountaineer. Stockily built, he is about five feet ten with the compact body of a wrestler. He is 45 and, in his own words, 'densely muscled'. There is nothing in his immediate demeanour to indicate that this man conquered Everest and has climbed the highest peak on each of the seven continents. His adventures have taken him to many remote places, including the jungles of Irian Jaya where he lived with Stone Age tribes, and Cho-Oyu in Tibet, the sixth highest mountain in the world. Nowadays he leads treks and expeditions to some of the world's highest ranges. In an earlier incarnation, Pat ran a construction property and finance business in Cork. It went broke when he was in his late twenties.

'I was a workaholic and very depressed, in fact almost suicidal,' he reflects. 'Someone asked me to go hillwalking so I came down here to climb Mangerton. I looked across and asked a friend about Carrauntoohil and it became my Everest. I climbed it later and after that my mountaineering life took off.'

Pat has an insatiable appetite for mountains: talking about them, climbing them, photographing them. He doesn't just love them, he has an emotional middle-age devotion to them which was so strong that this Corkonian upped trekking poles, moved county and built his home right in the middle of them. From his house, 400 feet up the side of Strician Mountain, you can see the Reeks – when the weather permits – as well as Tomies and Purple Mountains on the other side of the Gap of Dunloe. The mountains are a constant presence. The walls of his house are adorned with photographs of his travels.

Next morning I ask Pat what the wind measures on the Beaufort scale, the method of determining wind speed and strength by observing its effect on natural objects. He reckons it is five or six, with winds 'keen to freshening'; it is not a day for venturing into the Reeks.

I decide on a drive round the area. Eileen Cronin is a larger than life, talkative Kerry woman. She and her husband keep 70 sheep. She is known locally as 'Miss Carrauntoohil'. A stoutly-built woman, she wears a duck-egg blue cardigan over a brightly patterned floral blue dress. The laces of her white runners are undone. When I arrive she is hanging out her Monday morning washing in a barn beside a small shed with two picnic tables and vending machines. I sip a coffee from a polystyrene cup and we stand shoulder to shoulder in silence looking up at the mist. Several times Eileen ruminates with pursed lips; several times she shakes her head, and several times she shoots me a concerned look. For nearly 40 years she has lived at Cronin's Yard, or at what might be termed 'base camp'. Many times she has seen people setting off unprepared for the dangers ahead, returning defeated and frustrated. Eileen has witnessed the hopes, fears, elation and disappointments of climbers from all over the world. Her backyard used to be the nerve centre for the mountain rescue team.

'If the clouds are in there, it generally doesn't shift for a day or two. I think you'd need your head examined to be going up into those mountains today. It would be the height of nonsense. It's supposed to be like this for the rest of the week.'

Eileen recaps on the four deaths since Christmas. The last person to be killed was just a week ago. He was a 28-year-old man from Cork who slipped and fell from the Fibrahy Ridge.

A German couple pulls up in a hired Punto. They stretch their limbs, smell the air and check the conditions. The woman asks to use the toilet. The pounding rain is getting harder. We move inside the shed. Screaming swifts, with their scimitar wings, dive-bomb back and forward from a nest in the eaves. Eileen talks about winters.

'We get a lot of rain but very little snow. But people are here at all times of the year. They come from Europe, Australia, New Zealand and Canada. The majority of them are nice people but most aren't fully prepared for the walk. Some go up in track shoes and don't have any gear. There used to be a ridge walk on the June bank holiday but it was called off ten years ago because of insurance problems. In July there will be more than 300 taking part in the four peaks challenge covering England, Scotland, Wales and Ireland.'

I ask if she has ever climbed the mountain. She giggles. 'I made three attempts and I didn't get there; I nearly got there once, but the fog came down and I came down with it.'

A television crew once interviewed her for a programme called 'Wilderness Walks'. They took her up in a helicopter.

'It was brilliant,' she recalls. 'Absolutely beautiful and they flew me over the top. 'Twas a frosty day and I was looking down on the cross at the top. We flew over the Gap of Dunloe, the Black Valley and the lakes of Killarney, so it was quite a trip. 'Tis something I'll never forget.'

Eileen waves me off, relieved that I have decided not to risk it. As a parting shot she reminds me of an old Kerry saying: 'If the weather today is bad, don't worry, next week is another day.'

I drive round to Lisleibane to reconnoitre another entry point into the mountains. Three miles along a pot-holed track, I look up to see if there is any hint of the mist shifting or the prospect of a tinge of blue showing through in the sky. But the Reeks are reluctant to reveal themselves and it looks equally as bleak as Cronin's Yard; in fact it's getting worse. The air is grey, the sky drab.

The Ring of Kerry is 100 miles in circumference. Within the Ring is an inner circular mountain road that circumvents the Reeks – a magnificent mountain cloud-locked ring road that does not form a complete tarmaced surface. On the southern side, at the Black Valley, it ends in a cul-de-sac. Apart from a couple of cyclists struggling uphill against the elements, the roads are peaceful. At Lough Acoose a lone walker laden with a rucksack that would capsize a mule plods along slushy roads. The main news item on Kerry Radio is the fact that Tralee is one of the most heavily littered towns in Ireland. It has come third from bottom in the annual litter survey organised by 'Irish Business Against Litter' and carried out by An Taisce.

Back at Beaufort, Pat reckons the weather should clear by Wednesday. After all, he chirrups, it's only the day after tomorrow, so I won't have too long to wait. We discuss routes and look at maps. He praises my patience, saying it shows I have respect for the mountain, not risking going up by myself in dangerous conditions. The thought of sub-zero temperatures and the prospect of not seeing anything, even if I reach the top in one sodden piece, put me off. But for three days I have given in to the elements of nature and can't wait indefinitely for an improvement. Pat has just had a phone call from a Japanese friend, Seiko, who lives in Kinsale. She wants to climb Carrauntoohil on Wednesday. Would I like to tag along?

Is the Pope Polish? Can a duck swim?

The very mention of the name 'Carrauntoohil' sends a shiver down the librarian's spine in Killarney.

'Watch yourself,' she warns me, 'if you're heading up there, and don't on any account go up on your own. There have been four deaths since Christmas and we don't want any more.'

I have come into the library through sheets of driving rain to plunder the Irish section for information about Carrauntoohil. Given the number of travellers and writers who have visited the county, surprisingly little seems to have been written about the mountain. There have been descriptions of climbing it or gazing at it by a variety of authors and poets, including Wordsworth and Synge. Since the time of the Welsh bishop Giraldus Cambrensis in 1186, scores of visitors have been moved to write about their time spent in the 'Kingdom'. Kerry has seen them all. From Elizabethan soldiers to Vatican emissaries, from political economists to French royalists, and from German princes to American missionaries, they have all penned their opinionated views. Novelists, poets, travel writers, antiquarians and historians have also offered theirs. Some refer to Carrauntoohil but few ever climb it. For all its fame it has been dwarfed in terms of symbolism by other mountains.

There is also disagreement on the anglicised spelling of Ireland's highest mountain. I muse over a dozen different phonetic renderings, starting with Isaac Weld, an eighteenth-century topographer's transcription of it as 'Gheraun-tuel', to the following attempts by a variety of writers: Carranthuouel, Carrantuohill, Carrantuohil,

Carrantouhill, Carrantouhil, Carrauntuohil, Carrauntuohill, Corrauntuohill, Carrauntual, Carrantual, Carrantohill, Carrauntaul.

The Ordnance Survey plumps for Carrauntoohil with the Irish spelling, *Corran tuathail*. While there is confusion over the spelling, what is not in dispute and is etched into the mind of every schoolchild, is that it's the highest place in Ireland. I have also seen it used as a synonym for 'mountain' by a Sunday newspaper columnist writing about 'having tea with a Carrantouhil of ham sandwiches'. Writing in *Footloose in the West of Ireland*, the English hillwalker Mike Harding quotes one guide as saying the mountain is named after a hairdresser in Killorglin called 'Karen O'Toole'. In the 1950s Hayward describes the ascent to the summit in his book *In the Kingdom of Kerry*. He took the tourist route but Pat Falvey has promised me a better way – 'when the mountain is ready', of course.

A non-stop deluge clears shoppers from the lunchtime streets. Even the jarvey men leave their horses standing in the rain to shelter under trees. In Plunkett Street a notice in the window of the Rí-Rá Internet Café entices me in to the warmth and dryness:

Best Rates, Comfy Seats, Great Coffee, Fastest Connection and Cute Staff. (Except the Boss).

The 'cute' Canadian girl sitting by the till tells me Rí-Rá means 'Chit-Chat'. She seats me at booth number six logging me on to the Google search engine. Rí-Rá is a pleasant environment. A lava lamp in the window adds a relaxing ambience. I type in Carrauntoohil and within two seconds the website of the Kerry Mountain Rescue team pops up; it is a team that has seen much activity this year. The headlines scream out alarmingly at me:

Daring Rescue on Carrauntoohil

Visitor Killed in Cliff Fall

Dawn Rescue for Stranded Mountaineer

Girl Freed after Five Hours Trapped Under Rock

Doctor Dies on Kerry Mountain

Three Climbers Cheat Death in Avalanche

Stranded! Night of Terror for Germans on Kerry Mountain

Saved! Teenagers Found After 24-Hour Mountain Ordeal

Over the Christmas and New Year period the Kerry hills claimed the lives of three climbers. One man died at the Heavenly Gates on Carrauntoohil and a man and woman died in a climbing accident when they fell on their way down a steep gully in the Lough Duff area in the Black Valley south of the MacGillycuddy's Reeks. It was the first double fatality that the mountain rescue team had attended since its formation in the 1960s. And, as Eileen Cronin reminded me, another man died in the middle of May bringing the tally to four in less than five months.

I wander round a couple of trinket and gift shops. The paddywhackery of old Ireland sits comfortably with the mobile phone shops and cyberspace cafés. Shelves overflow with mini shamrock cottages, 'Danny Boy' music boxes, Rock of Cashel candles, 'Genuine' Connemara marble rosary beads (with extra strength double link chain), and the authentic Blarney luckstone. Smiling leprechauns are ubiquitous: on 'magic' towels, cushions, handkerchiefs, keyrings, lighters, fridge magnets, boxer shorts, chocolates, and on the 'Top of the Morning' Lucky Leprechaun alarm clock. It's satisfying to find, in the midst of all the kitsch, that Reidys sweet shop in the main street still sells mint fondants, friendship rings, Everton mints, sherbet strawberries, liquorice torpedoes, coconut mushrooms and clove rock from the Exchange Toffee Works in Cork.

The 'Carrauntoohil Stew' in Ma Reilly's Bar does not make amends for not getting a crack at the real thing but meets my need for warm food. The Gem sugar bowl fulfils a fitting prophecy: 'He who runs away lives to fight another day.'

Two well-upholstered American women with treble chins waddle in, taking seats at the table beside me. With an appalling lack of finesse, they squeeze on to chairs with trousers far too tight for their waistlines. When they order steak and chips, they complain that there are no iced Coke, no milkshakes and no sunshine. They examine their purchases, scrutinising a scarf, some pottery and a crystal vase. They are still uncertain about the euro, and with a calculator work out how much it has cost them in dollars, ending with much tut-tutting about money, holidays and the fact that the Irish Coffees are not decaf.

Wednesday morning at eight o'clock: at last Pat decides Carrauntoohil is ready and we are ready. There is an edge of quiet excitement. It is an overcast day with a calm wind.

When Pat's friend Seiko arrives we drive along with her to Lisleibane and park in an area enclosed by stone walls. For fifteen minutes we sit in the Falveymobile – a brightly coloured Mitsubishi – until a torrential downpour ends. Our spirits lift. Under a sepulchral sky we walk along a path running beside the Gaddagh River flowing and foaming at a furious pace. The incessant rain of the past few days has left it brimful. We return nods to the cheery hello of two men walking around Lough Callee. Cautiously we make our way over slippery rocks richly coated with mosses and lichen at Coomcallee, 'the Hag's Glen'. Pat takes us along a route known as the 'step of the goat'. He tailors the hike to our interests – some walking, a little light scrambling and a ridge climb with special relevance to goats thrown in for good measure. Seiko, I discover, shares the same January birthday as me. We step across Corraun and come to the lower coum of Corraun. Pat explains basic scrambling techniques: study the rock and visualise your route, take small steps, look for three points of contact, always depend on the handholds and footholds.

'On the more severe climbs some people refer to them as "thank God" holds,' he says. He tests our ability to work out a safe route as we move up the rock. Pat goes first, with a smooth easy aplomb. Seiko follows, making steady and nimble progress that would grace the Tokyo Ballet Company. I take on the unglamorous role of a goat sweeper or perhaps scapegoat. Having successfully negotiated the 'step of the goat' Pat tells us when he first climbed Carrauntoohil there was a mystical look about it.

'Many years later I wrote an article about climbing it and called it "My journey up into hell". It was about the Devil's Ladder where most people are killed or injured and it was very blustery.'

I ask about the deaths. Pat says there has been a huge increase in calls in recent months because people are more reluctant to attempt going up on their own.

'People still want to do it and, although they have confidence in their own ability, they ask for advice just to increase the margin of safety. The deaths have not put people off; in fact in a funny way, they may have had a reverse effect. If there were no fatalities and no publicity you would get fewer people but there is a curiosity. It becomes more of a goal to succeed where other people have failed and it enhances their ego.'

We slip into silence twisting our way up to the central coum, Comerlar, and on to Cummeenoughter, 'the Eagle's Nest', the highest lake in Ireland. Crags surround us on three sides. Gradually we pick our way higher, knitting in and out of the cliffs. Seiko is enthralled with the colours of the rocks, especially the pink ones.

He leads us a sheltered and picturesque route. For most of the three-hour walk to the top, we are out of the wind. Pat has deliberately not taken us the standard tourist route but a much longer way; this gives us a better feel for the Reeks, the oldest red sandstone mountains in Europe. We take a breather from our exertions, sitting on stones, admiring the views of Killarney and Lough Leane. Water pours down the cliffs in a frenzy from a dozen different streams splashing across moss-covered rocks.

The next stage takes us along Brother O'Shea's track, a pathway beaten down to earth and rock because of the trampling of walkers. The track was named after a religious brother who died following a fall. It leads up to the Beenkeragh ridge, 'the hill of the sheep', where we are confronted with a bank of mist. It is a steep ascent. Pat and Seiko lag behind. I wait at the top before the final assault across the arête joining Beenkeragh to Carrauntoohil. A storm is raging; it is a gusty final fifteen-minute trudge. Pat takes Seiko's hand and delicately guides her through the mist over rocks. Take it slowly, he advises, one step at a time.

'We're not in any hurry,' he reminds her. 'We've all day. Climbing a mountain is a bit like eating an elephant. You can't bite into it all at once. Just bit by bit in easy pieces.'

As a fellow mountain goat, Seiko has great staying power, determination and a stubborn ability to make the summit. Like the local people she has an indefatigable spirit. In freezing conditions we shake gloved hands at the top. The remains of a cairn provide shelter but Pat has come prepared. Like a magician pulling rabbits out of a hat, he whips a kisu (an emergency shelter) from his rucksack. We pull it over our heads, making it a tent. To keep it firmly in place on the rough rocks we sit on its ends. In its warmth we are safely ensconced from the wind at the top of the highest point in Kerry, the pinnacle of Munster and, at 3,414 feet, the roof of Ireland. Pat produces a flask of tea and passes it round. I stick to my chicken soup while Seiko devours a hard-earned bowl of Japanese rice. In this rarefied atmosphere we munch a late lunch. Seiko wears a large crystal ring on her index finger. It is the first ring her husband bought her. I produce my obsidian stone. We share kinship, exchange Capricornish qualities and mull over the goats' usefulness to society through the centuries: providing milk, wool, parchment and bodhráns for musicians.

Seiko asks Pat if he thinks Carrauntoohil is a handsome mountain.

'It's a rough rocky barren outcrop that to me is beautiful. Its beauty is in its ruggedness, with dangerous imposing features that in ways threaten you but at the same time pull you into it. Because I have learnt to love the mountain for its dangerous aspects, I have also gained the respect of it. Mountains can fool you; a calm day can suddenly turn vicious, and for me that is the attraction.'

Carrauntoohil has an inexhaustible allure for Pat. He reckons he has climbed it as many as 1,500 times – probably more than anyone else in Ireland. Some weeks he walks it two or three times a day as part of his training. He loves the buzz and energy the mountain gives and the variety of stimulating scrambling, climbing and walking routes it offers.

'It's an amazing thing but only about 25 per cent of local people have climbed to the top. The indigenous people are working the land so they are part of it and don't see the significance of trying to reach the summit.'

We are missing the mountainscape that lies all around us but we are happy; we happy few, a contented trio, huddled together for warmth and far removed from the cares of the world – until the mobile phone moment. Pat's is first to ring. He launches into a business discussion on leasing cars and properties. Seiko calls her husband and tells him of her triumph. I indulge in an un-Thoreauvian activity: texting my wife and a couple of friends, saying I am the highest man in Ireland (fleetingly at least), then get out for a walk around. Unhurried, I want to savour this moment. I have waited a long time for it. The flat summit, with a twenty-foot steel cross that replaced a wooden one, is over 100 feet long; I can barely see from one end of the summit ridge to the other.

From the top we cross a sloping shoulder and emerge from the mist down a path to a grassy saddle leading on to the Devil's Ladder. From here we look south into Cummeenduff, 'the Black Valley' and in the distance, across sunlit fields and smaller hills, make out Kenmare. For 45 minutes we squelch and slide our way down the 600 foot vertical gully made up of unstable wet, mucky stones and rocks. I fling my arms out sideways for balance. In snow and ice conditions, Pat says, it can be treacherous. He once slipped on a section, and fell 50 yards. He escaped without breaking any bones, just some bruises and an even more badly-damaged ego; the conqueror of Chomolungma, as Everest is known to the people who live around it, should not be expected to lose his footing on the Devil's Ladder of Carrauntoohil. With a name like Chomolungma, it could almost qualify as a MacGillycuddy's Reek, were it not for the fact that it is 29,028 feet. On cue, some rocks on the Devil's Ladder give way, taking others tumbling along with them for twenty yards in front of us like a mini avalanche. We laugh like children. Crystal clear Kerry mountain water threads its way downhill, running across large, flat, blue stones, filtering between smaller ones. We pass withered, large-flowered butterwort and weather-beaten milkwort. Pat regales us with stories of Everest.

We stumble through Coomcallee again. On either side of us the lakes of Lough Gouragh and Lough Callee lie serenely in the sun. With pride we look up at our conquest. Pat points out the blunt pinnacles of Hag's Teeth. He talks us through our route that looks daunting from ground level. Momentarily the mist moves from the very top of Carrauntoohil. Sunshine lights up its summit. I rummage in my rucksack for my camera to capture this unusual sight. This is the first time in four days I have seen its summit exposed – a serrated sickle shape; its translation of *Corran tuathail* becomes obvious – 'a left-handed reaping hook', or 'an inverted reaping hook'. It's also clear that Carrauntoohil doesn't dominate its surroundings since it is connected by ridges to other mountains; its near neighbour, Beenkeragh, at 3,314 feet, is exactly 100 feet shorter.

With the cool, early evening sunshine on our backs, we make our triumphal return along the valley, walking across springy moss, splashing our way over stones on the gushing Gaddagh River. On some occasions, Pat says, the river was so high he had been forced to swim across it with walkers. Weary but elated, we arrive back at Lisleibane car park after our six-hour hike. Seiko looks exhausted and drained. My knees are starting to complain. It has been a day of fun and excitement. Some people would probably brag of going up and down Carrauntoohil in two hours or less. It has not been difficult, or even dangerous, but Pat's expertise and mountaineering knowledge brought it all safely alive. The Reeks are an open book to him. He knows every peak, chasm, gully, ridge, lake, valley, waterfall and stream in these mountains; he knows their tops and tips, their secret ledges and hidden routes, their short and long cuts, their infinite enjoyment and fickle moods.

Pat sums up his opinion on Carrauntoohil. It has everything to stimulate his sense of sight, sound, smell and touch.

'It can throw everything at you from hailstones, wind, snow, sleet, rain, and some days, even the sun. It is a place to view the landscape, the seascape, and a place to escape to as well.'

PART III

16

Ballymore Useless to Stupidstown

We know the pathways that the sheep tread out,
And all the hiding-places of the hills.

W.B. Yeats, *The Dreaming of the Bones*

The woman in Murph's coffee shop in Kilcock holding court about her holidays is an authority on Egypt. She is talking to, or rather at, three women about her recent trip to Alexandria. They listen to an animated, one-woman, illustrated talk show, recounting the details of her tour with her husband. She is dressed in a brown, pinstripe trouser suit, the archetypal no-nonsense schoolmistressy type. She passes round a compact digital camera with pictures, accompanied by an uninterrupted well-rehearsed commentary.

– That's the Citadel in Alexandria – it's a very famous building.

– That's me standing outside St Catherine's Cathedral in the centre of the city.

– And that's what they call Pompey's Pillar – it's a really rough ride to get there by taxi but it's worth it.

– That's Joe standing at the tram station; we took some trams but it's far better to walk around the streets.

One of the women stifles a yawn. The other two respond with a few polite oohs and aahs. I pour a Leinster Gem sugar quote into my weak coffee: 'A good word never broke anyone's teeth.'

For those wishing to hear it, it has been a formidable Egyptian mistress class. The whole café could easily have been involved. One of her friends calls to the waitress for the bill. But there's no stopping Kilcock's very own Cleopatra. She loves a passive audience.

'I'll just finish off with these last few. Modern Alexandria, of course, really dates from the early nineteenth century and the reign of Muhammad Ali who introduced cotton and built a canal. Did you know it's the second largest city in Egypt, with more than 6,000,000 people? That's me again at the catacombs – now there's an incredible story about them …'

She gives me a curt nod as they leave. I refocus on the local scene, asking the waitress about the Hill of Allen. She says it is unquestionably the highest place in County Kildare. For confirmation she turns to a customer who agrees. They add a rejoinder that more of Kildare is below sea level than above. Although there are what they call a few 'lumps' and 'bumps', they are only 'wannabe mountains'.

Contrary as it might seem, I had decided to begin my Leinster summit-bagging trip in one of the flattest parts of one of the flattest counties of all – the Bog of Allen in the north west of the county. This part of Kildare looks wealthy and healthy. Large detached houses, concealed behind high hedges or fifteen-foot wooden fences and walls, bristle with imposing steel security gates, burglar alarms, intercoms on gateposts, warning signs of guard dogs and pictures of vicious-looking bulldogs with menacing signs in red: 'Beware, I live here.'

This is big sky country, with a wide-open landscape; the horizon is free of hills or any charismatic landscape features. The road is thick with shiny Range Rovers. Several 4WDs pass me at speed. From Kilcock I glide through what are known as the 'turf towns' of the northwest, a mellifluous quartet of villages: Timahoe, Coolearagh, Allenwood and Lullymore – all unknown places to me, marooned in the Bog of Allen. Curiosity gets the better of me and I stop at Lullymore's Peatland World, a park celebrating the bogland. The villages depend almost entirely on the peat industry for survival. In the 1950s Bord na Móna opened up the peat bogs and the Allenwood power station began burning up to 60,000 tons of sod peat a year. It closed in the early 1990s.

The park consists of exhibitions, replica ancient dwellings, woodland walkways and theme gardens. An unscientific straw poll amongst the staff in the shop at the nearby Lullymore Heritage Park throws up some intriguing information and shows that the Hill of Allen may not be the highest point. Olive the tea lady casts doubt by suggesting Dunmurry Hill while Jim the caretaker says I should check on a place called Cupidstown Hill near the Dublin border. He says he is 'pretty sure' that is the place I want.

I drive over to the Hill of Allen, barely noticing it before I have passed its tree-covered slopes. I check the map. Dunmurry Hill is smaller, and Cupidstown seems higher but it is not clear if it is in Kildare or County Dublin. My map does not delineate the county borders and there is no height listed for it.

South Kildare is stud farm country. My route takes me from Milltown through Newbridge, Kilcullen and into Ballymore Eustace. In the road structure of Ireland, Kildare is a conduit and has a pivotal position. Dublin is linked to 80 per cent of the territory of the Republic by roads that run through Kildare.

It is a county of closely juxtaposed road contrasts. I cross a motorway bridge and glance down on the traffic roaring beneath. A few yards beyond a roundabout, a cattle grid signifies that I have entered the Curragh. Every mile or so, diamond-shaped yellow road signs warn of horses crossing. This is serious horsey territory, reflected in the names of the pubs in the towns: The Horse Tavern, The White Horse Inn, The Paddock, The Stirrups, The Beaten Docket.

All Kildare, like the entire country, is in the throes of World Cup fever. The county is en fête on the eve of Ireland's next crucial match against Saudi Arabia. Car windows, radiators, bonnets and roofs are plastered with bunting and flags. Houses, offices, pubs, taxis and lorries display flags with the words 'Pure Magic'. Cars and vans pull over to allow right of way to a hurtling, siren-flashing ambulance, emblazoned with flags. Every telegraph pole, tree, wall and flagpole is pressed into service, with pennants fluttering in the breeze like clothes on a line.

It is early evening by the time I arrive in Ballymore Eustace. The village is sequestered into the eastern corner of Kildare with views of the Dublin and Wicklow hills to the east. Ballymore is served by the double-decker Dublin Bus No. 65 which sits with its engine thrumming in the centre. A regular service operates between the village and the city centre but for all its proximity to Dublin, Ballymore Eustace does not keep late metropolitan hours and seems to have drifted into a deep early sleep. At seven o'clock the only petrol pump in the place is closed; the Ballymore Inn does not serve food on Mondays; the solitary public pay phone has been vandalised; the only papers left in the newsagents are *Racing Post* and *The Irish Field*, and all five beds in Dennison's B&B are booked; most alarmingly of all, Aspel's Centra Foodmarket has run out of Tiffin. Public phonebox-less, petrol-less, food-less, paper-less and Tiffin-less; small wonder that I rechristen it 'Ballymore Useless'.

I set off early the next morning from my B&B three miles outside the village in the direction of Cupidstown to see if I can find some information about the hill before the World Cup match starts at 12.30 p.m. On the way over to Kilteel the Bluebird brushes through cow parsley. It rises on the hedges to more than ten feet threatening to overwhelm the back roads between Eadestown and Rathmore. The verges are bordered with purple vetch, lesser stitchwort, wood sage, hart's tongue fern and greater celandine.

By 10.30 a.m. Kilteel is still closed; in fact, the Kilteel General Stores closed many years ago. Brennan's Inn is also shut and there is a forsaken look about the village's bungalows and houses. I ask an oil delivery man about Cupidstown. He says, 'I never heard tell of it'.

I set the map and look across to Cupidstown, an unremarkable hill of modest size rising in uninspiring fashion which people pass every day and disregard. At 1,248 feet it does not have the requisite height or bulk to make it a mountain. There is nothing in its appearance to indicate sexual or love connotations. Unlike some Irish hills, it does not rise voluptuously, sensuously or in an anthropomorphic shape. It does not have a bosomy or female image as its name, associated with Aphrodite the goddess of love, implies. High-speed aerial chases are underway between swifts and chaffinches on the road from Kilteel. I watch their acrobatic display. Four swifts circle around, wheeling and swerving, scything through the air, skimming the road, hedgehopping and weaving to and fro in pursuit of insects. They rarely settle in one place for a second. Eventually, after more screeching and flipping around rooftops, they drop out of sight. The chaffinches are much more restrained, quartering the road quietly at an even pace.

Lamb's Hill Road, when I get there, is a severe test of nerves. It is an unlikely find in flat Kildare; one of those

GMRs on which I am not sure if I will make it to the top. I contemplate reversing but, once committed, there is no going back. It is so steep the idea of reversing is impossible. A strong driving resolution is required. There is no turning place and the road narrows to just wide enough for one vehicle. If I meet another car someone will have to turn. It is not so much pot-holed as heavily rutted, with the entire side gouged out in places. After much nervousness, and an equal amount of nausea, I reach the brow of the hill and drop slowly down the other side, which is fortunately in much better shape. I call at a bungalow to check on parking access. The woman asks if I am the man from Dúchas.

'You have that look about you and I thought you may have wanted some information about Kilteel Castle.'

'I am looking for information about Cupidstown.'

She asks me to hold on, saying John can probably help me. She shouts his name twice.

'He's a bit deaf y'know, but he is 87. I'll go and get him.'

She disappears into the kitchen. A minute later a doddering old man wearing a navy V-neck jumper and oatcake-coloured cords comes shuffling into the hall. He smiles inquiringly at me.

'I want to find out something about Cupidstown.'

'You want to find out about Stupidstown?'

'No, no CUPIDSTOWN – the mountain.'

'Oh Kew-pidstown,' he bellows, emphasising the 'Kew' as if it were Kew Gardens. He fiddles with a hearing aid. 'It's my left eardrum. What are you doing?'

'I am here on a quest.'

'You're here for a rest?'

'I saw Cupidstown on some maps.'

'You saw it in snaps?'

'Have you any idea how Cupidstown got its name?'

'Well, it's been called that for a very long time,' he readjusts his hearing aid. 'When Cromwell came here, he had a base up there.'

'So Cromwell was here?'

'Yes, the English lad, y'know who I'm talking about? You probably heard of him.'

I had indeed heard of him but it was the first time I'd ever heard of him referred to by anyone in such convivial terms. Images of sixteenth-century lager louts are conjured up; or those English footballers 'the lads', Michael Owen and David Beckham, but Oliver Cromwell – the English lad? Maybe I misheard him. Perhaps he meant to say 'cad'; the man long regarded as a genocidal maniac and religious fanatic, a man alleged to have killed thousands of defence-less men, women and children as a result of his 'scorched earth' policy. Unperturbed, John's getting into his stride.

'There's a place in the next townland called Cromwellstown Hill, above Cupidstown. I can remember being told that Cromwell had a gun when he was sacking Kilteel from his high command post up there. The pet name for his gun was "Cupid" and that's how the mountain came to be called Cupidstown. And to this day the name lives on.'

'What sort of gun was it?'

'Huh?'

'Cromwell's gun, do you know what it was?'

'Och, I dunno about that, but I do know that's how the mountain got its name.'

I walk back up the hill. A track, wide enough for a Land Rover, leads from the road past a young forestry plantation. It runs directly to the mobile phone mast at the top of Cupidstown. An unadorned trig point in an adjoining field marks the highest point. Sweeping views of the flat lands of Kildare open out across the midlands. The countryside is at a standstill. Not a tractor, trailer, lorry or delivery vehicle is to be seen. It is a rare, transit van-free landscape. Not a single Eircom, Coillte, or An Post van threads the country roads. Life has ground to a halt. It could be 7.00 on a Sunday morning. I scan the eastern high ground to the Dublin and Wicklow hills. Several ridges, with three or four elongated rounded humps, dominate the horizon. The undersides of the clouds are in harmony with the tops of the hills.

The early summer sunlight flickers fitfully. Shafts of light bring out soft greys and glittering greens. A cool breeze tempers the heat. Looking west, I suddenly see a long, cone-shaped funnel of milky air. It appears to be a small-scale whirlwind but is in fact a dust devil – something I have never seen before. It is spinning slowly in the direction of Cupidstown Hill, moving in an unhurried fashion across the land reminiscent of the twisters in American movies – albeit on a smaller scale. I watch the colour ebb away from the countryside. A storm starts to whip up. The skylarks stop their rippling chirrup call. Buttercups dance in the field. The wind rustles the milkwort, cuckoo flowers and herb robert at my feet. The dust devil moves to the north of me and gradually disappears. It's time to be gone. I can hear a whistle blowing.

The 'olé, olérs' are in full voice in Brennan's Inn. About 80 people have squeezed in and are in party mood, celebrating Ireland's opening goal against Saudi Arabia. The bar is festooned with green balloons. Everyone, from a baby of six months in a pram to a 70-year-old on a stool at the counter, wears green. Jerseys, green caps with orange wigs and Viking-style hats are the order of the day. A man is wrapped in an Irish flag that he calls his kimono. Even the Kilteel dogs are kitted out with green coats for the occasion.

When the second goal is scored, men hug each other and dance around, cheering and clapping. After a third, they explode into good-natured euphoria. Middle-aged couples, who haven't done so for years, embrace. Young men punch the air with clenched fists. A woman beside me says she has no nerves left. The supporters launch into 'There's only one Mick McCarthy'. Kilteel hasn't experienced so much raucous noise since the days when Cromwell sacked it.

After the match I drive over to the library in Naas in search of hard information. The sceptic in me can't get the idea of Cromwell's gun being called Cupid out of my head. John's emphatic conviction impressed me. The football excitement has reached orgasmic levels on the car radio. A man phones a local station, calling the result 'masturbatory'.

Naas library is a football-free zone. I ask for some books

on Cromwell, running through indexes of *Cromwell in Ireland* and *Hell or Connaught: The Cromwellian Colonisation of Ireland 1652-1660*. There is no mention of Cupid. Doubt returns. I flick through Taylor and Skinner's *Maps of the Roads of Ireland*, published in 1777. It gives nothing away. A woman checks the Griffith Poor Law Valuation, looking for the name Cupid. A helpful man looks up other maps. On one it is spelt 'Cupiestown', possibly a cartographic error.

I draw a blank everywhere. The staff give me the numbers of a local historian, an archaeologist who writes a weekly newspaper column, and a teacher. I call all three; none has ever heard of the Cromwell/gun hypothesis, but they do not discount it. It is possible, although one man thinks unconvincing. He casts doubt on whether Cromwell was in Kilteel. It may have been his Roundheads who were there. The story may be apocryphal but the idea is enticing and I stick to my guns.

Several people that I had come across in Kildare mentioned the name of a man in the Curragh whom they thought I should meet. I had driven across bits of roadway, skirting it for several days, and wanted to find out more about this area renowned as one of Ireland's ancient landscapes. Percy Podger, I figured, should be worth meeting, if only because of his name.

The Curragh is flat terrain. It is a curiously alien countryside, a level landscape not part of my vision quest, a side-trip and deflection. A heap of decaying machinery and implements litters the yard of Percy's home at French

Furze, more scrapyard than farmyard. Half a dozen rusted, beaten up and dilapidated second-hand cars add to the disorder. Percy, who looks about 45, wears black wellingtons caked with mud, dirty brown trousers and a coffee-coloured zipped fleece heavily stained with the detritus that comes from sheep shearing. The word PUMA is on the arm and a headless design of the animal is on the front.

He drives a ten-year-old Polo Jetta held together with bits of bailer twine and wire. He has four or five days' unshaven growth on his face. He offers to take me for a drive across the broad plains of the Curragh. His collie, Sue, in the back tries unsuccessfully to lick my face. We rattle across the grass, startling the carrion birds known as 'scall-crows' and a flock of plover. Sheep, daubed with yellow patches on their shoulders, roam freely without fences over the grass and roads at a leisurely pace. The Curragh, he says, has a unique status as a pasture for sheep. It is made up of 2,000 hectares and is the largest commonage in Ireland. The grasses include purple moor grass, sheep's fescue and mat-grass. Chariot races, athletic contests and fairs were once held on it.

Percy is a controversial figure. He is officially banned from driving across the Curragh – a comforting thought as we lurch across the long grass and bumpy ground. Earlier in the year he lost his High Court claim that the Department of Agriculture acted unlawfully when it ordered him to move his sheep off the Curragh during the foot-and-mouth scare. More than 50 sheep died from starvation and malnutrition because he had to take them to his farm, which is not suitable for grazing. The ewes and lambs had eaten bare all the grazing available on his farm and he had to supplement their feed by buying nuts and hay.

We reach speeds of up to 25 mph which seems excessive for the terrain. We bounce across the ground, jolting over bumps and tussocks. I ask about his sump and back axle. The car's well used to it by now, he laughs. We park behind gorse bushes, hiding from the soldiers' binoculars. Percy is wary of the army patrols around the camp. He speaks in a whisper.

'They have often chased me off this land and have threatened me.'

He swerves and dodges his way around more dips and hollows.

'The ground's a bit elastic in places. They call me Podger the Dodger. As regards high places, which is what you're after, you can see Dunmurry Hill with the mast on it, and over there the Hill of Allen. But some people say the highest point in Kildare is probably the top of the flagpole in the Curragh army camp.'

There are all sorts of nicknames for the county: 'the short grass county', 'the thoroughbred county', but the one he likes best is 'sss' which means 'soldiers, shit and sheep'.

Percy is an active member of the Friends of the Irish Environment. He travels all over Ireland, campaigning and helping people to contest planning applications. He fights many battles on his own doorstep. He is opposed to the Kildare by-pass on environmental grounds. He is against the planners, the developers, the council, the army and the horsey set. He is also opposed to many other things in the Curragh: horses galloping across the grassland leased to him, the army driving their jeeps and lorries around, 'cutting up the fields', and the jockeys on their horses who are 'out to get me'.

'The damage they are doing and the extent of their abuse is outrageous. You can go and look at the files in Kildare County Council. You can see a video of some of the verbal abuse where they have threatened to burn me out.'

His life seems to be a roller-coaster of confrontation and agitation, fighting for what he believes are his rights in an increasingly menacing world. Percy has led a multi-faceted life, mostly in the United States and Ireland. His occupations have included barman, mechanic, deer capturer, lift operator, hotel doorman, hardware store manager and stockbroker.

'I worked with a stockbroking firm in the twin towers in New York a few years ago, so I think I made the right choice to leave it all behind.'

Moving from the world of Wall Street stocks and shares to the world of sheep farming in the Curragh was a big leap.

'I would be getting on to a carriage on the subway in Manhattan where they were packed like sardines and thousands more were queuing to get on trains. I used to wonder what it would be like on the open fields of the Curragh herding sheep.'

Percy's mule sheep have blue-faced Leicester bloodlines and are a Swaledale breed. They have another significant advantage in that they are extremely resistant to scrapie. He owns the grazing rights stretching back to 1870. He takes mild offence when I ask how many sheep he has.

'The papers say I've 1,000 sheep so who am I to contradict the media?'

'So you are something of a mongrel or hybrid – a bit like your sheep?'

'Those would be some of the more polite names compared to the level and number of things I have been called. I'm an Irishman, but my grandfather was from Jersey in the Channel Islands.'

'What else have you been called?'

'I would be better off not saying. You should ask the jockey boys and horse trainers; they have a unique language when it comes to dealing with me.'

'I get the impression they don't like you?'

'I don't know what their personal feelings are toward me. I have never done anything to harm them or put them in danger. But as recently as the day before yesterday I was actively herding sheep when the trainers permitted their jockeys to come on to the gallops. When I waved to try to get them to slow down, they just put the pedal to the metal. It didn't matter what was in the way, they were going forward.'

'It seems to me you have been persecuted. Does it feel like that to you?'

'I have nothing against the horse industry. We have bred horses for a long time. My great-grandfather was a champion jockey, my grandfather was a jockey too so we have an attachment to them but it is the incessant destruction of the Curragh that has been happening in the past five years which is the big problem. These lands are exclusively for grazing sheep. A lot of developments have been detrimental to the Curragh. For grazing reasons I have stood up to them and said I will fight back.'

'Who are they?'

'The state and the horse industry – they seem to think they are outside the law. The Curragh should be properly protected. The law is there but they are extremely selective in how they enforce it. My livelihood has been destroyed by the machinations of these people. If I'm not allowed to have my sheep here I may have to sell the flock.'

'So you are staying here as long as you can?'

'I am still here and I don't plan to move. They may as well get that message. They have tried every which way to get me off: through the courts by order of a Department of Agriculture senior veterinary inspector and by ministerial orders, which they tried to get the gardaí to enforce. Maybe they will be a bit more creative in the future but I don't mind how creative they are, I ain't moving. In the nineteenth century local farmers fought to retain their rights of way and commonage and those rights are enshrined in the 1870 Act for the better management and use of the Curragh. As a statutory commoner I stand up for my grazing rights in the same way as my ancestors have done. This is my own dung heap and everybody fights best in his own dung heap.'

'What does your surname mean?'

'Talk to a lorry driver and he will tell you it's "a thick plank". A podger is a plank that they put on their wheels. I think the name derives from Padgersky and Padgerski – sky is Russian, ski is Polish. In Chicago there are huge numbers of that name. So most likely it is a bastardisation of it.'

'What's the reaction of people when they hear your name?'

'I often joke about it and people have a smile on their face, just like the way you have now. I take it lightheartedly. I could end up being a crank over it but I don't believe I am. I always say it's just like dodger, but with a P; a jammy dodger, that's me.'

My flat senses refreshed, I take the road over to County Dublin. As the 'scallcrow' flies, it's a short hop across the Poulaphouca reservoir into the southern part of the county. The road from Ballymore Eustace leads through Blessington, Manorkilbride and on to the Sally Gap. The hills of Dublin and Wicklow are lit up with the sunshine of a bright summer evening. The road starts with two wide lanes but deteriorates along stretches into a much narrower track with sharp bends and twists. Signs warn that it may be impassable in winter. Grass gives way to thick heather along the hillsides. Yards and yards of a multiplicity of high ferns deck the roadside. Red poppies, tall stands of foxgloves, buttercups and ragweed are all interwoven.

My research has produced the fact that Kippure Mountain is the highest point in County Dublin. When I turn left just before the Sally Gap, Kippure, with its tall television mast and signals radiating from the skyline, lies in front of me, its slopes covered with purple heather. A road snakes to the top. At the entrance a yellow and black locked barrier and sign halts my progress: Private Road, No Vehicular Access.

Other signs ban shooting and camping. I could walk up, but reckon that as a tarmac-bashing slog it is too long. The evening weather is turning, storm clouds are churning, and a wind is brewing. A better option I feel will be to leave Kippure until tomorrow when with luck the barrier will be open. On this occasion the mountain can wait until I am ready. Pat Falvey would be proud of me. The road to Glencree, and on to Glencullen is barren. The only sign of civilisation in this part of south County Dublin is a line of telegraph poles. A couple of camper vans and half a dozen cars pass. It is a road of mountain surprises. When I turn a corner at Glencree, the conical white peak of Great Sugarloaf jumps out at me.

Johnnie Fox's pub is overflowing at the seams. The bar that claims to be the highest in the land is also one of the busiest. The barman says it will be at least 45 minutes before he can get me a table, unless I do not mind sitting in what he calls 'the pigsty'.

Fox's pub is 1,000 feet above sea level. It is reached by ascending steep roads with hairpins. According to a notice over the door, the pub can trace its origins back to 1798. The stone-flagged floor is strewn with sawdust. Bric-a-brac, including kettles, crockery, sewing machines, farm implements, horse tackle and old prints, crowd the rooms. A log fire crackles in a huge grate. Several hundred people are dining, drinking and discoursing. A leaflet about the pub's history informs me that it featured prominently in the social evolution of Ireland. Daniel O'Connell used it for secret meetings when he lived in Glencullen, and Michael Collins set up an ammunition factory in one of the outlying buildings. In the 1950s Fox's hosted programmes of traditional music and storytelling broadcast on radio on Sunday nights.

The other diners in the pigsty include an ebullient bus driver and tour guide with a group of delegates attending a European business conference in Dublin. The driver, Noel Moran, knows Fox's well; it's his third visit this week accompanying tours. He has been to it more than 300 times. Noel, who is from Kevin Street in the Liberties in Dublin, was a bus conductor for twenty years before leaving in the late 1970s to become a chauffeur for a businessman who went bankrupt.

'So I started me own business, taxiin' and ferryin' people around on their holliers, and it's a grand life. Junowharrimean?'

Noel likes indulging in tourist-industry gossip. He runs through the international character traits of the people whom he has chauffeured. The Scandinavians are the best. They arrive early in December as the drink is cheaper than in Denmark or Norway. They are very clean and don't leave any litter. The Germans are always squabbling with each other, causing a hullabaloo, but they are always on time. The French talk amongst themselves, worry about the quality of the food, and how Ireland is generally not authentic enough for them. The English love it, although they miss some of the jokes and they can be a bit arrogant. The Americans adore it but it goes a little over their heads. They like to explain where they are from and compare life here to their own world across the Atlantic.

Noel saws hard on a tough steak. 'It's all prearranged here and some people like more spontaneity. Junowharrimean? It's marketed as a typical Irish pub, which it is not. It's not a country pub, but people love the idea of being high up and getting out of the smog and dirt of Dublin.

'But you still get the locals drinking in here as well, so it's not just a tourist trap. And the music is good, although I've heard all de jokes and gags that the guys do many times now and they're wearing a bit tin. De best time up here is probably Sunday afternoon about four o'clock when dey sit outside at de tables. They're all bleedin' locked by nine o'clock and I often wonder how dey get themselves ready for work on Monday morning. Junowharrimean?'

Noel drives a sixteen-seater Merc Sprinter. 'Brand new,' he boasts, 'and it's grand for deese mountain roads. Sure I know dem like de back a me hand.'

He talks about Kippure, locally called the 'Dublin needle'. He warns me that it's a dangerous road, not because of its state, but because cars are vandalised. Young Dublin hooligans go there at weekends in stolen cars, setting them on fire.

'Oive driven everyone around,' he gushes, 'from Neil Diamond to the Pope's doctor, and from Santana to the Sheriff of Dayton County in the Yew-noighted States. Then there've been Canadian policewomen, African heads of state and their entourage, Russian politicians ("strange fellas" some of them), card sharks, chancers and knackers, jokers and actors, as well as sportsmen and spoilsports – I've had 'em all in de back o' me wagon.'

In the main dining area a two-man band strikes up the first of the evening's musical offerings. They begin with 'Dublin City in the Rare Oul Times', working their way through 'Raglan Road', 'The Town I Love So Well' (Dublin of course, says the singer) and a selection of traditional songs and ballads.

After my meal of mountain chowder followed by smoked salmon I wander round the bar. A notice on the wall setting out the 'Life of a Mountain Publican' intrigues me. It says he must be an aristocrat, a diplomat, a democrat and a doormat ... similar attributes to a Dublin taxi-driver. It concludes: 'He must be outside, inside, offside, glorified, sanctified, crucified, stupefied and cross-eyed.'

A long fat Dublin rat sprints across the road, scuttling into the verge just past Glencree as I make my way back up to Kippure the next morning. I pass a dead badger and the burnt-out shells of two cars in a lay-by overlooking Lough Bray. Curiously, a sheath of mid-morning mist covers only the needle, but the mountain is clear. Kippure does not look particularly high and belies its 2,475 feet. The barrier is open and I follow the gravel road, passing cuckoo flower and swathes of heather. Fence posts with red reflectors line the side of the road for the two miles to the top. On either side, clumps of bell and ling heather grow in profusion while globes of bog cotton wave in adjoining fields.

The television mast is cordoned off with a grey fence. There is a small hut containing maintenance tools. Signs warn of danger from overhead work, falling objects and riggers working on the mast. The debris associated with keeping a television mast in place includes the remains of discarded concrete stay-blocks dotted all around. The newly strengthened anchor blocks hold the taut cables in place. Piles of granite rocks and white granite stones surround the fence. Steel ice protectors, shaped like an umbrella, encircle the mast which, with its dish-cluttered addenda, also serves Esat, Eircell and the gardaí.

Kippure means 'trunk of the yew tree'. There are no yew trees in sight, just hundreds of sitka spruce on nearby hills. Half a dozen sheep contentedly munch their lunch as the mist moves in around the posts that mark the county boundary between Dublin and Wicklow. A fierce wind is gathering force. My car door swings on its hinges. In the summit building – part house, part shed – Herbert Barradell sits in crowning splendour, the highest office worker in Dublin. From this cold and isolated outstation, he runs the maintenance mast show. A quiet, unassuming man, Herbert can look back with a rich fund of stories about the changes that have taken place during 40 years of his working life spent at the apex of County Dublin. Today he has a lot of callers. A man from the fire service has come to check the alarms.

Herbert boils the kettle. 'Every day's not like this,' he says, 'with all these visitors.'

He opens a bag and unrolls a foil-wrapped cheese sandwich while I break out the Tiffin. Over a pot of hot tea in his office, he tells me about his involvement in building the road to the mast in 1959. The weather was bad and the work was heavy and tough. It took between six and eight months and involved a team of twenty.

'It was built with timber as there is timber across the bog. We put down 30,000 poles, using the same method as in prehistoric times. Then we put hard core and tar and chippings on top of that. It has stood the test of time well although there are a few potholes. The bog is 30 feet deep at the gate but we just built the road on top of it and levelled it with sand.'

Herbert also worked on the building of the mast which took four months.

'When we came here to put up the mast there was a lot more bog than there is at the moment. It's mostly granite now around the top, but there was nothing else here except for the trig point.'

Herbert's job is general maintenance. 'The mast was brought up in sections and assembled by specialists from Norway. It is fully automated these days but we do bits and pieces of anything that comes up. I don't climb the mast myself but help the riggers, and look after the running of it. In the winter the winds up here often reach 100 miles an hour which means you can't do any outside work. But the fog is really the worst as it slows you up so much, travelling up and down the road. It hasn't been too bad in recent years, but the winters of the early 1960s were the worst.

There were times you'd be gasping for breath. The longest I stayed up here was seven days. I can't remember which year it was, but it was one of the worst winters and we were marooned for the entire week. There were five of us, including a night watchman. It was impossible to get down the road because of the violent whirling snow. You couldn't see anything. In those days we had accommodation but we don't have beds any more.

'Another night, a few years ago, the watchman and myself were stuck down the road. We got halfway up and couldn't get any further, so we had to stay in the car all night. It was very cold although we kept the engine running. I would have chanced it and walked back up but the watchman was elderly and I couldn't leave him alone in the car. It was an experience I wouldn't like to repeat.'

'What have been the highlights of your time here?'

'On a clear night the lights of Dublin are spectacular. The changes have been remarkable. Dublin has spread out at least twice as much since the early 1960s. There were only a few lights on one spot in Bray when I came here at first and now it's a town in its own right; in fact it's almost joined with Dublin.'

'Why do you think people are attracted to come here?'

'Compared to most people's lives it is an unusual place to spend your working days. People like yourself who come up are knocked back by the view. It is spellbinding when you first see it, but I've seen it most days so I suppose I am used to it. These mountains mean a lot to people and they are important to them because they are so close. We get a lot of walkers at weekends. Solitude is so rare nowadays and it is a contrast to be so high up and yet so near such a huge city.'

The wind has calmed. We venture outside and stand beside the mast. Dublin lies in a hollow, partially lit by the sun. We look over to Howth Head north of Dublin, and Three Rock Mountain, another hill with a mast. South, towards the soft outlines of the diaphanous Wicklow Mountains, lie Lugnaquillia and Turlough Hill. Herbert and I exchange handshakes. I wander around on my own, listening to the noise of the mountains: a helicopter clatters beneath me, heading southwards; the sharp, short rat-a-tat punctuation of artillery fire echoes from a rifle range; a couple of larks sing in the distance; the television mast hums in the wind.

I head over to Glencree, where the only building of any size is the Reconciliation Centre. The walls of the café carry an article about a cycling trip through the Dublin mountains. It is by T.P. Le Fanu, based on a paper published in the *Journal of the Royal Society of Antiquaries of Ireland* for 1893. I like his description of the sounds he recorded in the area:

> There is little to describe the silence of this wild region, and the ear soon becomes accustomed to the stillness that, as we stand and listen, we almost resent as intrusions the various sounds which reach us at this great elevation – the cry of a bird winging its way over the moors, the bark of a distant sheep dog or, occasionally, borne on the breeze sweeping across the desert solitudes, the faint whistle of a train, softened and mellowed by distance.

I bite into a scone that is like a lump of dried cement. Despite having been microwaved, it is rock hard and inedible. It is so solid, it could have been made from the granite of the surrounding Dublin mountains.

The road takes me south. I browse a dozen different Dublin radio stations: Atomic Kitten, Ozzy Osbourne, David Gray, some Country and Western classics, Percy Sledge's 'When a Man Loves a Woman', a snatch of Beethoven's piano concerto No. 5, an advert for sliderobe wardrobes in wood finish with Japanese doors. I'm transferred back in time with hits from the 1980s: 'Kids in America', 'Red Red Wine', 'No More Heroes', and even more enduring hits from the 1970s: 'The Boxer', 'Lyin' Eyes', 'Maggie May'.

17

The Tug of Lug

The whole mountain appeared as one glorious manifesta-
tion of divine power, enthusiastic and benevolent, glowing
like a countenance with ineffable repose and beauty before
which we could only gaze in devout and lowly admiration.

John Muir, *Picturesque California*

Two New York honeymooners, Brian and Tracey, are
tucking into a late supper of scones, toasted teacakes
and thickly buttered brown bread at the Bridge Meadows
B&B near Donard in west Wicklow. Brian is a reporter with
a local newspaper in Rochester City, New York State, and
Tracey is a social worker. For the past two weeks the newly-
weds have been touring Ireland. They've picked up a
quaint transposition of names that make the places sound

more attractive. They've been in Upper Donegal, Castle Trim, Cashel Rock and the Island of A-Chill.

We discuss the September 11 attacks. It made little impact on their lives, Brian explains, as they live so far from it.

'New York State, especially upstate, is a world away from New York City. Fact I've only been in the city once or twice in my entire life. If anything, I know Toronto much better as it is nearer us. You'd like it out there. We got plenty of mountains. The Adirondacks State Park is on our doorstep. There are more than 2,000 mountains and some pretty big ones too. More than 40 are higher than 4,000 feet.'

Lily O'Reilly, who runs Bridge Meadows, is a thin, slightly built woman. Her house overlooks west Wicklow and part of Kildare. A metal sign on her front door says *Céad Míle Fáilte*. She greets me warmly with 'that's great wedder ye brought wid ye'.

For the best part of a week, driving the roads of Kildare and south Dublin, the Wicklow Mountains have been a taunting presence. Wicklow is high country. It contains a greater area of elevated land than any other county in Ireland. A quarter of it is over 1,000 feet. South from Dublin, granite peaks run through the centre of the county rising to the mountainous navel of Lugnaquillia, Ireland's third highest mountain, whose name means 'the hollow of the cocks'. Compared to the Adirondacks, it is a relatively small mountain range, but there are over twenty points rising above 2,000 feet. Lug, as it is referred to in mountaineering parlance, is part of the Glen of Imaal and borders an army shooting range. Access is often closed during the week. I

276

had phoned from Dublin to check that I was able to get in to it on Saturday.

The top of Lug is under a mantle of cloud as I approach from Donard. Signs warn that I am entering an army artillery range and should not leave the main roadways. Near Fenton's pub I check the route with a man getting out of his car.

'Your best way in is along what we call the banana road because of its curve,' he says. 'Mind you, there's some brutal craters on it, so you shouldn't take your car up there. It's best to park at Fenton's and walk from there.'

A signboard with bold red lettering says:

Firing in progress in the Glen of Imaal will be indicated by the display of a red flag by day and a red light by night. All movement beyond this point is prohibited. It is dangerous to enter the army ranges at any time. You do so at your own risk. Any person finding a projectile or any part of a projectile is warned not to touch it but report its location to the range warden services.

Large-scale maps on the wall of the army information centre indicate the extent of the range. The centre is based in a cottage beside Fenton's. A soldier is frying bacon under a grill and dealing with telephone calls. He gives me a copy of a map produced by the army with details of where not to walk outlined by a broken red line. Blue lines show the routes through military lands. It outlines the dangers, helpfully pointing out that, 'any persons near an exploding shell or projectile are almost certain to be killed or maimed'.

If I keep to Camara Hill, the soldier points with a fat finger, and follow the rough track on to Lug, I can't go wrong. The army has been using the area as a firing range for almost a century. I ask about the shooting. He says he is not at liberty to disclose any information about the army's activities. He stands in front of a blackboard outlining firing practice details for the year, his khaki arms folded across his chest in a militarily defensive way. His short black moustache bristles on a lugubrious countenance. To live near Lug, I figure, you have to be lugubrious.

'Why do you want to know?'

'I am a journalist doing research.'

'I never trust a journalist.'

'Quite right. Neither do I.'

He is anxious to get back to his bacon sizzling in the kitchen. He lapses into army jargon and initialisms to bamboozle me.

'This area is also used by FCAs and we have some OPs out there. We use artillery rifle, 25-pounders, 105mm mortars, machine guns … now, if you'll excuse me, I'll have to go and attend to the kitchen.'

I walk round to the banana road – a dirt track of oval-shaped craters filled with thick brown water and access only to military vehicles. A mud-spattered army Nissan Patrol 4x4 passes. Two soldiers give me a nod and a wave. The hedges are sprinkled with tormentil, herb robert and buttercups. I fix my gaze on the way ahead. A clearly defined broad path wends its way up Camara Hill leading to a vaguer path up Lug. It is a tough pull up Camara, after which the massif of Lug appears. Even though it is 3,039 feet, it does not look pre-eminent. It is huddled in with many other granite mountains and has a long plateau.

Hayward was positively purple in his prose about the Wicklow Mountains. He called them 'a breathtaking tumble of everlasting hills – a great conclave of unimaginable giants rubbing shoulders in elemental conference'.

Stationary palls of mist, like wispy smoke, hover above it this Saturday morning. Sheep wobble about in search of titbits or projectiles. What happens, I wonder, if they turn over one of them. Halfway along, trudging across bog, heather and moss, I catch up with three high-spirited women struggling upwards and cheerfully complaining about the weather. They are not struggling, they tell me, just taking the mountain at their own pace. Una, Lorraine and Geraldine introduce themselves. They regularly come from Dublin to walk in the Wicklow Mountains. They have climbed mountains all over Ireland and tackled Snowdon.

'We call ourselves the lovely ladies of Lug,' says Una. 'It's a special place for us because it's the highest point in Wicklow as well as Leinster. We often come on Saturdays as it's a great day to get out of Dublin. I would much rather be standing on the top of Lug than standing at the kitchen sink or walking along Grafton Street.'

Huffing and puffing, we jointly make our way to the top, shrouded in mist. A cavalcade of ten shadowy figures silently files across the summit plateau known as Percy's Table. The size of a football pitch, it is a mixture of short grass and ankle-high heather. Over a warming flask of tomato soup, sitting beside the cairn, I watch the mist slowly dissipate, carving holes for rounded mountains to appear out of nowhere. With the aid of the map, and help from the threesome, the surrounding peaks are identified. We discuss the names of some of the closer hills: Cannow Mountain, Camenabologue, Table Mountain, Conavalla and to the west, Keadeen.

'I am brutal wid names,' admits Una, 'but I know for certain dat's Tonelagee over der. Dat's moi Wicklow Waterloo. 'Twas the first mountain I climbed ten years ago and I went on me arse several times walking up it one snowy New Year's Day. Jaze, it nearly killed me. They say its name means "Arse of de wind".'

They quiz me about my trip. The inevitable question comes up about why I am here. The answer comes when the mist clears and I look out over a topographic tableau of mountains with the landscape laid out exquisitely. Lorraine says I'm lucky with the weather. Most of the time there is low mist on Lug; today is exceptionally good. They talk about what walking in the hills means to them. Lorraine says it is a great outlet and gets them away from the kids.

'My husband goes fishing, so we have something to talk about when we go out on a Saturday night. My children are able to look after themselves now although I call them boomerang kids as they keep coming back to us and don't seem to want to leave.'

Geraldine has given some thought to her hillwalking. There is a certain satisfaction for her in reaching the highest point in Leinster. She stares across the hills of Wicklow and Dublin marching off in all directions.

'In its own way it is humbling to be up here. I think it brings out the child in all of us and confirms how inconsequential we are. Walking through the clouds is a romantic thing to do. You get a fresh insight, and I believe we understand ourselves better if we walk up mountains. If you're climbing Lug, there are many different approaches to it. I suppose that's part of the attraction for walkers as well as the fact that you are away from civilisation. The grandeur is exhilarating. I heard someone once talking about "the tug of Lug" and to me that sums it up. It tugs at your heart, calling you up for regular visits.'

A troop of six men treks purposefully past us at the top, without as much as a pause for breath. They give us enthusiastic smiles. Beside the large circular cairn a square concrete plinth has been erected by An Óige to commemorate the Association's twenty-first birthday. A toposcope, with a 360-degree view indicator, shows the layout of the principal mountains, rivers and features of the countryside. I read the names of some local peaks: Moanbane, Duff Hill, Djouce Mountain, Mullaghcleevaun; also included, across the Irish Sea, are the mountains of Wales: Snowdon in the north, Cadair Idris in mid-Wales and to the southwest the Preseli hills of Pembrokeshire. None of them can be seen today. Several years ago I climbed Cadair Idris and tell the women about a legend that applies to those who have conquered it; after you've climbed it, and slept the night on it, you're said to be either mad, dead or a poet.

Una says there's a variation of that saying about Lug. 'After you've climbed it, you're in brutal need of a double vodka, double bacardi or double brandy.'

We set off on the downward route. The conversation wanders. Una tells of a handy way of remembering their names.

'We're known to neighbours as the "rambling house-wives". The first letters of our names – Lorraine, Una and Geraldine – spells Lug, so that's why we feel such affection for this mountain.'

As my pace is faster, I leave the lively ladies of Lug, returning over Camara. On my solitary return trip I meet several other walkers heading to the summit, including a barefoot couple. A woman is being towed uphill by a Great Dane. When I reach the heavily-cratered banana road an exotic Wicklow treat awaits me: a charm of goldfinches, with their conspicuous red, black and white foreheads, sits on the stumps of trees chanting to one another for five seconds. With their twittering 'ptswitt-witt-witt' call they leap off at speed to a hedgerow.

It is a rich reward for an afternoon of dry, sunny weather and good company in the Wicklow hills feeling the emotional tug of Lug.

If I hadn't stopped at the Mountain View Stores on Sunday morning to buy the papers, I would have missed Bill Cullen.

'He'll tell ye all ye want to know,' says the woman, folding my thick bundle of papers in two. 'I couldn't say a bad word about him, but just make sure you've plenty of time on your hands 'cos he's the gift of the gab. We call him the old man of Donard; don't tell him I said that.'

Half a mile away, at a signpost for the Castleruddery standing stones, I pull the car over to the side of the road and walk through an open gate into a flat field where a man is driving out. He stops, his window already down.

'I am looking for Bill … Bill Cullen.'

A stooped figure with disarrayed black hair squints up at me through black, thick-lensed spectacles.

'Mm-hmm, who'd be wantin' him. Are you an explorer?'

'Not quite, just curious about the area and the stones here.'

Bill gets out of his navy '89 Opel Kadett hatchback. A hammer, saw and pickaxe lie in the back. He is the unofficial custodian of the stones that stand erect on his land. We walk over to them in a corner of his field, speckled with daisies and violets. A flat-topped earthen bank surrounds an impressively arranged circle consisting of 30 stones of varying size. The circle is 100 feet in diameter with an interior and exterior facing of stones and a bank in between. Some lie on the ground, others are upright. Most are made of granite, but two bigger boulders that Bill describes as entry stones, are white quartz portals. He says the quartz is significant since it reflects light without absorbing it. Whitethorn trees surround the stones.

'The history of the site is that it is druidic in origin,' Bill says effusively. 'The people who lived here adored the rising sun. Their entrance faced east. On 21 June the present-day druids gather here for their rituals. I have seen as many as 80 down on their knees or lying on the ground. They chant and make signs known only to themselves as they forage the ground.'

Bill talks with his head bowed, looking at the ground and occasionally lifting it with half an eye closed and his mouth pulled back to one side. The stones hold a great appeal for visitors. People come from all over the world to see them.

'Last week there was an Australian woman here with her daughter. They came from the Northern Territory. She was amazed at it and at the greenness of Ireland. Some people also see parallels with their own country, although not as pronounced. There was a Dutch fellow here a couple of years ago with charts and maps. He told me that the stones were built over a source of energy and ley lines, and they have magnetic energy.'

Bill is 82 and lives on his own. Fifty of his Cheviot sheep are sprinkled over fifteen acres. He lives beside Sugarloaf across from Lugnaquillia, which stands as a backdrop to his house. We look east in the direction of Lug.

'That's the world I live in and the world I am familiar with. I was over in Birmingham last month at my brother's house and it's all go, go, go over there. It's very noisy too. The Irish long to be back here. They're over there, but they are really here in spirit.'

'Did you never fancy getting married?'

'There's an old Irish proverb, "marry a mountain woman and you will marry the whole mountain". It's as simple as that. The way I look at it is I have no one to give out to me. My father lived to be 90 and my mother was 83. But as time moves on, the desire for women decreases and I am happy living on my own. I like the peace of it. I have a few quid at my back and I am freewheeling down to the end. I don't want to be a burden on anyone. I am well used to cooking on my own – it is no bother. I cook good steak and a neighbour makes good bread for me, so what more do you need?'

'Do you never get lonely?'

'Happiness is in being lonely. You grow into a position where any noise is interference. I like reading, and the quiet, although I do like having a yarn with people like you. I don't want for money. I have a television and radio, but unless there is something exciting on I wouldn't put the television on. I read the newspapers because I'm interested in world events.'

We walk over together into the centre of the stone circle. As we ponder their cryptic purpose, Bill puts his hands flat, palms down, across the stones.

'Sometimes when I do this I get a pulsating tingle in my hands, like magnetism. I get it in my fingers, a kind of trembling. It feels like an electric shock. It is coming out of the ground and is electro-magnetic. Some people don't believe me when I tell them this, but then I suppose we didn't get our imaginations for nothing either – we are supposed to use them. Different people who come here get a tingling sensation.'

He asks me to put out my hands. I hold them in the

same position as his. I feel no tingling, no trembling, no sensation; not a tremble, not a shake, not a shiver, nor even a minor quiver. Perhaps today is not a good day for experiencing the secrets of the stones. I do feel some spits of rain. Bill surprises me when he says the stones don't really mean a lot to him, although he understands their fascination for other people.

'They were there before my time and they'll be there when I am long gone. What puzzles me is how many human beings were here to pull them into shape. Some of those stones weigh a ton or more and I marvel at that.'

No one knows the exact meaning of the stones. Down through the centuries they have become loaded with legend. There is bizarre speculation about them, and the quartz portals are an enigma. They stand in silent testimony to the skills and craftsmanship of their builders, 5,000 years ago. Like the Slieve Blooms, like the ancient Loughcrew rock carvings, and many other places on my travels, their secrets remain unscrambled and locked inside them.

18

The Carlow Pterodactyls

And dearer the wind in its crying,
And the secrets the wet hills hold,
Than the goldenest place they could find you
In the heart of a country of gold.

Seumas O'Sullivan, 'Lullaby'

The military road out of Laragh qualifies as a GMR. It rises through a rugged landscape before plunging into a long, curving, steep descent to Drumgoff Bridge; it quickly rises again, dropping down to Aghavarragh; then it's a slow, second gear uphill climb to Croaghanmore. Regimented forests of trees cover the slopes. A line of crawling vehicles slows my progress through Baltinglass. A Renault tractor, a Volvo dustbin lorry and the Baltinglass touring and recovery lorry service lead a long tailback of cars into town. Two yellow visual delights enliven the journey on back roads through Graney, Knocknacree, Palatine and into Carlow town. The first is a field full of yellow flag iris at Palatine. Farther along, I pause to watch two yellowhammers perform a merry dance on the road. They flit up to a singing perch on a high twig, launching into their characteristic 'little-bit-of-bread-and-no-cheese' song. This is the best view I've had of these small birds which, seen through the binoculars with a background of porcelain sky, are the colour of golden sun.

In Caffe La Scala in Carlow I scan an article in the day's paper under the headline '20,000 left homeless as monsoon rains trigger flash floods in India'. It grabs my attention partly because of an accompanying map of the country. I am struck by the curious resemblance between the shape of India and Carlow. I spread out *Carlow Through the Waters of Time*, a brochure designed to entice more people to stop in the county instead of simply passing through on their way elsewhere. The two-page spread contains a map. I compare the outline with the map of India in the paper. I remark on the similarities to the statuesque waitress. Cocking her head to one side, she describes it as uncanny and eerie. She has never noticed it before. She calls over a couple of other waitresses. One, wearing a black top with Kookai on it, says she lives in Tullow, which is roughly equivalent geographically to Calcutta; another lives in Borris, more or less where Bombay (now Mumbai) is, and the third lives in Carlow town, or Delhi. The headline in the paper interests the girl who shops in Kookai.

'It's banjaxed, that country ... mind you they said the same about Carlow a couple of years ago, so maybe they have more in common than just their shape.'

La Scala Gem sugar sachet provides enlightenment: 'Faraway cows have long horns.'

The people of Carlow are waiting patiently for their summer to begin. The weather has moved from a description of being 'brutal' to 'bitter'. Women tut-tut about the winter clothes on display in shop windows before the summer has even arrived. My knowledge of Carlow could be contained on the back of a postage stamp. It's one of Ireland's smallest inland counties with a population of 42,000. The county is only 27 miles long and fifteen wide, yet within the confines of this small area there is a wealth of topographical and historical interest. Its motto is not – but might well be – *multum in parvo*, 'much in little'. The liveliest titbit I come across is that its people are known under the classy nickname, 'the scallion eaters'.

People who look at mountains often remember the first view they had of them. It is something that sticks in the mind. Sometimes, mountains pounce on you as you turn a corner, round a bend or drive over the crest of a hill; when you least expect it, they suddenly appear without warning. Such is the case with my first sight of Mount Leinster. It comes through the unlikely setting of the graveyard of Bennekerry Chapel on the Tullow Road a mile outside Carlow. I pull over and park at a five-foot high wall running along the side of the cemetery. Through two yew trees, I can see the Blackstairs sweeping up to their highest point with a mast. White haloes of dove-grey clouds sit on top of some peaks.

Children emerge from a primary school next door for their lunch break. High-pitched communal screaming, shouting, laughing and name-calling ensue as boys chase a football. In another corner of the schoolyard, giggling girls skip over a yellow and black rope, whilst others throw an orange ball into a basket. Song thrushes vigorously and repeatedly belt out their long, melodic triple call: 'chip-chip-chip'. A man hammers nails on to lathes on the roof of a partly constructed house across the road. A John Deere trundles by and a motorbike zooms past. Through it all the faint strains of 'Be Thou My Vision' emanate from the chapel as a young girl laboriously practises for Sunday mass. For half an hour I absorb the early afternoon Carlovian sounds. A man walks past and asks if I am heading for Tullow. If so, he would appreciate a lift. I clear a small mountain of accumulated maps, guidebooks, leaflets, files and yellowing newspapers from the passenger seat, and taxi him the ten miles to Tullow. Mick Stynes knows Mount Leinster well.

'We call it MLC which stands for Mount Leinster Carlow, but in Wexford they call it MLW. It's part-owned by both counties. Mind you, if you're in Carlow and you say ML is in Wexford, you're dead, and if you're in Wexford, and you say it's in Carlow, you're dead again – so you can't win.

'Bedad, 'tis a grand view from up there. Mind you,

you'd need one short leg and one long leg to get to the top although you can drive most of the way, but it's a tricky road. I'll tell you something – you're steeped in luck, having a day like that. You must have St Peter on your side. So many days you can't even see it from the road. I've been up some days and inside five minutes the weather has changed. Search parties are going up all the time to bring people back as it's easy to get lost. One of my friends even burst a lung up there.'

Mick jumps out at the Square in Tullow. 'God bless and good luck, and take care up above,' he says as he taps a double thank-you with his fingers on the roof.

Mention of Mount Leinster seems to immediately trigger a happy recognition with people. Their face lights up and a grin, like a Carlow (or Wexford) cat, spreads over it. They talk about it with real affection; it is somewhere that seizes their imagination and is more than just a convenient symbol. They automatically break into a smile at the sound of the two words that creates associations of ideas – perhaps an emblematic reminder of childhood with a personal history that gives meaning to the mountain. I hadn't before noticed the evocative power of this reaction in other areas. Neither can you fail to be conscious in south Leinster of the towering hill barrier of the Blackstairs with Mount Leinster *summum bonum*. Its name is celebrated in sporting life. There's the Mount Leinster Climbing Club and the Mount Leinster Rangers Football Club. It is also the only mountain that I have come across that has a 'Friends of ...' attached to its name. A group known as the 'Friends of Mount

Leinster' was formed more than ten years ago to combat a plan by a prospecting company to carry out open cast mining in the area.

I pick up a sign for the Mount Leinster Drive and follow a long and winding GMR. A row of short standing stones is perched on the roadside verge at the turn off to the mountain. I join a steep road to the summit. Over on Slievebawn Mountain I make out what I think to be a kite sailing halfway up the hill. When I reach the top I find a group of men huddled around a van sheltering from the wind. I mistake them for site engineers working on the mast but it turns out their minds are on much greater heights. They are paragliders and hang-gliders – men who risk all to jump off mountains.

'We're in our mecca,' one of them says to me. He introduces himself as Dara Hogan from Rathfarnham in Dublin. He organises the paragliding and hang-gliding from the top of Mount Leinster.

One of the men is putting his feet into a harness and struggling to try to take off but the wind is gusting too strongly. A student called Fernando has just finished his finals. He says he wrote a thesis on aeromodelling and aerodynamics. He is keen to try his hand at paragliding but the wind is not in his favour.

Dara walks with me over to the cairn on the Carlow-Wexford border, enthusing about the mountain and his chosen sport. He has been indulging his passion since 1995 in a variety of high places all around Ireland. On a busy day, he says, there could be up to 25 people gliding off the mountain. There are a number of smaller sites in the Dublin area but Mount Leinster, at a height of 2,610 feet, is Dara's premier paragliding pilgrimage.

'One of the best things is that you get thermals blowing up the side of the mountain. There is a road all the way to the top and that is essential for the hang-gliders as they can't carry their equipment. We can climb the mountain carrying our paragliders but my rucksack weighs 22 kilos.'

'What exactly is a thermal? I always assumed it was a warm type of underwear.'

Dara splutters with laughter, turning it into a cough. 'A thermal is a column of rising air. When the sun heats a dark field just like those we are looking down on in south Carlow, rising air will come off that field and if you get into that you can spiral up to the cloud base which is flat. You glide off that and try to find another thermal. A couple of weeks ago a friend was paragliding from here and flew the whole way to Moone in Kildare, a distance of 42 kilometres. I managed only seven kilometres that day.'

Today is poor for Dara and his mates because the winds are too strong and are prevailing.

'The hang-gliders might just about be able to fly but it is not suitable for us paragliders. We need between twelve and eighteen miles an hour. The hang-gliders would want at least sixteen and up to 23. Some days you get lucky and get what you need, other days you don't. On those days we just curse it when it's either too big or too little, and enjoy the views from the mountain. The trouble is you have to rely on the wind conditions being right and given the summer we're having, it can be depressing.'

'So where is the best spot to glide off from on the mountain?'

'We find the ridge that faces into the wind and fly off from there. It may not necessarily be the highest point. The key thing is to stay up, to make sure you catch a thermal lift. Earlier this afternoon there were two guys here who were hang-gliding and flying for an hour and a half.'

I had arrived too late to see them but in my mind's eye the images of hang-gliders from television programmes is an indelibly imprinted one of pterodactyl-style flyers, soaring and turning their flimsy wings with effortless ease. Dara talks about the difference between hang and paragliding.

'The hang-gliders use an aluminium and sailcloth dart-shaped aircraft like a small light plane. A paraglider is like a parachute, but a parachute is designed to bring you down while a paraglider is designed to fly and stay up.'

'What's it like soaring with the ravens and buzzards?'

Dara smiles with a faraway gaze. 'It is just obsessional. It can take over your life. It is quite amazing. There's also a bonus as pilots learn to spot pubs from the air so that we can land beside them.'

'What about the risks involved?'

'You certainly have a lot of fear to overcome and a lot of personal courage comes out of learning to fly. When you get over that, you just want to do it whenever you can and build up the experience and knowledge required. I have a very understanding wife.'

'Most people I've met are walking up the hills or

working on them, but you are different because you are jumping, or perhaps, running off them?'

'I think we are unique. Pilots always like looking down and part of the sheer joy is just looking at where you are going and navigating. The beauty of this high mountain is that it takes so many wind directions. Once you've got a good jump-off it takes twenty minutes to fly into a valley, so you've a great chance of catching a thermal once you fly out.'

'What is the best thing about it?'

'It's the freedom that I love. You are completely on your own, in your own personal aircraft, and I am in ecstasy at the pleasure the mountains provide.'

Apart from a place to enjoy his airsport, Mount Leinster doesn't mean much to Dara and his friends, as far as any symbolism is concerned. I ask if his connection with the mountain has led to any romantic attachment with it.

'Not really. I think it is practical. Lots of us appreciate the countryside, especially soaring thousands of feet up. It is high, it is efficient, the flanks on it are classic, but aside from that, it is really the utilitarian nature of it that is important to us.'

The cairn commands impressive vistas stretching across Carlow, Kilkenny and over to the Comeragh Mountains in Waterford. There are views to the south across the spine to Knockroe, Blackstairs Mountain and Slievebaun. We also make out the coastline around Arklow and Gorey. Apart from a portion of burnt forestry scarring a hillside in the foreground, it is a landscape of well-groomed fields of varying sizes, most of which are bereft of animals. Only a few cows and sheep dot the landscape but on this windy day not a stray paraglider is to be seen. We pick out Myshall, Bunclody, Bagenalstown, Borris and Graiguenamanagh, their edges embroidered with bungalows and small estates. The horizon is a mix of prosperous farmland, forested small hills and imposing mountains. Lugnaquillia and its Wicklow brethren rise prominently to the north.

Another glider, Jim, comes over to join us. For him hang-gliding is addictive.

'You get a great buzz from being high up in the sky,' he says. 'The adrenalin really flows and you feel a bit like a bird. It's a great feeling, just hearing the wind blowing round you. It can be hard to maintain the balance and you are so reliant on the thermals.'

Jim talks about the Nine Stones of Leinster where the club members rendezvous before each gliding gathering. He says it is an appropriate place since the stones have always been regarded as a symbolic meeting point. It was supposed to represent a place where the nine chieftains of the area used to meet, or where shepherds met when they were collecting their sheep and bringing them down after lambing. There is another story, Jim says, that after the Battle of Bunclody, the United Irishmen went across the mountain. When they lay in the heather to rest at the Nine Stones they were overtaken by British soldiers and nine of them were killed. Legend has it that the people who lived up there buried their bodies and put the nine stones to mark the nine graves.

The frustrated paragliding pilgrims prepare to leave their mecca. They fold their unused sails and pack their equipment into a van, disheartened and disappointed. They wave their farewells. On the way down I pull in the Bluebird's wings to look at the Nine Stones. They sit at drunken angles; in fact one errant stone has fallen over, sprouted its own wings and rolled off downhill.

I have vague plans to head over in the direction of Kilkenny but decide to stay another night in Carlow. Clonegall and its twin village Watch House aren't large enough to justify any B&Bs so I tick off another GMR – the Scullogue Gap – running between Kiltealy and Borris in the southwest of the county. A strong sun blinds me on my late evening drive. Mount Leinster from the western side has a different aspect, its stones and rocks brightly lit. In a sweeping movement of which Dara and his winged friends would be proud, a sparrowhawk slow-flaps over the road verge on the lookout for its supper before gliding out of sight.

Dusk has fallen over Borris when I ring the bell at Step House, an early Georgian town house that has been transformed into a B&B by Cait Coady. We share a joke about one of those misheard misunderstandings in which the traveller delights. I had phoned earlier and asked her son if I could speak to his mother. He thought I had said I wanted to sleep with her. Obviously wary, she directs me straight away to the Green Drake Inn. 'You'll find plenty of women down there,' she quips. 'I am not sure if they'd wanna sleep wid ya, but they'll certainly wanna dance wid ya.'

An old-time *céili* is swinging into top gear. Women of all ages, from teenage girls to grandmothers, sweep around the dance floor in tight tango. Old-style traditional dancing survives in this part of south Carlow. More than 50 women in bright floral dresses waltz around the floor – the octogenarians as energetic as the fifteen-year-olds. Quick-steps, jives and set dances are particularly popular. 'The Walls of Limerick' and 'The Siege of Ennis' get them going with much stamping of the floorboards.

Following a rendition of 'Happy Birthday to Annie Ryan', the two-man band 'Crystal Sound' launch into what they classify as a 'Mixed Music Grill': a rousing military two-step, then the Gay Gordons and finally the Highland Fling which turns into a mixed muddle of women flinging themselves at each other. They become uproariously entangled and a small crowd ends up at odd angles on the floor, reminiscent of the Nine Stones of Leinster.

After a couple of clear favourites, 'The Humour is On Me' and 'Shoe the Donkey', it's slow-waltz time, and songs with titles such as 'A Right to be Wrong now and then', 'Nearest to Perfect' and 'Reason for Living'. Women in their seventies and eighties shuffle around the floor, some with much more finesse than others. A couple of men emerge from the bar next door and are dragged on to the dance floor. The maladroit men are not interested in dancing and quickly prove it is not the place for them.

I am asked for a waltz but decline the kind offer, claiming sore legs and knees sustained through an overdose of fresh air. Women choose their partners for what turns out to be a free-for-all incorporating songs well known, but seldom heard, such as 'McNamara's Band' and 'Home Boys

Home'. A tweed-capped man takes on the role of self-appointed engine driver, leading a train of 40 women of all shapes and sizes, each clinging to the other's waist, chugging in a tipsy, meandering fashion around the room. Much hand-clapping and singing along to 'Cotton Fields' and 'When the Saints' brings the evening to a magnificent finale.

The first indication that I have crossed into Wexford is the purple and gold pennants strung across the road from telegraph pole to telegraph pole. The colours are the purple of the heather, and the gold from the gorse of Mount Leinster. In my omnium gatherum of useful/useless facts, Wexford is called the 'Model County'. The title presumably stems from the fact that it's a neatly manicured county with well-maintained roads and hedges, fine beaches with excellent water, good housing and a thriving economy. Boring, some would say. Leaving Bunclody, I rattle over a complex series of country roads, battling against signposted danger warnings of bad bends, oil spillages, cows and horses crossing, silage cutting, concealed entrances, dangerous junctions, 'loose' children, and the best hand-painted sign I have seen: 'Slow Down For Fox Sake'. At Killann a solitary cow swings her tail and slouches along the road in no particular hurry to get anywhere.

For a few miles I have detected a noise coming from the back of the Bluebird which seems abnormally loud. My usual manner of dealing with this problem is to close the car windows, turn up the radio and step on the accelerator, blocking out extraneous noises; but when people start pointing and nudging I realise it is more serious. I pull over. The bracket holding the exhaust has broken, leaving a hole in the back box. Luckily the anti-roll bar is preventing the pipe trailing along the ground, creating an even more uproarious din. More than 5,000 miles on great mountain roads, dirt tracks, country lanes and untarred boreens has taken its toll. I need to find a garage for a new exhaust. New Ross seems to offer the best option because it is the only size-able place in the area. I roar my way into town. The woman in charge of Ross Repairs shakes her head. There is nothing she can do today. She smiles sympathetically and apologet-ically.

'It's Thursday y'see, the mechanic's day off.'

Of course, I mutter under my breath, I should have guessed. At the next garage, a small man who could pass for a dwarf, his face buried in an engine with a filter in his hand and stained overalls, says he's a one-man band. Four cars are waiting to be looked at.

'Could you come back on Monday?' he asks.

At JCE tyres, they put the car on a hydraulic ramp. A moustachioed mechanic runs his fingers along the exhaust pipe, feeling for holes. I join him underneath and point out the hole in the back box. The prognosis is not good. He sighs heavily.

'You could get away with it for a while, but have you tried Jimmy's place? He might be able to tide you over with a welding job, although it's alloy and it might be difficult.'

If only someone had mentioned Jimmy's place earlier it would have saved a lot of trouble. When I find him on the outskirts of town, Jimmy is working on a VW Vento. Red and black jump-start leads run from the battery to a Thor Booster battery tester. He asks me to wait five minutes. Jimmy's is one of those rapidly disappearing time-warped garages from a different era, a different century and a different world. Small jobs can be done with no trouble. For collectors of the genre, it's also a place richly evocative in motor signage.

'A Dagenite Start: Music To Your Ears' proclaims a sticker on the window of the sliding door. A tin sign screwed on the wall at the back advertises a piece of long-forgotten collecting history from the 1960s: 'We Give Green Shield Stamps'. Underneath a Uniroyal Tyre Pressure chart are the words: 'Uniroyal Tyres: Tread and Shoulders Above the Rest'.

Jimmy rubs his hands on a dirty cream cloth. He drops to his knees to inspect the damage. No sharp intake of breath, no shaking of the head, no rubbing of chin, no problem. A friendly grin and Jim'll fix it. He reckons he can do a patch-welding job and should be able to stretch the bent bracket back into shape.

'It'll probably take a coupla hours, but it'll be cheaper than a new exhaust. There's nothing wrong with that exhaust anyway. Come back about half-five and it should be ready.'

At the tourist information office the town's arms trumpet New Ross as the 'Norman gateway to the Barrow Valley'. A reading of the town's history shows that it was a meeting place for merchants, sailors and pirates. It used to be a bustling port of tall, sea-going sailing ships, with the old Royal Hotel, dating from 1790, a hub of activity. A notice board outside informs me that the town was once known as *Nova Villa Pontis*. This is news to the woman inside wrestling with a party of schoolchildren.

'I never heard that name,' she gasps in astonishment. 'I know it used to be called Ross of the Bridge, but there y'are, you learn something every day.'

A large party of children from Our Lady Queen of the Universe School in Bagenalstown queues up to board the major tourist attraction – the emigrant ship *Dunbrody*. I decide to give it a miss. I walk along the quayside in the direction of the Norse-named Tholsel, the tollhouse, and now town hall. Like most small towns in Leinster, the 1798 monument opposite the Tholsel is the focal point – in this case, for the town's cider drinkers. Half a dozen mildly bohemian-looking *Villa Pontis*-ians lounge around slugging bottles of Bulmers cider and circulating a large can of Dorfmeister. Long ponytails, black T-shirts and black wrap-around shades reflect the romantic fashion attached to *Nova Villa Pontis*. One lies half-collapsed against the base of the monument, double chin on his chest, arms lying limply by his side.

A plaque on the monument dedicates it to 'Our heroic ancestors who fought and fell at the battle of Ross in 1798. From a grateful posterity'. Graffiti scars the monument with multi-coloured paint and chalk marks scrawled along its base. One reads: 'No topless bathing'. The owner of the Tholsel Inn pops his head out the door to keep an eye on the street life. He gives me a wry grin. Nodding uphill in the direction of Mary Street, he says 3,000 men were killed there in 1798. The town was the epicentre of the bloodiest battle in the entire Rebellion.

'The battle of New Ross was decisive in the failure of the Rebellion. It was a terrible slaughter.'

The Tholsel was built in 1749 on the site of the medieval market cross of 1320 and has remained largely intact. It was the centre of the Crown forces in the defence of the town and was known as the 'Main Guard'.

One of the *Villa Pontis*-ians, his hair flying behind him like Beethoven, struggles to stand up. He sways from side to side, rubs the stubble on his face, kicks an empty can of Pilsner across the pavement, and mutters a few incomprehensible words. Another of the winos, with a wonderful Wexford wobble, stumbles over to his very own *Ponte Vecchio*, straddling the River Barrow – this one more prosaically named O'Hanrahan Bridge. A bronze statue of a Wexford pikeman carrying a flag stands on the top of the monument. From his front door the publican points skywards. 'That's Kelly the Boy from Killann up there – do y'know the ballad? John Kelly was a local hero from '98.'

I had driven through the village on my way into town. I crane my neck and look up at the top. With arm outstretched and fist clenched, the eighteenth-century pikeman looks, for all the world, like a twenty-first-century Irish World Cup fan or player; more like Keane the boy from Japan, than Kelly the boy from Killann.

The New Ross of today is an attractive thriving town

laid out in a grid pattern, with steep streets of three- and four-storey yellow, cream and indigo terraced houses. It retains its old aura. Three teenage boys while away the afternoon fishing for eels at the bridge. One of them tells me he once caught a nine-pound cod at Kilmore Quay. I look back along the waterfront. Tall thin houses – many of them pubs of irregular height – predominate; each has its own slogan. I make an inventory of the strip of names and their alcoholic claims. The Hilton for '*Poitín* & Porter'; Katie Pat's for 'Best Ales and Lagers'; Prendergast's for 'Finest beers, wines and spirits'; Roches' 'Specialising in Guinness extra stout', and Hanrahan's 'Purveyors of the finest drinks from grape and grain'. I walk back to pick up the car, pay Jimmy €10, thank him for saving me the price of a new exhaust, and purr off, forgetting to collect my Green Shield Stamps.

In the dungeon of Huntington Castle the chemical blessings are being hand-delivered when I arrive. Although Kilkenny is my final Leinster destination, I have detoured to a summer solstice party in Clonegall to which I had inveigled an invitation. A local historian had told me to contact Olivia Robertson who lives in the castle and ask her about Mount Leinster. When I had phoned she had invited me to the party.

More than 50 people are gathered to celebrate the solstice. I adjust my eyes to the semi-darkness. The dungeon is a low room lit by candles giving off a strong scent of incense. I bump my head on the lead water pipes running across the ceiling. The occasion is the annual knees-up of the Fellowship of Isis, an organisation founded in 1976 with thousands of members all over the world. In Egyptian mythology Isis is the goddess-queen of magic. The Fellowship claims to be multi-religious, multi-racial and multi-cultural. The summer solstice is one of the most important events in their calendar. The village of Clonegall, on the Carlow-Wexford border, is the unlikely setting for the headquarters of this little-known sect.

The 'high priestess' Olivia is delivering the blessings in a barking voice. There is a chiselled edge to her accent. Each guest is individually splashed with water. Some laugh at her comments, others close their eyes mumbling a few words. When she reaches me she says my chemical balance and polarity are very good.

'Your yin and yang are excellent and you love everybody, but you could be harder with people.'

She invokes the goddess of mountains, rivers, waterfalls and seas for me. Before I have time to produce my obsidian stone she has moved on to the man standing beside me with a Jesus beard and a silver earring through his eyebrow. She gives him a short lecture on the values of love, beauty, truth and abundance. The druid dream magic music is turned up and a series of invocations and prayers follow. Other gods are invoked: the goddess Aphrodite, the goddess of midsummer, the goddess of love and the sun god. A noisy baby is hushed by its mother. I bump my head again on the pipes and look up at the cobwebs covering them. The next item on the packed itinerary is what is described as an 'alchemical wedding'. The blushing bride, with a bright orange fleece and her groom with a gaudy purple one, step forward hand in hand.

'In the name of the God of Isis I tie the eternal knot between you,' Olivia wheezes. She asks each to make a personal statement. The bride wishes for peace; the groom for harmony and love. The newly-married couple walks around six times in a small circle while a woman sings about them 'being one' and asks for balance for their children. The wedding is followed by a 'magical summer solstice journey' whereby all those present embark on their own individual trip, eyes closed and hands in the air as if under arrest. Olivia, her voice now dropping to excited football commentator level, leads them. The music is turned up and the lights turned down.

'We are off on a spiritual adventure. We leave through a dark tunnel, with pale green light at the end. We are now in the land of heart's desire, *Tir na nÓg*. You are in the Elysian Fields, a heavenly paradise. All your worries leave you and you forget earthly things. We have now moved to a seashore covered with jewels. Then we climb a hill and reach the Temple of Zodiac with the stars all around. You meet some old friends here. Then you are on your own with the silence. You have always wanted to climb that hill and now you are up there. You come eventually to the World's End. An angel is guarding you and dealing with any problems that arise. The veil between our worlds is thinning. We start to come down the hill and if we look back we can see only mist. We see a lake and swans flying over it in a V shape. They glide across the lake and then we enter a garden and a cave. We must enter it to return to earth and go down a long dark tunnel again with a candle. When we come back to earth we become small and we know that all this life is a dream. We come back into our earthly bodies and send out peace and harmony, love and beauty.'

I am dizzy. I am not used to such hectic zipping around at breakneck speed without a few leisurely coffee breaks and a newspaper, or a couple of pints to restore the tissues. It has been a long-winded, ear-splitting journey. When we have 'landed' safely back in the dungeon, the time-travellers open their eyes, lower their hands and switch the balance of weight on their feet. The woman in front of me licks dry lips, looking as though she has passed into the next world. She indulges in some heavy in-breathing and out-breathing. Comments are exchanged on how it felt and what way the earth moved. Some send healing messages. They include ones in support of the environment, the anti-globalisation protesters, harmony between India and Pakistan, and a special one to an 'old Romany' in Glastonbury.

After the main business is dealt with I walk upstairs with Linda who has come down for the occasion from Coleraine, far away on the north coast. She has travelled the length of Ireland, nearly 300 miles by train and bus, especially to witness the Clonegall summer solstice party. Together we wander around the castle, losing ourselves in narrow corridors. We walk up and down short flights of stairs lined with wainscot and half-timbered studding. Like burglars, we pop our heads into a dining room with oak panelling, a dark drawing room with a tapestry and tattered furniture. We end up in a small bare hall where people are preparing to set off for Osbourne's pub.

Tea, ham and salad sandwiches, along with slices from a tiered wedding cake, are on offer in Osbourne's. Linda is not disappointed, although she takes most of it with an extremely large pinch of Isis salt. She is a fortune-teller and spends half the year in Egypt and the other half in Coleraine.

Over a glass of chilled Sancerre, I speak to Olivia about Mount Leinster. She regards Huntington Castle as a holy place of the Tuatha Dé Danann. It is built around an ancient well and its outlet is at a neolithic bullaun stone. Mount Leinster, for her, is the hill of the goddess Tara.

'When we were children it was always a beautiful blue. My brother and I wanted to walk into the blue. It meant spirituality to us. From Huntington Castle nowadays we see the colours of the foothills which are violet, pale blue and indigo. I use those in my art when I am painting. The mountain also gives us perfect symmetry and balance.'

Olivia was a member of the Friends of Mount Leinster who ran a campaign in the 1990s to stop a mining company prospecting for andalusite on Tomduff Hill, a small spur near Mount Leinster. Andalusite, she explains, is used in the iron and steel industry and to make bricks. It originated in Andalusia in Spain.

'It would have been an environmental disaster,' she says. 'Open cast mining leaves all sorts of hazards and scars the countryside. It is a filthy business and a danger-ous industry. We fought a long and successful campaign to preserve our hills and mountains. The Order of Tara is a friend of Mount Leinster and of mountains all over the world. We always link with a local hill or mountain and in an emotional, not intellectual way, we try to help the environment.'

Olivia raises her glass, swallows the last of her wine, and bids a final toast:

As an bhean O Tara, 'All glory to Tara'.

19

Murder on the Hill

One climbs a mountain, drawn instinctively by the magnetism of the highest point, as to a summit of personal
awareness, awareness of oneself as a point in relation to as
much of space as can be grasped within a maximal horizon.
Thus a mountain top is one of the most sensitive spots on
earth, of our feelings for the earth in all their depth, elevation and comprehensiveness.

Tim Robinson, 'Listening to the Landscape'

A tall, urbane and ebullient Englishman comes down to
breakfast shortly after me in my B&B near
Thomastown. He carries himself in a dignified manner.
With a cultivated voice, he orders Earl Grey tea, 'crisp
toast', and tells the woman in charge she looks fifteen years

younger since he last saw her.

Anthony Tighe (pronounced tie) is the last trustee of the Woodstock Estate which owns a large slice of Brandon, Kilkenny's highest hill. As I provide a résumé of my project, Anthony leans across the table, making a steeple of his hands. Within one minute he is pouring out the reason for his visit. The Tighe family lived at Woodstock for 150 years. They used to own 22,000 acres of grazing rights on the hill. They now own around 2,000. He has come over from his home in Northamptonshire to try to sort out controversial ownership rights. Anthony's ancestors arrived in 1703 and bought lands from the forfeited estates of Ireland which were confiscated by Henry VIII. The Tighes developed Woodstock House and its surrounding estate, building up a substantial farming and fishing industry on the River Nore. They still own more than three miles of fishing rights. From the depths of a black briefcase Anthony unfurls a bulky, 1927 six-inch linen valuation office map. He spreads it across the breakfast table, propping the corners on toast racks, teapot stands and milk jugs. He speaks in a placid manner. Running his fingers up and down sections of the map, he talks about the mountain and shows me the remaining lands owned by the Tighes.

'Brandon Mountain,' he says, 'has an individuality of its own and is an important landmark for local people. We have 1,400 acres on it and we own a portion at Ballygub around the foothills. A lot of this land is gorse and is used by foresters.'

'So who owns the rights?'

'The farmers have grazing rights, which in Ireland are like fishing rights, and are a tricky subject. We own the fee-simple title. We sold part of it to the government in 1972 but we still own the shooting rights on Brandon. We have an agreement that we maintain the shooting rights even though we don't use them nowadays. Change is a very emotional subject here. I do not know what to do about the lower slopes of Brandon. I am trying to talk to the graziers about what is best to be done. They can buy the title from me but I suppose they won't because they are so entrenched.'

'Entrenched in what way?'

'Well, it took some time to get the message across that we own the land. Sheep grazing rights have nothing to do with the fee-simple title; the difference between that and a grazing right is a murky area, although the word through the local grapevine is that they know the Tighe estate owns it.'

'How many farmers are involved?'

'There are about eight farmers and they got an affidavit to say that they have grazing rights. They get large subsidies from Brussels called REPS, so they don't do too badly. But they certainly are a bit concerned about what I'm up to because I've appeared out of the woodwork, so to speak.'

'Will they be meeting you?'

'They don't want to meet me. They went to a solicitor who advised them not to have anything to do with this bloke Tighe. Unfortunately, they didn't realise what I was up to. I am quite happy to put it in writing that they have grazing rights. I want to clear up things because there are too many loose ends, but I have to take things gently. I would like to put up a cottage here and still have the salmon fishing rights. The locals say we haven't been around so we've lost it, but you can't lose that. The rights don't lapse.'

We talk about Woodstock House, destroyed during the Civil War. The Black and Tans requisitioned it in the spring of 1920 and used it as a barracks.

'When the old IRA decided they had had enough of what the Black and Tans were doing, they burnt the house on the second of July 1922 shortly after independence. I know some grisly things happened in there involving the Tans. They did an enormous amount of damage and destroyed the house contents, including chopping up the Chippendale furniture.'

'So how was it burnt?'

'A gang – that as a matter of fact did not come from Inistioge at all – carried it out. They were given instructions to burn it from the IRA high command in Dublin. The gang arrived during the night after nicking a gallon of petrol from the only petrol pump in Inistioge. They broke in, spread petrol around and had a roaring fire that burnt for two days. Apparently, they got away very quickly, and all that's left to this day are the walls.'

'So was it burnt solely in retaliation for what the Black and Tans had done?'

'Yes it was. I am sure of that. If I'd lived here in those times I think I would have understood the difficulties the people had to put up with.'

'Do you know who did it?'

'I do know who did it and I have met them. I wouldn't want to name names of course but no later than yesterday I had a telephone call from someone in Dublin and we talked about this. I get on very well with the people who were on the other side of the fence so to speak. I try to see it from their point of view.'

'What did the local people think of the burning?'

'They were very loyal. The employees of the estate were tremendously supportive at that time. It was known as the Big House because the Tighe family provided all the employment in the area. The old matriarch was Lady Louisa Tighe. She was very good and looked after people and didn't mind what religion they were.'

'What relation was she to you?'

'She would have been a great-great aunt. I come from the Wicklow Tighes.'

'So once you get the rights sorted out, what does the future hold?'

'There is a big problem of trying to sort out what is left. We need to work out the final solution of the remaining land. The bulk of the land is leased to Coillte. We are cooperating with them to turn it into a heritage park. The big thing I want to do is look to the future and to what will be happening in 50 or 75 years' time and see where the young people will be employed.'

Kilkenny has always been a deeply silent county for me. I had looked forward to it with anticipation. Frank O'Connor summed up his feelings for the hills of the county in one word: 'sensuous'. Pondering on this, on the road between Inistioge and Graiguenamanagh, I brake sharply to let a dithering Kilkenny rabbit live. Fifteen yards farther along his mate was not so lucky and the remains lie splattered along the verge. I swerve and disperse a cloud of flies.

The epitome of pastoral tranquillity, this is a county of hilltop churches, Norman castles and abbeys, deep valleys, luxuriant green fields and country lanes; it has a pleasing otherworldliness about it. Three buff-coloured Shetland ponies munch their way through the long grass in a field with a tethered donkey near Thomastown. In the Riverside Café in Inistioge an affable black Labrador called Rusty lies lazily under my feet as I sip my strong coffee and peruse the wit and wisdom of the sugar offerings: 'Don't show all your teeth until you can bite.'

Rusty is so quiet that when I accidentally stand on him as I leave he can't be bothered to yelp.

Reigning supremely on the way into Graiguenamanagh and, like the Uniroyal Tyres in New Ross, standing 'tread and shoulders' above everything else, is Brandon Hill, an implacable presence looking aloofly down on the town. My eyes are drawn to its profile, filling the skyline, yet intimate and inviting; its significance, like so many Irish hills, out of all proportion to its physical mass – a mere 1,703 feet high.

The first man I meet at lunchtime in Graig, to give it its shorthand moniker, lives up to the town's image of being gregarious. Simon McDonald, sometimes known as Seymour, is cleaning out his barge.

'Where you from?'

'Belfast.'

'*Béal Feirste*,' he smiles, giving a low whistle in admiration of my trip. 'How's Belfast this weather? Do you know Jim McClean up there? I rowed with him on the Lagan many years ago.'

We look up at Brandon rising abruptly above us under a pale sun. Grey clouds hang low. In his own words, Simon was 'bred, born and reared' in Graig. As a child he used to pick small, dark bilberries known as fraughans on the mountain's lower slopes and sell them in town. He recalls his youth on it with a hushed reverence.

'You would get seven shillings and six in old money for a stone of them which was a fair price. In the 1940s we used to have brown bread and made fraughan sandwiches. They were beautiful to eat. The whole town would have been up picking them on the bottom slopes along by Freney's Well. Did ye ever hear tell of Freney – Captain James Freney?'

'No, who was he?'

'Freney was a robber who lived 250 years ago or more. He robbed the rich all around south Kilkenny and into Wexford and Waterford. Unlike Robin Hood he didn't give to the poor but kept most of the money for himself. He had a gang and a bay mare named Beefstakes. Freney is supposed to have hidden part of his gold hoard on Brandon Hill. There is a stone up there and if you sit on it at a certain time of the day when the sun is setting on part of the hill you can see where the treasure is.'

'Have you ever seen it?'

'No, I think meself the treasure was the fraughan – any

money that was got came from picking the fraughans. Freney's name lives on in a big way in folklore. They say that in his first hold-up he earned about 50 quid, but he gave his victim back a pound or two to cover his expenses home.'

'What did he look like?'

'He was a small man with only one eye. He lost the sight of the other through contracting smallpox.'

Simon can remember when there wasn't a tree on the hill 60 years ago.

'There were gorse bushes and loads of heather that the women gathered and they called them a *"bresna"* from Brandon. There is a cross up there but I am not really in favour of it. I think they should not have interfered with the hill and left it alone.'

'What does it mean to local people?'

'Brandon Hill made us, to a certain extent. You can't escape it, not that we want to. But looking at it now, it is unique, standing to attention, towering over the town as an ever-present reality. Roaming round it when we were youngsters, laughing, walking up to the summit … it's a part of our history and of what we are.'

'Is it a steep climb?'

'Put it like this: you wouldn't want to have a weak heart and you'd need strong lungs. It is surprising though when the emigrants come back from America, Australia or England, the first place they head for is Brandon. Whatever kind of feeling they have, they make a beeline for that hill. It's a symbol of stability and they honour and respect it. If they don't make it to the top when they come home on holiday then they weren't properly home in Graig or Inistioge.

'By the way,' he adds almost as an aside, 'two men were shot on it once. There was a fracas between a gamekeeper and the poachers. The gamekeeper shot one of the poacher's dogs and after that one of the guys shot the gamekeeper.'

'Dead?'

'Dead as a maggot. One of the poachers was shot as well. No one was ever arrested for the shooting. They got back and swam across the River Barrow. One of them went into a pub for an alibi, and they put the clock back an hour.'

Simon sums up the relationship between Brandon and Graig.

'It's simple. You can't have one without the other. I get on me boat, brings a few cans of Smiddericks and sandwiches with me, me dog Captain, and I spends all day on the river with the mountain up above. If there is a heaven that is where I want to be. That is Graiguenamanagh to me.'

My own heavenly base, the Waterside Guest House on the quay, is a converted, nineteenth-century four-storey corn store. 'Medieval Rivertown' is how Graig styles itself. This is the smart side of Graig. While the quaysides have been gentrified the town itself has resisted being prettified. There is a tatty yet comfortable feel to its tightly compacted streets. It does not have a decent café; I feel a Gem-less, quote-free afternoon coming on. A notice on a supermarket window advertising summer classes catches my eye:

Kick-boxing for men and women
Realistic self protection with close quarter combat
Head-butts, knees, elbows, take-downs, chokes.

After dinner, I engineer the discussion in Ryan's pub to talk of Brandon. One man, who has lived and worked on the Thames Barrier and Docklands developments in London, says he's climbed Brandon 'umpteen times'. A scruffy, check-shirted man joins us and talks about Woodstock. He listens intently when I tell him about my fortuitous meeting with a member of the Tighe family earlier in the day. He thinks I'm part of the family.

'The Tighes were well respected in Inistioge and gave a lot of employment to the locals. Some people used to genuflect to them in the street.'

Scruffy check-shirt asks what Anthony Tighe had said to me. I tell him the story of the men getting a gallon of petrol from the pump in Inistioge and setting the house on fire. Without blinking an eye, he casually corrects one factual point.

'It was two gallons of petrol,' he says. 'I know that for a fact because my great-uncle burned the place.'

I pause and take a sip of my pint, listening with renewed interest, pretending not to be too absorbed.

He continues, 'I remember him telling me a bit about it. It was mainly because the Black and Tans had been using it for awful deeds.'

'What else did he tell you about it?' I ask casually.

'Not much more. He never really liked talking about it. It's like the Civil War itself, the old people don't like speaking about it.'

I detect a slight chilling in scruffy check-shirt's manner. He fires me a threatening look. He says when I came into the bar some people thought I was a detective looking for drug pushers.

'You'd need to watch yourself around here,' he warns. 'This is a small town and people talk a lot. They don't miss much that goes on. My advice to you is to get outta town as quickly as you can and don't come back.'

He takes another swig of his stout and thumps the bar counter. His speech is slurred and his profane words are sodden with a hint of menace.

'For your own bloody good, I mean. There's only so many questions that you can ask in a place like this before people become suspicious and wonder what you are really up to.'

I acknowledge that I am a stranger in town but protest that my interest is in the mountains. Sometimes that involves delving into history.

'Well, I am tellin' you, you'd better look over your shoulder as long as you're in Graig. People have been beaten and even shot around here for less than askin' a few questions.'

Scruffy check-shirt is becoming argumentative. I get the impression he thinks he has said too much. I feel other eyes looking at us, and sense a disquieting atmosphere. It's long past midnight. I gulp down my beer and decide not to prolong the discussion, thanking him for his information. Exiting hastily into the cold night air, I keep a nervous eye over my shoulder lest an overly gregarious Graigite decides to test out his head-butting or close quarter combat skills on me.

Sunday morning river traffic is an easy-going affair in

Graig. Tentatively, I pull back the curtains in case any of Graig's gunmen, guerrillas or gangsters are lying in wait. From my vantage-point, high up on the fourth floor, all I see is an aerial view of some timid and unarmed birds. A dozen barges and small boats are tied up. Across the top of the water a heron flaps at a steady speed and two pairs of Graig mallard paddle upstream. Quietly, so quietly you hardly notice, a rowing boat steals past. A restless pied wagtail, its long tail constantly dipping, alights on the *Barrow Commodore* then shifts to the *Carib Princess* before briefly settling on *Miss Aoife*. A slate-grey barge chugs leisurely past. Its occupants peer out through net curtains, waving at two children playing at the water's edge. A congregation of greedy rooks gathers, not for morning mass, but to squabble around left-overs of late-night Graig spilling out of an overflowing wheelie-bin for the use of 'Visiting Boat Owners Only'.

From the water my eye moves over the graceful, granite arched bridge, up to the dormer windows of the spanking-new quayside town houses all pastel pinks, lemons, ochres and aquamarines; then upwards to Deerpark Forest and Gorlough Wood, through the grassy slopes to the cynosure for all of Graig – the cross on Brandon's summit, serving as a high reminder of the day's objective.

'Where do you go to my Lovely?' blasts out on Radio Kilkenny as I make my way out the Inistioge Road. People scurry to eleven o'clock mass. I turn on to a country lane and after a short distance reverse into an opening to let a farmer in his Zetor 4718 pass. He gives me a toot.

I singalonga Peter Sarstedt.

Hedges high with nettles, briars and ferns run along both sides until I come to a spruce forest with densely packed trees. A break in the trees affords views of the open countryside. A network of forest tracks shakes the car to pieces. I jolt along, trying with little success to dodge the potholes and loose stones. At the end of a lane closed with a forestry barricade, I park at a gate and climb over a stile. It is not the easiest of walks. I wade through fields of knee-high heather on to another slope, eventually picking up a stony path to the summit. Sarstedt lingers with me along the route.

The top is crowded with furniture. A 40-foot steel cross, bolted to a rusted orange tank housing the generator that powers the light bulbs, is the focal point. All roads lead to Graig: from the town centre I count eight radiating outwards like spreading tendrils. On a clear day it is said you can see at least nine counties. This is the clearest of clear days; an uninterrupted spectacle looking out over silent, neatly parcelled farms, sparsely populated straight fields and forests of pine. The texture of the landscape is a mixed palette of beiges and golds, a result of the silage cutting. It is rolling and dipping countryside, an amalgam of hills, mountains, rivers, valleys and bays.

I look across to a triangular hillside, identifying some of the near hills: Coppanagh Hill, Tory Hill, Slieve Coiltia near New Ross, or *Nova Villa Pontis*, if you prefer. In the middle distance the River Nore wriggles through fields. I watch the interplay of land and sea at Wexford Harbour and make out Hook Head lighthouse. The long ridge of the Blackstairs and Mount Leinster stands to the east. Rippling away to the west is a greater concentration of the soaring Munster mountains, stretching from the recumbent Slievenamon, over to the Galtees, blending into the Comeraghs and Knockmealdowns.

A young couple arrives behind me. We discuss an ugly six-foot square concrete shelter, its door lying in a dank pool of water. It contains empty bottles of Coca-Cola and high-energy drink cans. I muse over what it may have been used for. The man asks if I know.

'It's the Temple of Zodiac,' I reply. 'It's where you meet old friends before you come to the World's End down there at *Nova Villa Pontis*.'

He looks at me with a peculiar smile as though I'm suffering high-place hysteria or an overdose of magic mushrooms. He says it's getting cold and promptly disappears with his girlfriend, without so much as a backward glance. I get the distinct impression, like Sarstedt, that he 'wants to look inside my head'.

Talking to Anthony Tighe fired my imagination about Woodstock. Having heard so much about it, I feel it would be remiss not to visit the grounds. The only views of how this Georgian mansion looked 100 years ago are found in the walls of the Woodstock Heritage Museum in Inistioge. The front was elaborate and ornate. After the main section was built, two wings of lesser height were added. A broad flight of steps led up to the front door and entrance hall.

On my way over to the ruins in the Woodstock

Demesne a downpour erupts. I shelter under the dome of a multi-limbed Monterey pine on the newly-shaven croquet lawn, watching the droplets trembling on the leaves. All that is left of the big house is a doorless, windowless, roofless shell with exposed red-brick walls. Here and there is evidence of a door frame architrave. The crumbling remains are ringed off with a high, green mesh fence. A sign reads 'Danger, Building Unsafe, Keep Out'. Plasterwork hangs perilously loose. The interior is covered in plane trees, creepers and weeds. The ground beside the fence is an unsightly weed and wildflower wilderness, drowning in a morass of overgrown ferns, long-dead nettles, thistles, dandelions, ox-eye daisies and holly bushes.

I try to visualise what a magnificent house it must have been in its heyday: the parties, the pleasure and the picnics; the guests arriving for dinner by horse-drawn carriage; the drama, discussion and drinking, as well as the dancing, socialising, gaiety and music.

Nowadays most people come to look at the gardens. Few bother to cast as much as a sideways glance at Woodstock's decaying façade. An elderly couple wanders up, pausing to look at the ruin. The woman stops beside me, saying she's a bit of ruin herself. She's more interested in the gardens. They were renowned, she says, for their vast array of exotic plants, shrubs and trees.

With their immense girth, the stately trees are an architectural delight, standing like gigantic pieces of sculpture. I check their name tabs: Western Red Cedars, Wellingtonias, Deodar Cedars, Japonicas and Japanese Thuja. Upright and solemn in their brilliant green summer foliage, they are enduring symbols, having lasted in some cases for 200 years. Most are healthy, but one or two ancient ones in this grand ensemble look as though they are living on borrowed time.

Back in Inistioge a swarm of twenty black leather-clad bikers emerges from the Woodstock Arms. Some of them also look as though they are living on borrowed time. Four squat about a yellow Ducati. Others board their gleaming Yamahas and Suzukis, waiting for the rest to join them. Like a party of swallows or swifts, at an unknown signal, they rev up startling the whole village, and head off with a collective deafening roar.

'They're awful yokes them,' says the petrol attendant at Reddy's foodmarket, jerking his thumb at the bikers. 'And an awful price too. One of them fellas was telling me that they cost €22,000 each.'

At 89.9 a litre the petrol prices have risen alarmingly since 1922. As I drive back to Graig I think of the damage that twenty litres can do. Inistioge is invested with an intense historical presence. The essential character of the place hasn't changed much in 100 years. It has a continuity rarely seen in Irish villages. I am not sure if people want to reinhabit the past but they do not like to forget it. It seems to weigh on them. The dramatic events of the early 1920s took place amid a time of strife, conflict, ambush and revenge. People talk about the burning of Woodstock as if it were last month or at most last year, instead of 80 years ago. The spirit of this place is inextricably linked to the past. It is a village long on memory.

I return to my waterside watering hole, tired from a long day. I want a night of television surfing but the set produces only fuzzy pictures. Sitting by the window I watch a moon climb, full-orbed, in a starless sky and hang above Brandon, lighting up the slopes. From my high garret, I listen to a chorus of yelping dogs. At midnight the Anchor Inn throws out its rumbustious revellers.

My last late Kilkenny evening turns into a night of two full moons. One shines serenely over the shoulder of Brandon, guarding Freney's hoard of hidden treasure; the other, a perfect reflection, glistens in the serenity of the Barrow. A young man and teenage girl walk on the quayside holding hands. They are having a Leinster lovers' lunar tiff. He pleads with her to stay while she begs to go home.

'I am going now,' she says. 'I really am going home. Seven o'clock comes very early. Now please let me go.'

Three drunks shout-sing their night-time tunes at the moon: 'Come on Ye Boys in Green', and howl a couple of half-hearted 'olés'. A man staggers into the street and vomits into the gutter. Another stands on the bridge and hurls a can into the river, shattering the moon's reflection and leaving a ring of concentric circles.

When I'm alone in my bed (as Sarstedt would have phrased it) the final sounds that surround me are the click-clacking high heels of a woman walking alone along the quay, screaming into her mobile.

'Omigod forget him, put him outta your head, he's only a man forgodsake, Marie; he's only a man.'

20

Mighty Trostan

'Tis distance lends enchantment to the view,
And robes the mountain in its azure hue.
                    Thomas Campbell, 'Pleasures of Hope'

It is high summer by the time I approach the northeast-ernmost part of my itinerary. Brazil has won the World Cup, the name Roy Keane is forgotten, and Carrauntoohil has claimed another victim – a walker who collapsed from a medical condition. The only true constant is the rain which continues to pour down in bucketfuls. The statisticians from the Irish Meteorological Service confirm that May was the wettest on record and June was not much better. The wet weather has left a crisis in the countryside and a sad legacy now being quantified in the summer: crops are rotting, milk yields have fallen, tourism has plummeted.

Up in the North the annual summer timetable of trouble is underway. On BBC Radio Ulster the newsreader goes through a litany of nasty overnight incidents: rival gangs of rioters clashed in north Belfast, ambulance crews were attacked with petrol bombs, stone throwers smashed windows in three houses, a man was shot in the knees in the west of the city – a fairly normal night in post-ceasefire Belfast.

Driving towards Broughshane in north Antrim, my attention is caught by a sign in red letters on a church notice board with a profound proclamation: 'Blessed are those who can tell a mountain from a molehill.' Psalms 121.

Along the roads of the area God and death are companions: 'Jesus is Lord', a billboard advertises; 'The Wages of Sin is Death', warns another, and a church noticeboard, 'Look unto me and be ye saved, all the ends of the earth'. Free-range eggs are on offer at a two-storey farmhouse, 'Monday to Saturday' and underneath in emphatic capital letters: 'NO SUNDAY SALES'.

The mountains of Antrim are more correctly hills. They are rounded rather than pointed. I reflect on my time in the past four months spent walking up mountains. It has often been compared to a religious experience. It is, after all, an act of faith of sorts; there are times when your legs hurt, your breath will not come, your eyes sting with sweat, your feet ache, and the only way you are going to get to the summit is by reciting a creed. Once you get there you feel better when the pain gives way to euphoria and you lift your eyes heavenward, although you may feel you are in purgatory.

To complete the religious symbolism I close my eyes, touch my obsidian stone, and say a prayer for drier weather to St Michael, the patron saint of high places.

The long straight road to Broughshane is full of hidden dips. Every few miles, signs warn of swells and rises. A couple of tractors pass and a few farmers raise index fingers. On Big Collin, the flailing arms of wind turbines dominate the landscape. The road runs parallel with Slemish where St Patrick tended his sheep. It is County Antrim's best-known hill and a dominant landmark for miles around. A volcanic peak, it rises from flat land, looking like Ayers Rock. Slemish may look as though it should be the highest place in County Antrim – and many people in the Braid Valley think it is – but then appearances, as I have come to learn, are deceptive in the mountain world. The highest point is, in fact, Trostan buried away in the middle of the glens of Antrim.

Road signs point to quaint-sounding place-names: Buckna, Cullybackey, Aghnadore, Lisnamurrican. Broughshane is drowning in a sea of flowers. Every window ledge, hanging basket and tub overflows with geraniums and other plants. Purple, pink, red, white and blue flowers hang from telegraph poles, the fronts of houses and from every building. From MacGregor's Corner the glens eventually come into foggy focus. The two broad outlines, partially visible through my windscreen, are Slievenanee and Slievenamaddy. When I stop for petrol at the Glenravel filling station in Martinstown I feel I have strayed over to western Scotland. The attendant, a man with sky blue eyes, shows me the way but warns 'sneer a dozen miles away frae here, and 'tis a brave wheena steps to the top o' it'.

'I definitely wouldn't advise you to go up there today. Ye'll not see a haet and you'll get pelted. I was only up Trostan onc't when I was at school twenty years ago. It was a charity walk called "Operation Rising" and all I remember is that it rained most of the time and we called it "Operation Raining".'

He quizzes me on the Bluebird's performance: 'how many miles are ye gettin' to the gallon?; what's she 'lack' on corners?; is there power steerin'?; they're powerful motors these.'

The route into the glens takes me through the Orra Scenic Drive. This one may not qualify as a GMR but comes near the definition. I pick out the names of some hills as reference points: Carnanmore, Cushleake, Oghtbristacree, Crocknamoyle, Gruig Top, Crocknacreeva. They are only lumps in the countryside, no more than 1,000 feet. I check the map. A spider's web of narrow roads and tracks leads invitingly in all directions. The minor roads are marked yellow. Scores of them cut across the chequerboard north Antrim countryside at all sorts of curious twists, linking up with each other at crossroads and T-junctions where they join the main roads in red.

The contours seem easy on the eye. In fact, the contours of Trostan and Slievenanee look identical; only fifteen feet separates them in height. The scenic drive crosses an expanse of open moorland through Slieveanorra Forest and over to Trostan, now shrouded in midday cloud. Sheep, their shoulders daubed with scarlet paint, wander across the moors. A sign promoting section five of the Moyle Way is fixed at an angle to a large stone slab by the roadside:

> Here you are overshadowed by the mighty Trostan which
> stands an impressive 550 metres above sea level. Having
> defeated the O'Neills and MacQuillans at the Battle of Orra,
> the MacDonnells celebrated their victory at Trostan's summit
> where they built a cairn to commemorate the victorious
> leader, Sorley Boy.

Two fat raindrops, like balls of stone rolling from the
eyes of a crying child, run down the front of the signboard.
'Mighty Trostan' looks mighty misty and mighty murky. I
can just about make out some of the lazybeds on its lower
slopes, but its top half is obscured and looks likely to be for
the rest of the day. I follow a mighty twisty road into
Cushendall, dropping down along the Glendun River.

Cushendall is a compact town of 1,500 people, where
four roads and three glens converge. In the early 1800s it
was known as 'Newtown Glens' and was a place of little
importance. The Irish name *Cois-Abhann-Dhalla* means 'the
foot of the River Dall'. A well-preserved red sandstone
tower of unshiftable solidity, known as Turnley's Tower,
stands as the architectural focal point at the crossroads. It
dates from around 1817 (a memorable figure around these
parts as the digits make up the same height as Trostan).
After making his fortune in China, Francis Turnley
returned and bought Cushendall. A notice says the tower
was intended as a 'place of confinement for idlers and rioters'. It is known locally as the Curfew Tower, and curfew

was still being rung from it during the Troubles of the early twentieth century. The only idlers hanging around it today are three teenage girls waiting to use the nearby phone box. There are no rioters in Cushendall, but I figure the tower could well be brought back into action to confine the riotous mobs on the streets of Belfast.

Three glens, Glenballyemon (Valley of Eamonn's town-land), Glenaan (Anna's Valley), and Glencorp (Valley of the corpse), roll down into Cushendall where at a sedate pace the River Dall trickles its way round discarded beer bottles, cans and plastic containers. The town has a dramatic set-ting. The sea surrounds it on one side, enclosing it within Red Bay, while it is ringed inland by mountains.

The conversation amongst the lunch-goers in Harry's Restaurant is dominated by sport. Five men sitting across from my window seat argue about sporting heroes of the past. Everyone from George Best to Nobby Stiles, and Jimmy Greaves to Barry McGuigan gets a mention. I order a cool glass of beer. Three other men are discussing the exploits of Antrim's hurling team. I ask about Trostan and if there are any old people who know something of its history. A man called Jimmy says I am about twenty years too late.

'All the oul' hands are dead. You shoulda' been here a wheena years ago, but they're all gone now.'

They discuss who owns Trostan. There seems to be gen-eral disagreement, but the consensus is that it is owned by a conglomerate of farmers. Jimmy, who was a forester in the glens, is nursing a Bushmills with a small jug of water. 'We call this stuff the wine of the county and the wine of the country,' he says, adding an equal measure of water to his refilled whiskey glass.

'Trostan is divided up between a lot of different people. I think the MacDonnells, Blaneys and McAlisters all have a share in it. You should look up Andrew McAlister or John Blaney out the Cushendun Road.'

For Jimmy, Trostan has always been a 'dark-horse mountain'.

'It's never had the importance in historic or folklore terms of some of its neighbours such as Orra or Slievenanee. Orra has much more history attached to it with the skirmishes between the MacDonnells and the MacQuillans. For most people Trostan is barren, dreary, treeless and unimportant. It's not very imposing, unlike Tievebulliagh or Lurigethan, so it doesn't really look anything special.'

With great summital exactitude, Jimmy says the one thing he is sure of is its height.

'It is 18-17 feet. I always thought that was an easy way of remembering its exact height.'

Over at the Glens of Antrim House, run as a Mace supermarket, Andrew McAlister explains that Trostan is not an ostentatious mountain. Andrew is a full-blooded glensman with a love of his native place. His family can trace their name back more than 300 years. They have been in business in the present site since at least 1790 and were in the glens long before that.

'I think we've covered nearly every occupation,' Andrew says. 'We're just a typical old country business. We have been farmers, grocers, caterers, undertakers, licensed victuallers, wholesale spirit merchants and a whole lot of other things. There seems to have been a family split around 1798, obviously an important date in Irish history. I am not too sure whose side we were on because we've always been a bit mercenary. Some of the family went to Westport, some to Dublin, while others moved only a mile down the road. Generally the McAlisters tend to be a bit parochial and don't move too far.'

There are 57 families of McAlisters within the glens and most are related to each other.

'Like many country areas they all have nicknames, usually after their grandfather. In my case it would be the Arthurs; sometimes they could be named after the townland they come from, or after the colour of their hair, or their occupation such as millers, weavers and so on. What happened in our family was that one generation was called Daniel, the next was called Arthur, and it passed on. For some obscure reason I'm called Andrew so my mother decided to break that tradition. But I'm still called Andy Arthur.'

I ask what Trostan means to him.

'Trostan is one of the lesser-known mountains. Tievebulliagh has a much more distinctive peak and Lurig is more spectacular while Trostan is a long low, slightly domed mountain. It's ironic that it is the highest. It should be the most interesting looking but it is a bit subtle, it doesn't emphasise its glories in the same way the others do. Some of the other mountains have more history in terms of Celtic forts, but Trostan never had that tradition, maybe because it was a bit higher and more difficult to make a living on.

'Before the famine there were probably six or seven times more people living in the hills than there are now. In the Battle of Orra in 1559, the MacQuillans and O'Neills were tricked by their enemy, the MacDonnells, who laid rushes on the boggy ground to pretend it was firm. The opposition's horses plunged deep into the bog and the army was easy prey for the MacDonnells. Since that day there's an old saying that lives on here, "There's no one but a MacQuillan would be fooled by a reed bed".'

By early evening the summer sun has come out. Over the wall at the car park, my eye falls on a dipper sitting on a boulder in the shallow River Dall. Bobbing and curtseying, the small bird shows off its gleaming white bib, raising its short tail several times. After half a minute it sets off at speed with rapid wing beats, banking left, then right, zooming fractionally above the surface of the river in the direction of the bridge where its nest may be.

Cushendall branch library beside the river opens late on a Friday night. After a hectic afternoon, the librarian is enjoying a quiet moment. A red-faced woman with glasses, she wears a burgundy cardigan and rust-coloured skirt. On her feet a pair of dainty blue shoes with zips are open at the front. She will need to put her thinking cap on, she says, when I ask about Trostan. She sets off on a fast-paced trot around the shelves, ransacking her brain and making a number of sucking and humming noises as she walks around the room, 'Trostan, Trostan, Trostan', then a long pause followed by 'Trostan, Trostan, Trostan'.

Her starting point is the history shelves. She checks the Cushendall Local Studies section which contains two files. She points out *The Glynns*, the Journal of the Glens of Antrim Historical Society; she checks a collection of articles called *The Glensman*, and other glens reference books, including *McCahan's Local Histories*. At a brisk pace she hares around the room again with more muttering and whispering; after several heavy sighs, some inspirational drumming on her desk, and much gazing out through the window, she produces a host of new and old photographic books, some spurned by the millennium. The glens also have inspired poets.

'We've got Moira O'Neill, Dusty Rhodes – he was a tramp poet of the roads – and John Hewitt, whom I am sure you know about.'

My research produces a couple of general articles on the glens, a piece about Sorley Boy MacDonnell and a page of information about the townland of Barrard, *Barr Ard*, meaning 'lofty summit' which incorporates part of Trostan. John Hewitt, who holidayed in the glens, wrote that every hilltop in Antrim wears a cairn. In 'Sunset over Glenaan' he described the view from his cottage:

> I stop to name the peaks along their dark array,
> For these are more than mountains, shouldered clear
> Into the sharp star-pointed atmosphere,
> Into the sunset. They mark out and bound
> The utmost limits of my chosen ground.

John Blaney has offered to act as a cicerone for the trek over 'my chosen Trostan ground'. We drive along Gaults Road the next day, passing rowan trees about to burst into bud. The hedges are in summer throttle with cow parsley, bracken, fuchsia and honeysuckle brushing against the Bluebird. We trail a Zetor 7745 and two New Holland tractors unable to pass on the twisty road. The sky is a blanket of milky white, without a hint of blue. It is turning into a warm day. John motions me to park at a stile beside sheep pens where we walk through a steel gate. He points out the ancient lazybeds for the potatoes. We wend our way across bilberries and rushes that are called 'sprit' and are widely found on Trostan. They are about eighteen inches high. John's father farmed here and he has known the mountain since he was a child. He used to run over Slievenanee and Trostan covering up to ten miles a day, to help with lambing and sheep herding.

'It was a natural thing for a young boy to do then, unlike today when they wouldn't know anything about the mountains or the sheep. I remember in the 1960s walking through some bits of bog near Trostan which had built up on a bed of rock and the ground would ripple as if you were walking on water; it was terrifying. It was a pond of water with a growth over it that became thicker over the years.

'This area has been farmed by our family since my great-grandfather, although he wasn't a dedicated farmer and liked telling a good yarn in the pub. In those days they herded the animals – including horses and ponies – on to the hills during the summer. During the war, my father snared rabbits on Trostan. In fact they made more from selling rabbits than selling lambs in those days. They were shipped to England for consumption. But over the years myxomatosis has cleared a lot of them out, and the buzzards have attacked them.'

John taught maths and science in the secondary school in Cushendall, later becoming principal. He took early retirement because he wanted to spend more time farming. We make our way past the site of the narrow gauge dismantled railway line with not a trace of a sleeper left. The track covered a ring around the base of Trostan and the railway was used to take the stone that was mined down to the bay.

A couple of skylarks lift off at hushed speed, weaving low through the air ahead of us; we disturb two frogs in rushes. John says he has also seen salamanders on the hill. We make our way over an area that he remembers his father referring to as 'the broken ground'. It is a mosaic of brittle stones, rocks, heather, peat and the roots of willow trees. We walk through purple bell heather, past abundant clumps of the yellow four-petalled flowers of tormentil, cuckoo flower and stag's horn moss. The flat summit, littered with boulders, stones and fallen fence posts, leads to a windswept peat mound with a three-foot trig point marking the highest point at 1,817 feet. Because of the haze, views are restricted, but north, south, east and west, mountains still fill the horizon. We have been lucky. The rain has stayed off and there is not the slightest zephyr. We pick out the flat top of Slievenanee, the gargantuan lump of Lurigethan, and the pointed peak of Tievebulliagh; to the north of us, lying through the haziness, are Wee Orra and Orra More, or Big

Orra, known to some people as the 'Begorrah mountain'.

As the wind rises, we drift down on to the east side of the mountain, passing the walled remains of the smithy which John's father called 'the smiddy'. It was used by the blacksmith for shoeing the pit ponies that were stabled there in the winter. Several layers of stones remain on the ground and the outline of what must have been a substantial mountain building. We come to the remains of a disused iron ore mine. Ferns and spiders' webs hang over the entrance. We peer down an opening of five feet in diameter. The hole looks just big enough for a man to slide down. A dead sheep lies in a pool of water on the floor of the dark interior.

'It must have been a harrowing job for local people,' he says, 'working all the way down with the ponies and carts in there as well. The stone that was mined was taken to the bay where it was transported by boat for the steel industry, mostly in the English midlands. They closed in 1939 at the outbreak of war.'

We walk along Barrard, another section of Trostan, following a well-defined sheep path. John explains that the sheep have sweat glands on their feet which enable them to find the path through their scent. He talks about the foot-and-mouth outbreak the previous year. Cushendall was a prime area of infection.

'We were unfortunate in that we were within the one kilometre zone. We lost all our cattle – about 30 in total – and all our sheep. They were culled as a precautionary measure. It was like a death in the family and there was a big fear it would spread even more. About 30,000 sheep were slaughtered throughout the glens. Replacement sheep were very expensive to buy and this year the poor weather has depressed prices.'

He talks about the Trostan sheep and the coloured marking fluid farmers use to identify their own animals. We halt momentarily by the entrance to a sealed up mine. He differentiates the graffitied sheep grazing below us.

'The ones with the blue left hips are Patrick MacDonnell's, the ones with the red right shoulder are James MacDonnell's, the ones with the red right hip are Hugh MacDonnell's – they're all colour co-ordinated cousins. Then you have the ones with the red rump below the base of the tail, which are Desmond McCollum's; the ones with the red across the top of the shoulder blades belong to Francis John McCaughan; mine have the royal blue across the top of the kidney, while my brother Liam's have red across the top of the kidney.'

Side by side at a steady pace, we crunch our way through ankle-high heather, knee-high 'sprit' and waist-high rushes. A cool mist rolls in. Spits of rain, which had threatened for most of the afternoon, make their first appearance of the day. On the way back to the car we are chased by dozens of small brown moths and a north Antrim highland clan gathering of energetic glens' midges.

21

Close Encounters of the Chopper Kind

The mountains gathered round me
like bandits. Their leader
swaggered up close in the dark light,
full of threats, full of thunders.

But it was they who stood and delivered.
They gave me their money and their lives.
They filled me with mountains and thunders.
My life was enriched
with an infusion of theirs.

Norman MacCaig, 'Below the Green Corrie'

A primeval atmosphere still lurks in south Armagh. It is a landscape with a long history of settlement. Human occupation of the area stretches back to neolithic times. Like north Antrim, historical memorabilia litters the countryside with a concentration of monuments: cairns, raths, ring forts, cashels, remains of medieval churches and castles, early Christian cemeteries, souterrains, passage tombs, portal tombs and *crannógs* are all to be found. But this is also high surveillance country. Juxtaposed with this antiquity is the military hardware of the army: square watchtowers, observation posts and lookout stations are scattered on many prominent hills; a military monopoly dominates the present-day high ground. The cult of high places in south Armagh is a cult of ceaseless army helicopter activity. Driving around the area I feel eyes scrutinising my movements, logging my journey along crooked roads, watching me stop and turn the car.

At first appearance Armagh does not seem a county generously endowed with mountains. It is neatly divided between the flatlands of the north – apple blossom country where the horizon stretches endlessly without peaks, and from where the 'orchard county' nickname comes – and the mountains of the south. The Armagh mountains are in fact one of the four main upland areas in Northern Ireland; and there is no dispute over the highest point in the county: for miles around, Slieve Gullion omni-presides, dwarfing the villages and small towns with its own imprint of history.

On the way into Meigh (pronounced 'Mike') a farmer leads a pack of Friesians across the road after milking. They turn an indifferent eye. The village is ablaze with the colours of the Armagh County Gaelic football team as they bid for all-Ireland glory. Strings of orange and white pennants and flags fly from telegraph poles to and from Murphy's pub and Owney's Corner Shop. Small groups of women, with restless children on their school holidays, stamp their feet at Gullion View, waiting for the Ulsterbus Translink service to take them to a morning's shopping in Newry. Meigh is a place where WVM reigns supreme. I had stopped to buy a paper and sandwich, and within ten minutes noted five different breeds: Betty's Home Baked Bread: So Fresh It's Famous (Renault Kargo); Forkhill Fireplaces Fit for Kings (Citroën Berlingo); Plumbing Heating Piping: One Call Covers All, Call Jim McCaul (Toyota Hiace); Tony's Tiles: If Anyone Can Tony McCann Can (Renault Extra); and the Water Service (Vauxhall Combo). It is a toss-up as to whether or not there are more varieties of WVM than mountain sheep throughout Ireland.

A noticeboard in the window of a closed up office in the Slieve Gullion Forest Park explains that the stone buildings are examples of early nineteenth-century architecture. A French family called Chambré, one of three main land-owning families in the area, built them on the southern slopes of Slieve Gullion in 1815. The buildings were originally used as a piggery, hayshed, and potato and machinery shed. In 1995 they were officially opened after being renovated and modernised at a cost of £1 million.

Apart from two helicopters buzzing high above, it all seems mysteriously quiet. There is no one around. I wander among the deserted offices, peering in through the windows of a locked shop. A man emerges from nearby trees and introduces himself as Noel Loughran, the caretaker. Some of the facilities, he says, are open only at the weekends.

The courtyard tourist literature styles the area as 'a land of horse-fairs where ancient landscapes cradle the remnants of our past, both Christian and pagan; where people still proudly value their relaxed lifestyle and are always willing to share it with others'. The 'Ring of Gullion' is in a region which in 1991 was designated an Area of Outstanding Natural Beauty, a classification acknowledging it as a unique landscape of national importance.

Noel's family has lived at Slieve Gullion's foot for generations. As the leaflet promises he shares a story with me from his family's skeleton cupboard. Nearly 200 years ago, his great-grandmother used to pick sticks, known as 'taries' which were the burnt heather from the mountain.

'In those days all the mountain was owned by landlords,' says Noel. 'She took down some bundles of black sticks that were used to cook on the open fire. They were good for cooking because there was no smoke from them. On one occasion she was caught by one of the landlords and taken to court for stealing. She was sentenced to 30 days in Armagh women's jail. The judge said he wanted to make an example of the women from Dromintee who frequently were stealing sticks for the fire from the slopes of Slieve Gullion. My mother told me that story, but she never really liked talking about it. You had to question her and drag the information out of her.'

From the courtyard, a one-way traffic system takes me along one of Armagh's GMRs, through a forested twisty road to a car park at the edge of a plantation. The roadside is lined with overgrown thorn hedges, fuchsia and dwarf gorse. The summer ling and bell heather are rich in dazzling lilac, bright mauve, vivid purple and deep crimson. A path leads up to the north cairn and a large mound of stones about 40 feet in diameter, from where I search out the way to the south cairn. Slieve Gullion is one of those mountains that returns a rich reward for little effort in attaining its summit. It takes no more than half an hour to reach the first cairn and another twenty minutes' walk to the bigger cairn, passing en route Calliagh Berra's Lake, its wavelets rippling in the light breeze but with no foam crests. According to legend, any man who swims in the lake comes out visibly aged.

Slieve Gullion – an extinct volcanic site – is an elongated mass forming the northwesterly end of a mountain belt stretching from the Cooley peninsula. When I arrive at the south cairn I disturb a meadow pipit busily engaged in a lunchtime insect and worm search. It flits off to a clump of heather and rapidly disappears. Underneath the south cairn is a large passage grave that was excavated 40 years ago. Fragments of cremated bone and worked flints were found. My guidebook tells me it is known locally as 'Calliagh Berra's House'. The Calliagh Berra, the 'hag or witch of Beara', is common in folklore and is often associated with passage tombs.

Sitting with my back against the triangulation pillar, I watch the progress of a circling helicopter. It flies above the course of the surrounding ring of hills, juddering briefly, then dropping with supplies for the Forkhill military barracks. Another appears from the direction of Camlough. It lands in a field and shakes itself, before dispersing half a dozen soldiers into the undergrowth. Despite demilitarisation and the dismantling of some of the army's paraphernalia on the hillsides there is still a huge aerial security force presence throughout the area. The roads are regarded as being too dangerous for the army to drive their vehicles.

The toposcope lists the names of familiar ranges of hills: the Mourne Mountains, Slieve Anierin, the Slieve Blooms, and some not so familiar such as Dead Man's Hill, ten miles to the north. I make out sections of two large portions of water: Lough Neagh and Carlingford Lough. There are few arable fields. This area was badly affected by the foot-and-mouth disease and no sheep are to be seen roaming free on the mountains; in fact there are few sheep anywhere in the countryside. Beef cattle have primacy.

This landscape is known to geographers as 'dispersed settlement'. Small farm buildings and white cottages predominate. The countryside is populated with *clachans*, or clusters of houses, hamlets, villages and small towns. Every few hundred yards flamboyant one-off houses have sprung up. Some look as though they could accommodate an entire battalion of helicopter pilots, if not most of an army regiment. Many of the modern houses are painted in glacial white, echoing the whitewash of the thatched cottages that once covered the area.

The striking feature of the landscape is what geologists call a ring dyke; it comes to life from the summit. The distinctive dyke is a complete circle of low hills covering a wide area and standing guard over the swashbuckling

Slieve Gullion. Covering a large arc of land, it embraces numerous sharp, steep and craggy hills with rocky ridges and hollows, ranging in size between 500 and 1,000 feet. I count at least a dozen – all bigger than drumlins but smaller than mountains – spaced apart in intervals of twos and threes, tracing them at the same time on my map: Croslieve, Slievebrack and Mullaghbane; Aughanduff Upper and Lower, and Slievenacappel; Courtney and Sturgan. The broad-shouldered Camlough Mountain, the highest in the ring at 1,389 feet, punctuates the northeast skyline. In some cases, where the dyke is breached or its topography broken, a forest of hazel, sycamore, oak or rowan has been planted.

The valley in between protects Slieve Gullion, a tall queen within the centre of her circular empire, standing aloof at 1,894 feet. It resembles a moat surrounding a fortress or castle, but without water, apart from the Forkhill River and the long, thin, blue strip of Cam Lough. Drumlin country lies to the west and north of the ring, while the southern rim of the dyke is a natural boundary of Ulster. The *Slighe Midluachra*, the ancient road leading from Tara to Dunseverick on the north coast, went through this area called the Moyry Pass, better known as the Gap of the North.

Suddenly, and without warning, my veneration of the landscape and historic contemplation is abruptly interrupted. Like a motorised dragonfly, a Lynx appears out of the sky, advancing head-on towards me at speed from the direction of Camlough Mountain. I would like to say it zooms at me with all guns blazing, but that would be actionable hyperbole. It certainly flies full throttle, swooping low with a thunderous clatter over the top of Slieve Gullion, and for a few short seconds sends Calliagh Berra's wavelets into pronounced crests. The pilot checks me over, quickly banking away to the south, presumably satisfied I do not pose a serious terrorist threat and ensuring I am fully aware of the army's presence. I stand bemused, raise my Westmeath walking stick, and receive not as much as a wave in reply.

For nearly an hour I had sat at the top of the cairn. I sensed that the soldiers' sights were trained on me from Camlough Mountain where they are encamped. With their listening devices and long-range cameras, they maintain round-the-clock surveillance. My 'subversive' activities obviously made them wary and attentive. I was writing up my journal, jotting down aspects of the landscape that intrigue me, such as the strip field patterns of Ballintemple to the east of Slieve Gullion where the farmland is neatly divided into rectangular fields by hedges or walls varying in length. Seditiously, I was logging the passage of white vans along the road to Forkhill, checking their progress with my binoculars, studying the map and land at intervals through my imaginary time telescope. I was also taking photographs. Undoubtedly, suspicious activity; enough to have a man arrested and detained for 24 hours. I remind myself I am in south Armagh, known under the term 'bandit country' in the 1980s when a phalanx of hilltop forts stood along the border.

For those hillwalkers not accustomed to it, watching a helicopter head in your direction at full steam is a transfixing spectacle. There is no hiding place on top of a mountain, especially since Calliagh Berra's House is closed. All you can do is stand and stare. In the after-calm I hear again the thin but distinctive call of the meadow pipit, presumably accustomed to the daily invasion of its territory. I hasten down, slithering over heather, anxious to return to the car for fear of another aerial assault. I have not swum in the lake but I feel visibly aged.

The owner of the Slieve Gullion Inn says it is common for the army to check on people walking the hills.

'You'll not get away with too much around these parts,' he says. 'You can be sure they'll be watching you closely. I've heard stories of walkers having the film taken from their cameras. They're sensitive about photographing any of the installations.

'As for the helicopters, the people are tortured with them. It's a continuous thing and goes on all day, sometimes until one or two in the morning. They've been known to collide with almost everything from treetops to power lines. They've brought down TV aerials, blown off tiles, and rattled windows in the houses. But they frighten the cattle, sheep and horses. A lot of money has been paid out for trauma and illness claims against cattle. One farmer was paid compensation because his hens stopped laying eggs when a Lynx swooped down over the hen houses. Apparently it sent them into a terrible frenzied state.'

I order a sandwich and coffee, washing it down with a summer spoonful of a brown sugar proverb: 'So many men, so many opinions.'

With darkness descending, I leave Slieve Gullion, its ring of hills and ever-watchful eyes. Escorting me out of the area, another helicopter moves across the countryside, hovering occasionally and following the course of my road for a short distance before departing into the evening sky. Slowly, I make my way from south Armagh – a secretive world of its own – and cross the fringes of the south Down countryside into the Cooley peninsula, where I dream of helicopters but sleep the sleep of a tired walker.

In front of Carlingford Yacht Club a large flock of oyster-catchers is enjoying an obstreperous free-for-all, unhurriedly picking their way across shingle and stones at the water's edge. Quartering their own small area, they delicately probe for worms and molluscs. From a distance these normally conspicuous birds are hard to make out in the watery sunlight; at first I count only a handful. When I move closer I discover more than 100. Most are beachcombing for titbits. Others stride around solitarily keeping to their own territorial patch, while some step into pools of water, dipping their brilliant orange-red dagger bills into the murkiness. They are adept at opening shellfish.

Across the top of the lough, a pair careers off from the marina with their striking white wing bars, black mantle and head, their shadows reflected in the calm water. Like the army helicopter, they are on a low-level reconnaissance. After their 100-yard dash they alight on long, fleshy-pink legs, joining their comrades for a vivacious lunch party, tête-à-têting around the rim of a pool of dark brown water. For the best part of an hour I watch as they pick their careful way over the stones. Their distinctive melancholy shrieky 'kleep kleep' whistle rings out around the harbour. The sight of so many in one place reminds me of an unforgettable description by the Scottish poet Norman MacCaig, who said looking at them was like watching 'a black and white minstrel show'.

The wildlife show is not confined to oystercatchers. I identify redshank on the margin of their territory, strutting noisily on their scarlet stilt-like legs. A couple of herring gulls tilt past. Observing all from its lofty seat a heron watches the proceedings, while three ducks shilly-shally out in deeper water. It is just an ordinary summer Sunday afternoon in Carlingford but this ornithological spectacle goes unnoticed by the hundreds of visitors flooding into the village. They are more interested in joining the long queue at Le Crêperie stall for 'sweet tasty crêpes' or 'fresh savoury crêpes', and browsing the instant pop-up shelters selling pottery, silverware, paintings and jewellery.

The other big attraction is a vintage car run organised by the Newry and Mourne Classic Vehicle Club. Flaunting their prize possessions along the waterfront, the owners compare notes on new chassis legs, mudguards and door skins. The line up includes Triumph Heralds, Humbers, Sceptres, early Volvos and Jaguars. Vying for attention with them are a cream Riley Elf Mark II, a buff-coloured Ford Anglia de luxe, a saffron MG, and a sky blue Zodiac Overdrive. The pièce de résistance for me is not the grey and purple Hornet Hudson, complete with Michigan registration plates, which attracts much interest, but the smoke-grey Morris Minor convertible, *circa* 1957. It was during this period that the classic 1,000cc engine was introduced. As a former Minor enthusiast I feel an affinity with the owner, a man called Harry.

We discuss some of its unique characteristics: the drop indicators, the split windscreen, the white interior trim, the cuddly jelly mould shape of the bonnet and clutter-free dashboard. Harry bought the car for £300 in 1986 and has spent £1,000 souping it up.

'I put in a reconditioned engine and gearbox as well as a new exhaust all within the past year. I had it over at a rally in the Isle of Man two months ago and a man offered me four and a half thousand pounds for it,' he says, placing more emphasis on the half than the four.

'Of course, I wouldn't part with it. I call it my Rolls Royce, even though I can't drive it at the moment as I had a serious operation six months ago.'

Harry had two cysts removed from his brain. He says he feels lucky to be alive.

'I really shouldn't be here at all today; at one stage it was touch and go as to whether I would make it or not. I've certainly seen the gates of hell.'

His wife now does the driving. He misses it but is thankful to be alive.

I wander along the footpath, peering in through the windows of the empty vehicles. Vintage car owners like to indulge in their caricatures. The shiny leather seats are covered with folded tartan rugs and red cushions. Tins of boiled sweets and toffees, as well as custard creams and packets of mini apple turnovers, litter the seats and floors.

The Cooley peninsula is the aural antithesis of its next door neighbour, south Armagh. Less than twenty miles from Slieve Gullion, yet light years away in terms of noise pollution, it is a helicopter-free zone; in fact they positively discourage noise here. Louth County Council warns that it will prosecute jet-skiers and those with the temerity to launch 'fast power-boats'. Half a dozen porcelain blue mussel boats are tethered at the harbour. Apart from the waders, the only water-based activity consists of several modest sailing boats with no particular destination in mind and a white motorboat puttering into harbour carrying two men in fluorescent yellow jackets.

From my quayside bollard I swing my binoculars skyward. Louth's loftiest point, Slieve Foye, or Carlingford Mountain as it is sometimes called, is shrouded in what looks like 'permamist', i.e. permanent mist rooted to it for the day. On its lower slopes a herd of cattle and two horses munch the grass; a Land-Rover crawls along a thin forest track. Above this line nothing is discernible. Across the broad stretch of Carlingford Lough the Mournes in south Down are also covered. Rostrevor stands out on the waterfront with ranks of newly-built white houses running up a hill on its outskirts.

The afternoon's peace is shattered by the strains of mellifluous music from the town centre. Following the sound of a trumpet, I stumble across a live jazz session in the beer garden at the back of PJ's pub. 'The Five Pennies' are entertaining a sizeable crowd sitting at picnic tables, on garden benches and white plastic chairs. I park myself beside a woman swinging her two grandchildren round to

'Alexander's Ragtime Band'. Over a cool pint of Cooley's finest beer, I listen to the five-piece band, comprised of bulky barrel-chested men. They entertain the crowd with 'I Wonder Who's Kissing Her Now', 'King of the Swingers', 'Drop Me Off in Harlem', 'If I Had You', and their own unique theme tune, 'Pennies from Heaven'.

People pass on the street, pause to enjoy the jazzy offerings and applaud rapturously. Spontaneously, two rangy men, accompanied by two women in cream cardigans, swingalong to 'Hello Dolly', and an impromptu dance session erupts. They may not be the Black and White Minstrels, but this melodious lyrical quintet livens up a lazy Carlingford Sunday.

Spirits raised by the music, I tour the authentic narrow and hilly medieval streets bursting at the seams with antique and craft shops. The town, a Danish foundation, grew up around the rocky outcrop of King John's Castle, built around 1200 to defend the coastal pass against the Ulster Irish. With its surviving old buildings and ancient street layout, it retains an intimate atmosphere. Unlike most Irish towns of its size, it has not spread its tentacles much beyond its old boundary. It has successfully managed to keep its historic built environment. Apart from the castle, it can boast a Dominican Friary, a Mint, a Tholsel, Taaffe's Castle, and a quaint assortment of churches, buildings and two-and three-storey houses tarted up in seaside colours.

Georgina's Bakehouse and Tea Rooms doesn't have such a long pedigree, but has been established for at least twenty years. A roaring trade is carried on in this small café. Despite the fact that she has had the mother of all hangovers, the woman and her boyfriend beside me are having a 'where-shall-we-go-tonight?' conversation. Her downfall, she claims, was the two Irish whiskey 'nightcaps' that followed an evening's drinking and a meal in one of Carlingford's restaurants. She started with several gins, followed by an unquantified number of beers, two bottles of wine with her meal, and a mix of liqueurs. The remainder of the night was a black-out. She smiles at me.

'When I go out with my friends on a night like that,' she says, 'we call it a CRAFT evening: Can't Remember A Flipping Thing.'

Although County Louth is in Leinster, culturally it was traditionally part of the province of Ulster. It has many links to counties Armagh and Down. There are geological and topographical similarities between this area and south Armagh, and to my surprise I find another ring dyke – the second in three days. The Cooley ring dyke is an outer ring of craggy hills that includes Slieve Foye. The landscape has also been monumentalised; portal tombs and court tombs are scattered across the countryside, and the passage tomb of Clermont Cairn crowns the summit of Black Mountain. This area was the scene of the *Táin Bó Cuailgne*, The Cattle Raid of Cooley, the oldest Irish epic, dating from the time of Christ. It tells the story of Cúchulainn's defence of Ulster against the forces of Medbh, the warrior queen of Connacht. The Táin Way folding map and guide that I picked up in the heritage centre explains that the hills of the Cooley Peninsula are heathland – open and uncultivated: the soils are acid and poor in nutrients.

By Monday morning Slieve Foye has made a partial reappearance from its secretive Sunday slumber. The mist still remains fixed on the summit. I walk from my town centre B&B into this heathland. This is the only county top on my travels from where I have been able to launch myself from the centre of town. Along Savage Hill I search in vain for signs for the Táin Way. I clamber over a barbed wire fence, ploughing straightaway into thick and unpleasant vegetation. I'm confronted with a chevaux-de-frise in the form of ferns with stalks as high as young trees, tall nettles and high grass. With my trusty hazel stick I beat my way through. It feels like swimming in a sea of plants as I flail my arms to create openings. Even the criss-cross pattern of stone walls is covered with the dense scrub. I re-route several times in search of an easier way but the whole side of the mountain seems covered in swathes of ferns, hazel bushes and plants. After 30 minutes of crashing through the undergrowth and sweaty battling, I reach shorter grass sprinkled with clumps of purple heather and boulders.

Like soldiers guarding the ruined walls, towers and arches of King John's Castle, three black-legged and black-faced sheep stand at the entrance to a broad, steep gully. The mist has come down with a vengeance and the wind swirls fiercely. The sheep stand aside as I pick my way up through crags. A long, serrated ridge, interspersed with a series of rocky outcrops requiring some scrambling, litters the way to the summit. A damp mist closes in. The only noise is the occasional blast of a horn from the boats at the shipping port of Greenore several miles along the peninsula. High up in the sky, the sun filters out when the cloud cover temporarily lifts and looks like a pale lemon moon. It has been a slog to attain the topmost height of 1,935 feet – but only because I could not find the proper path.

When he was compiling his *Topographical Dictionary of Ireland* in the nineteenth century, Samuel Lewis passed through the area. In those days the oysters found in the bay were 'highly esteemed' and sent in great quantities to Dublin and Liverpool. Large numbers of herring were also caught during the season. Lewis wrote that the town was beautifully situated, with the scenery of the bay being 'remarkably fine': 'Carlingford mountain, which overhangs the castle … from its height and position intercepts, during a great part of the summer, the direct rays of the sun, for several hours before sunset.'

I have to accept his 1837 description as my vista from the summit is obscured by miserable mist. On the downward route I regain the countryside views at the foot of the gully. A vivid and dramatic combination of mountain, farmland and sea lies all around. The low-lying farms spread along the main road and on tracks that weave in and out of the Louth landscape over to Armagh and beyond. On the lower slopes towards the Eagles Rock on the other side of St Patrick's River, a harras of horses has found a small green patch of hillside; some munch their way through the grass. Five chestnut brown and five piebald stand like mournful statues, with not so much as a wagging tail, appropriate as the Mournes themselves – my next and final challenge –

look equally mournful across Carlingford Lough.

Two helmeted teenagers generate their own two-wheeled horsepower on their Postman Pat red mountain bikes. On the crossbar of one machine it says 'Force', on the other 'Giant'. They wobble over to me and say they have come across from Ravensdale via Raven's Rock and are on their way along the Táin Way to Slieve Foye Forest. At least they found the trail.

On my way down I finally pick up the yellow walking man signs and join a track after crossing a shaky wooden stile. This is the path I had tried to find for the ascent, but it was so heavily overgrown at the bottom I could not locate its starting point. A wooden gate leads me on to a stony and watery track less than a foot in width. There is just about room to squeeze my rucksack past fuchsia bushes, over-hanging branches and hedges, and squirm my way down to the starting point. When I reach the road again I realise how extremely poorly signposted the walking path is. There is no indication as to where the trail starts – not a marker, indicator or sign in sight. A bit more effort into marketing this area would be helpful. It is one place where 'Waymarkitis' has not reached. Having got my 'Moanday' morning gripe out of the way I am serenaded by a blackbird on the way back to the car park from where, with a weak-ening sun descending, I make my way out of a bustling Carlingford.

22

Terrifying Covey of Giants

We shall not cease from exploration
And the end of all our exploring
Will be to arrive where we started
And know the place for the first time.

T.S. Eliot, 'Little Gidding'

The melancholy Mourne mist has moved by the time I
drive from Rostrevor to Hilltown. At 2,796 feet Slieve
Donard stands indubitably as the highest point in the
Mourne Mountain range, the highest place throughout
County Down and all nine counties of Ulster. The
'Kingdom of Mourne' is home to a compact range of mountains, divided by the Spelga Pass, a GMR that cuts them into
the western and eastern ranges. As I round a bend on the
way into Hilltown, they appear out of the blue without

warning: bald-pated hills, undulating upthrusts standing in silence – a fitting finale to the last chapter of my travels. The eloquent words of Hayward swim into my head: 'magic mountains, huddled in conclave like some terrifying covey of giants.'

I sense the onset of autumn. The heather is in full bloom and the countryside is beginning to clothe itself in russets and browns. Unlike the Donard in west Wicklow, the emphasis on the pronunciation of the County Down one is on the first syllable.

Hilltown, *Baile Hill*, which stands at the northern edge of 'The Gateway to the Mournes', is a crossroads village. In a reading of its 'recent history' on a colourful signboard in the central square, I discover one of its claims to fame is that the Irish Tory, Redmond O'Hanlon – the Irish Robin Hood – was killed nearby in 1681. Its name has nothing to do with the hills that lie all around but is connected to the Hill family. A member of that family, who was the first Earl of Downshire, laid it out in 1765. It was near the crossing place of the Bann and was previously known as Eight Mile Bridge because it was eight miles from Newry. In 1835 Hilltown had 21 houses of which ten were pubs. Goods such as wine, spirits and tobacco, as well as silk, spices, tea, coffee, sugar and soap, were smuggled in through the Mournes. They came from boats and were brought inland by turf cart to Hilltown which appears to have been a distributing centre. Estyn Evans, the connoisseur of landscape and author of the definitive study of the area, *Mourne Country*, in 1951, attributes this to the fact that the place had so many pubs. He says 'the turf carts sometimes carried more than fuel for the fires, and this may explain why tobacco-spinning had an early start in Banbridge'.

The Gaelic language could still be heard in Hilltown in the late nineteenth century. When Evans came here in the 1940s the last of the native Irish speakers had only recently died. Its population today is 400 and the tradition of maintaining a plentiful supply of pubs lives on, with the village now supporting six. The Downshire Arms Hotel retains the link with its founder. There was originally an inn on this site dating from 1765 and the present hotel was built around 1920. Like so many small Irish towns through which I have travelled, Hilltown has reinvented itself in recent years.

Before taking the road to Newcastle, a short detour brings me past Mary Margaret's pub and along the single track pot-holed Goward Road to a portal dolmen lying in the shadow of the western foothills of the Mournes. Goward, from *Guthard* meaning 'the resounding height', is a huge granite stone weighing 50 tons – another terrifying giant. The capstone is supported by three upright stones, but has slipped sideways from its original position. According to legend the Night Sower of Goward was a ghostly figure who used to be seen sowing seed from a white sheet in the moonlight. It was said to be the ghost of a farm labourer who had been murdered and buried nearby. A farmer ploughing the ground uncovered the crime and from that time on the Night Sower of Goward was seen no more. It is nicknamed 'Pat Kearney's Big Stone', after a farmer who owned the land beside it, and is also known as 'Finn MacCool's fingerstone'. The dolmen affords impressive views of the surrounding countryside. In a neighbouring field two hooded crows are joined by a rook while a small party of magpies with long, wedge-shaped tails natters its way in and out of trees.

Slieve Donard, *Sliabh Domhanghairt*, St Donard's Mountain, was a holy mountain connected with St Patrick's disciple, St Domangard. It is said that St Donard established a hermitage and oratory here, and until the nineteenth century there was a tradition of a mountain pilgrimage on 25 July, St James's Day. Various names were applied to it. From the ninth to the twelfth centuries it was known as *Benn mBoirchi*. Then it was called *Sliabh Slanga* after the Greek prince Slainge, son of Partholan, who was buried there. During the Ordnance Survey of Ireland in the 1820s it was used as one of the points of the main triangulation between Britain and Ireland.

Fast-forward to the twenty-first century and the anglicised Slieve Donard is unique amongst Irish mountains in that it is owned and mollycoddled by a charity, having been bought by the National Trust. The Trust's guardians set up a footpath team to tackle the problem of upland erosion, caused by too many people walking in the area and overgrazing. The initiative has improved footpaths along the Glen River, and helped restore and repair parts of the renowned Mourne Wall. Money came from many quarters to preserve the mountain and fund the work: the Environment and Heritage Service and the National

Heritage Memorial Fund helped the Trust buy the mountain, while the European Regional Development Fund and the Sports Lottery Fund contributed to footpath improvements. The RAF and private helicopter companies helped transport rocks and wood up the mountain.

As I pull on my boots in Donard car park I silently wonder what the fifth-century hermits would make of all the palaver about their sacred mountain. My route, from the car park along the Glen River now in full summer spate, follows a stony path. The ground is starred with miniature flowers: harebell, eyebright and heath bedstraw. At the edge of the woods I cross a stile and continue on a crazy-paved path and up to the saddle between Commedagh and Donard where I pick up the wall, used as a handrail by many, to the top. As I get higher, the summit vegetation changes to ferns and short-cropped grass. Over lunch at the top, the views lead out to the strand and sea at Newcastle, along the east coast, over to the Isle of Man and the hills of Cumbria. Across the lough lie the mountains of Carlingford, from where I have just come. A wheatear on a rock a few yards from me suddenly disappears. The last one I met was in the Sperrins more than five months ago on a warm April day.

The colours of the countryside running over to the farmlands around Castlewellan could grace a carpet from the souks of Marrakesh or the covered market in Istanbul: shades of dark tan, soft golds, deep ivy, mustards and tortoiseshell weave a lustrous combination. I dilly-dally around the summit for a long time. Two cairns, a short distance apart, are known as Great Carn and Lesser Carn.

Between them, the surveyors of the nineteenth century and the wall builders of the twentieth century destroyed one of the cairns. A Bronze Age one survives as a large pile of stones in the north-east corner.

This is the final uphill struggle, my last peak conquered and a closing melodramatic mountain meditation – one last indulgence of time and space as a solitary anchorite. I play with the focus knob of my binoculars, identifying the different smooth, sharp and shapely peaks; I roll the alluring names around my tongue: Commedagh, Bearnagh, Binnian, Lamagan, Doan. Place-names, all with their own stories to tell, jostle for space on the map: Hare's Gap, the Brandy Pad, Silent Valley, Pigeon Rock, the Devil's Coach Road, Maggy's Leap and Dunny Water. Commedagh, also known as Kiviter, is the northerly neighbour of Donard and the Mournes' second highest peak at 2,512 feet – some 284 feet lower.

The names have not changed over recent years and neither have the views, but there are new features in the landscape. Apart from mobile phone masts, the biggest new addition is the Millennium Stone at Killyleagh made of Mourne granite. It was erected in the summer of 1999 to celebrate the millennium.

I first walked these hills 25 years ago taking part in the celebrated Mourne Wall Walk in 1977. More than 3,000 people used to participate in this annual hike which covered 22 miles of ascent and descent and involved most of the peaks of the high Mournes. It was stopped because of the serious damage being caused to the wall by tramping feet. The huge wall, made of dry stone quarried on the mountains, was built by the Belfast Water Commissioners between 1904 and 1922 to define their catchment area. Like a granite ribbon, it threads its soaring way across the tops of fifteen mountains. In places it is up to six feet high. When the travel writer H.V. Morton came this way for his book *In Search of Ireland* in 1930, he wrote about the Irish mountains having 'a curious dream-like quality'. He gives an amusing description of Donard's granite masculinity:

> You attack him from Newcastle. He is a decent-minded, kindly mountain with no evil in him but sufficient hardness to make you respect him, and yourself, when at last you fling yourself down by the cairn on top.

Donard and the Mournes are still respected and at weekends they are a popular destination. I track the progress of a shepherd walking slowly uphill with his playful collie prancing in front. He walks with a rolling gait, swinging his hips and using the weight of his boots. His body is leaning slightly forward. A tribe of twelve figures, like matchsticks with baby rucksacks, stands on a distant peak. I think of the interaction between humans and hills; of what the mountains mean to the people and those that live and work around them; of landscape as a metaphor for the human condition, and of the Tuatha Dé Danann, the pre-Christian gods, who from their bunkers and raths hidden underground in the hills, have eluded me.

The sun melts and the last of the daylight fades as I drive away from Newcastle, slowly losing sight of Slieve Donard. Heading for home, I think about my months of travelling, looking back across more than 8,000 miles of motoring. I can lay claim to a title that few in Ireland hold: a 32-county summiteer (allowing for the poetic licence of the fact that some mountains share county tops). Climbing mountains could become an addiction. There comes a point in every summit-bagger's career when the incurable stage is reached.

For now, my mountainfest and quest is complete, my task done; the lore and the cult of high places have been explored to my satisfaction and to the point of satiation. I have enveloped and gorged myself on mountains. I think of a collective noun to describe them and recall the words of Sorley MacLean in his poem *'Ceann Loch Aoineart'* or 'Kinloch Ainort':

> A company of mountains, an upthrust of mountains,
> a great garth of growing mountains,
> a concourse of summits, of knolls, of hills
> coming on with a fearsome roaring.

I steal one last glance at the shrinking range of the Mournes – ineluctable and enduring symbols. On the dashboard my obsidian stone is a reminder of the many miles we walked together. It served well its stated purpose of keeping my energies stable, clearing blockages and bringing an experience and understanding of silence, detachment, wisdom and love.

Like Thoreau, I had never become 'lonesome or in the least oppressed by a sense of solitude'. Having 'plucked the finer fruits of life', I feel I know Ireland and its hills in a fuller and richer way. Mountains are inexhaustible lumps of rock, quartzite, schist and sculpted granite. Yet they are a vital resource to many people and places of inspiration, relaxation, escape, refreshment, recreation and challenge. It is the people who live on them who make them what they are. I reflect on the people who have shared their stories with me and opened up their hearts in describing how their culture is defined by their connection to the landscape. The mountains have always something new to offer and fresh stories to tell; but as the Hilltown shepherd remarked to me on my last night in the Shamrock Bar, 'too many people just take them for granite'.

Glossary

GMR – Great Mountain Road

REPS – Rural Environment Protection Scheme

WVM – White Van Man

An Post – Postal Service

An Taisce – The National Trust for Ireland

Bord Fáilte – (now called Fáilte Ireland)

Coillte Teoranta – Irish Forestry Service

Dúchas – The Heritage Service (now called The National
      Parks and Wildlife Service)

Eircom – Telephone Service

Eiscir Ríada – The Riding Ridge

Táin Bó Cuailgne – The Cattle Raid of Cooley

Tir na nÓg – The Land of Youth

Tuatha Dé Danann – The people of the Goddess Dana

Milesians – The Sons of Mil: Iron Age gods and rivals of the
      Tuatha Dé Danann

Select Bibliography

There are a relatively small number of books specifically dealing with mountains in Ireland but many references to Irish hills are contained in a variety of other sources. I have drawn on an eclectic range of books on related subjects, including landscape studies, walking guides, atlases, topography and travel, archaeology, geology, natural history, folklore, and mythology. The following is a selective list of books that were particularly informative, stimulating and entertaining.

Aalen F.H.A., K. Whelan and M. Stout, *Atlas of the Irish Rural Landscape*, Cork University Press, 1997

Andrews, J.H., *A Paper Landscape, The Ordnance Survey in Nineteenth-Century Ireland*, Oxford University Press, 1975

Bonwick, J., *Irish Druids and Old Irish Religions*, Dorset Press, 1986

Butler, H., *Grandmother and Wolfe Tone,* Lilliput Press, Dublin, 1990

Clann MacKenna, *Clann MacKenna Family History Society,* No. 7, Monaghan, 2000

Clements, E.D. 'Clem', *The Hewitts and Marilyns of Ireland,* TACit Press, Clackmannanshire, 1997

Coleman, J.C., *The Mountains of Killarney,* Dundalgan Press, Dundalk, 1948

Dames, M., *Mythic Ireland,* Thames and Hudson, London, 1992

Day, A. and P. McWilliams, *Ordnance Survey Memoirs of Ireland, Counties of South Ulster, 1834-1838,* Institute of Irish Studies, Belfast, 1998

Dempsey, E. and M. O'Clery, *The Complete Guide to Ireland's Birds,* Gill & Macmillan, Dublin, 1993

Dillon, P., *The Mournes,* O'Brien Press, Dublin, 2000

Dunford, S., *The Irish Highwaymen,* Merlin, Dublin, 2000

Durell, P. & C. Kelly. (eds.), *The Grand Tour of Kerry,* Cailleach Books, 2000

Ellis, P.B., *Hell or Connaught: The Cromwellian Colonisation of Ireland 1652-1660,* Hamish Hamilton, London, 1975

Evans, E.E., *Mourne Country,* Dundalgan Press, Dundalk, 1951
_____*The Personality of Ireland,* Lilliput Press, Dublin, 1992
_____*Ireland and the Atlantic Heritage, Selected Writings,* Lilliput Press, Dublin, 1996

Feehan, J., *The Landscape of Slieve Bloom,* Blackwater, Dublin, 1979

Fewer, M. (ed.), *A Walk in Ireland,* Atrium, Cork, 2001

Fitzmaurice, G. (ed.) *The Kerry Anthology,* Marino, Dublin, 2000

Flynn, P. J., *The Book of the Galtees and the Golden Vein,* Hodges Figgis, Dublin, 1926

Gosling, P., *Carlingford Town, An Antiquarian's Guide,* Carlingford Lough Heritage Trust, 1992

Gwynn, S., *The Fair Hills of Ireland,* Maunsel & Co. , Dublin, 1914

Hansard, J., *The History, Topography and Antiquities of the County and City of Waterford,* Dungarvan, 1870

Harbison, P., *Pilgrimage in Ireland; the Monuments and the People,* Barrie & Jenkins, London, 1991

Harding, M., *Footloose in the West of Ireland,* Michael Joseph, London, 1996

Hayward, R., *In Praise of Ulster,* Arthur Barker, London, 1938

_____ *In the Kingdom of Kerry,* Dundalgan Press, Dundalk, 1946

_____ *Leinster and the City of Dublin,* Arthur Barker, London, 1949

Heaney, M., *Over Nine Waves,* Faber, London, 1994

Heaney, P., *At the foot of Slieve Bloom,* Kilcormac Historical Society

Herman, D., *Walking Ireland's Mountains,* Appletree Press, Belfast, 1994

Hewitt, J., *The Collected Poems,* Blackstaff Press, Belfast, 1991

Inglis, H.R.G., *The Contour Road Book of Ireland,* Gall and Inglis, London, 1962

Jennett, S., *Munster,* Faber, London, 1967

Joyce, J., *Graiguenamanagh, a town and its people,* Graigue Publications, 2000

Joyce, T.P., *Bladma, Walks of Discovery in Slieve Bloom,* Glenbarrow, 1995

Kavanagh, P.J., *Voices In Ireland, A Traveller's Literary Companion,* John Murray, London, 1994

Kirk, D., *The Mountains of Mourne, A Celebration of a Place Apart,* Appletree Press, Belfast, 2002

Low, M., *Celtic Christianity and Nature,* Blackstaff Press, Belfast, 1996

Lynam, J. (ed.), *Irish Peaks,* Constable, London, 1982

Lynch, D., *Munster's Mountains*, The Collins Press, Cork, 2001

Malone, J.B., *The Complete Wicklow Way*, O'Brien Press, Dublin, 1997

Meehan, C. , *The Traveller's Guide to Sacred Ireland*, Gothic Image Publications, 2002

Mersey, R., *The Hills of Cork & Kerry*, Gill & Macmillan, Dublin, 1987

Mitchell, F., *The Shell Guide to Reading the Irish Landscape*, Michael Joseph, London, 1986

Morton, H.V., *In Search of Ireland*, Methuen, London, 1930

Mould, D.D.C.P. , *The Mountains of Ireland*, Batsford, London, 1955

Mulholland, H., *Guide to Ireland's 3000-foot Mountains*, Mulholland-Wirral, 1988

Murphy, D., *Cromwell in Ireland*, M.H. Gill, Dublin, 1897

Murphy, M.J., *Sayings and Stories from Slieve Gullion*, Dundalgan Press, Dundalk, 1990

_____ *Mountain Year*, Blackstaff Press, Belfast, 1987

MacManus, D., *The Middle Kingdom*, Colin Smythe, Gerrards Cross, 1993

MacNeill, M., *The Festival of Lughnasa*, Oxford University Press, 1962

McKeever, P. J., *A Story Through Time, the formation of the scenic landscapes of Ireland (North)*, Geological Survey of Northern Ireland, Belfast, 1999

McMann, J., *Loughcrew, The Cairns*, After Hours Books, Oldcastle, 1993

McNally, K., *Standing Stones and other monuments of early Ireland*, Appletree Press, Belfast, 1984

O'Connor, F., *Irish Miles*, Macmillan & Co., Belfast, 1947

O'Connor, P.J., *Some Guides to the Irish Scene*, Oireacht na Mumhan Books, 1992

O'Faoláin, S., *An Irish Journey*, Readers Union, London, 1941

Ó Ríordáin, S.P., *Antiquities of the Irish Countryside,* Methuen, London, 1968

O'Sullivan, S. (ed.), *Folktales of Ireland,* University of Chicago Press, 1968

Pennick, N., *Celtic Sacred Landscapes,* Thames and Hudson, London, 1996

Poucher, W.A., *Ireland,* Constable, London, 1986

Praeger, R.L., *The Way That I Went,* Hodges Figgis, Dublin, 1937

_____ *A Tourist's Flora of the West of Ireland*, Hodges Figgis, Dublin, 1909

Roberts, J., *The Sacred Mythological Centres of Ireland*, Bandia, 2000

Robinson, T., *Connemara, Part 1: Introduction and Gazetteer.* Part 2: a one-inch map, Folding Landscapes, Roundstone, 1990

Sheehan, J. , *The Eskers of Ireland*, Moate Historical Society, 1993

Smith, D.J., *High Ground Wrecks and Relics: Aircraft Hulks on the Hills and Mountains of the UK and Ireland*, Midland Publishing, Leicester, 1997

Swan, H.P. (ed.), *Romantic Donegal*, Carter, Belfast, 1964

Taylor and Skinner's *Maps of the Roads of Ireland*, Murray, London, 1777

Warner, P., *A Visitor's Guide to the Comeragh Mountains*, Blackstaff Press, Belfast, 1978

White, M., *Mount Leinster: Environment, Mining and Politics,* Geography Publications, Dublin, 1992

Index

Index